LEGISLATIVE LABYRINTH

Congress and Campaign Finance Reform

Diana Dwyre
California State University, Chico

Victoria A. Farrar-Myers
University of Texas at Arlington

CQ PRESS

A Division of Congressional Quarterly Inc.
Washington, D.C.

CQ Press
A Division of Congressional Quarterly Inc.
1414 22nd Street, N.W.
Washington, D.C. 20037

(202) 822-1475; (800) 638-1710

www.cqpress.com

Printed and bound in the United States of America
04 03 02 01 00   5 4 3 2 1

Designed and typeset by BMWW, Baltimore, Md.
Cover by Karen Doody

Library of Congress Cataloging-in-Publication Data

Dwyre, Diana.
   Legislative labyrinth : Congress and campaign finance reform /
   Diana Dwyre, Victoria A. Farrar-Myers.
     p. cm.
   Includes bibliographical references and index.
   ISBN: 1-56802-568-8 (pbk.)
   1. Campaign funds—United States.   2. United States. Congress.
 I. Farrar-Myers, Victoria A.   II. Title.
   JK1991 .D99   2000
   324.7′8′0973—dc21

00-046830

This book is dedicated to

Joe Picard

and to

Jason Myers

CONTENTS

FIGURES AND BOXES

PREFACE

The American Political Science Association (APSA) each year selects a few political scientists to put their Ph.D.'s to work in Congress. We both served as APSA Congressional Fellows in the U.S. House of Representatives from November 1997 to August 1998 (the second session of the 105th Congress). Our interest in campaign finance led us independently to seek positions with House members working on campaign finance reform. Our training as political scientists led us to ask questions about the various theories and models of politics, policymaking, and government, and we set out to relate the theoretical to the practical.

One of us worked for a Republican and the other for a Democrat. Victoria Farrar-Myers was a legislative assistant to Rep. Christopher Shays of Connecticut. Shays was the primary Republican cosponsor of the Shays-Meehan bill, the leading campaign finance reform bill that passed the House twice in two years. In the 105th Congress Shays was a senior member of the House Budget Committee, a member of the House Government Reform and Oversight Committee, the chairman of the Subcommittee on Human Resources, and a member of the Tuesday Group, a coalition of moderate Republicans who meet weekly to discuss their party's policy objectives. He had developed a strong and supportive relationship with his party's leaders, who were directing a party now in the majority after four decades of minority status. Yet that relationship was severely tested by Shays's leadership on campaign finance reform in defiance of his party's leaders. This dynamic was one of the most interesting aspects of the effort to pass a campaign finance reform bill. Farrar-Myers was assigned to work with Shays's legislative director on the bill.

Diana Dwyre was a legislative assistant to Rep. Sander Levin of Michigan. Levin, a Democratic cosponsor of the Shays-Meehan bill, worked closely with the coalition of reformers to help pass the legislation. He was an effective liaison between the reform coalition and the Democratic Party Caucus and helped build Democratic support for the bill. Levin is a senior member of the powerful Ways and Means Committee and during the 105th Congress served on the Human Resources and Social Security Subcommittees of Ways and Means. He has a reputation for working effectively with House members from both parties and for wielding significant influence within his party. Dwyre was Levin's staff person responsible for campaign finance issues.

Both of us worked for pro-reform members of the House, and our experiences reflect that view. Yet as a bipartisan team we bring insights to this case study that most other experts about policymaking cannot, for we each saw the effort to pass campaign finance reform in the House from different perspectives. For example, Shays went against his party's leaders by championing an issue that they wanted to bury, whereas Levin worked cooperatively with House Democratic leaders to help pass campaign finance reform. Moreover, our direct involvement provided us with extraordinary access to the process, the players, and the events that shaped this contentious and hard-fought legislative battle. We were, so to speak, on the front lines. We both were afforded extensive contact not only with our own members of Congress but also with other House members, party leaders, White House staff, Congressional Research Service experts, legislative counsel, interest group lobbyists, think tank representatives, members of the media, constituents, and high-level committee and personal staff from both the House and the Senate.

Additionally, our daily (and sometimes nightly) involvement with the issue put us at the center of numerous meetings and discussions about campaign finance reform. We attended meetings with the reform coalition members, party caucus meetings, party leadership and whip count meetings, private meetings with House members, campaign finance reform task force meetings, reform staff meetings, issue briefings, strategy sessions, meetings with top White House staff, press briefings, sessions with allied interest groups, press conferences, and other gatherings. We assisted in crafting legislation, produced supporting documents, conducted extensive background research, wrote numerous floor speeches for our House members, composed press releases, and made posters, voting cue cards, and other materials for use on the House floor during the campaign finance reform debates. Finally, we both spent a good deal of time on the floor of the chamber during the many hours of debate over several months to provide ready assistance to our bosses and other pro-reform House members.

This opportunity to be immersed so deeply in the process as participant observers encouraged us to combine our experiences on Capitol Hill with our training as political scientists to write this book about policymaking in the contemporary Congress. As college professors who teach courses on

American government, Congress, political parties, and interest groups, we have noticed the lack of readable, interesting, and lively books about the modern legislative process. We hope that our book will help fill this gap. We offer an approach different from that of other legislative case study books, for we focus not only on the chronology of the legislative process but also on what this legislative battle can teach us about the roles of policy leaders, political parties, interest groups, and the media. Moreover, unlike other case studies, this one covers a bill that was not enacted into law, thereby demonstrating another important lesson about contemporary congressional policymaking: sometimes legislative proposals take many years to pass, if they pass at all.

While working on the Hill, we met regularly to discuss our experiences and plan our project. We kept careful records of the events surrounding consideration of campaign finance reform and collected various documents—such as "Dear Colleague" letters sent between House members, internal memos, minutes from meetings, letters from interest groups, press releases, and newspaper clippings—to help us piece together the story once we returned to our teaching jobs in California and Texas. Our experience as congressional fellows gave us both a deeper appreciation of the complexities of the policymaking process and the nuances of politics at the national level. We aim to share this appreciation through this over-the-shoulder view of the congressional effort to pass campaign finance reform. Finally, although while writing this book we have put our political science hats back on to analyze the process, we do not claim that this is an omniscient narrative. Instead, we believe it brings together the best of both worlds—a scholarly approach and an insider's view of Congress.

We could not have written this book without tremendous help from many people. First, we are grateful to those individuals who helped shape our approach to political science, our teachers. Diana Dwyre earned her Ph.D. from the Maxwell School at Syracuse University, where Linda Fowler, Jeffrey Stonecash, and Kristi Andersen taught her not only how to do political science but also how to have fun doing it. Victoria Farrar-Myers earned her Ph.D. from the University of Albany, State University of New York, and would like to thank all there who helped her obtain her goals, with special thanks to Scott Barclay for offering perspective and continuous encouragement. She also expresses her deep appreciation to Ira Carmen (University of Illinois), who taught her to be a good soldier and never to give up. We also thank our colleagues in the Departments of Political Science at California State University, Chico, and at the University of Texas at Arlington, who have been supportive and encouraging.

The APSA Congressional Fellowship Program provided us with the opportunity and the means to take leave from our regular teaching jobs to serve as congressional fellows during the 105th Congress. Special thanks go to APSA executive director Catherine Rudder and APSA Congressional Fellowship director Jeff Biggs. Many people in Washington helped make our D.C. experience invaluable. In particular, we would like to thank Allison Rak, Representative Shays's legislative director during the 105th Congress; Amy Rosenbaum and her boss, Rep. Martin T. Meehan, D-Mass.; and Hilarie Chambers and Dan Jourdan, of Representative Levin's office, for being such wonderful tutors on the Hill. Most important, Sander Levin and Christopher Shays made us part of their teams and gave us the chance to be on the inside of campaign finance reform. They are two of the most intelligent, talented, and hard-working members of Congress, and we are forever grateful to them for allowing us the honor of working for them.

Although we take full responsibility for the contents of this book, many people helped make it a better work. Tony Corrado of Colby College encouraged us to pursue this project and served as one of our most helpful, and toughest, reviewers. Mary Grisez Kweit of the University of North Dakota and two anonymous reviewers also provided useful insights and comments, many of which were incorporated into the book. Thanks also to Paul Herrnson of the University of Maryland for his insightful suggestions on the organization of the book; Barbara Sinclair of the University of California, Los Angeles, for her early support; and Meredith McGehee of Common Cause for her comments on the manuscript. The APSA Political Organizations and Parties section provided us with the opportunity to present our thoughts on campaign finance reform at a short course in August 1998. In addition, we would like to thank Amber Frier for her research assistance. The team of professionals at CQ Press deserves many thanks for making this book possible. Brenda Carter, Director of College Publishing, and Associate Editor Gwenda Larsen expertly shepherded us through the process, and our thorough and able copy editor, Joanne S. Ainsworth, helped make the book more readable and understandable.

Finally, we thank our husbands, Joe Picard and Jason Myers, for their enormous amount of support and encouragement. They give meaning and purpose to our personal and professional endeavors, and we dedicate this book to them.

1

CAMPAIGN FINANCE REFORM
A Catalyst for Policy Innovation

*Once begin the dance of legislation, and you must struggle through
its mazes as best you can to the breathless end—if any end there be.*

Woodrow Wilson, *Congressional Government* (1885)

The *Nightline* reporters and camera crew waited with anticipation for the triumphant return of Congressmen Christopher Shays, R-Conn., and Martin T. Meehan, D-Mass., from the floor of the House of Representatives. It was July 30, 1998, in the second session of the 105th Congress (1997–1999). With few legislative days left on the calendar before lawmakers turned their attention to the upcoming midterm elections, the final hurdle for passage of the Shays-Meehan Bipartisan Campaign Reform Act had been cleared. The last set of amendments designed to sink the effort had been defeated. Fellow proreform House members, staffers, and interest group activists were gathered in Representative Shays's office. They erupted in applause as the lead sponsors of the reform bill and their entourage of staffers entered the room and were momentarily blinded by the bright lights of the television cameras. The heady exhilaration of victory consumed everyone. It all seemed like a glorious dream for those who knew how close to defeat the campaign finance reform measure had come. Yet, although this battle might be won, the war would wage on. This night, however, was for celebration, for relief, and for believing one can make a difference inside the Beltway.

1

The intricacies of congressional policy debates seldom draw the attention of late night television news shows. Moreover, campaign finance reform is not a new issue. In fact, congressional efforts to counteract the influence of money in politics can be traced back to the Appropriations Bill of 1867. Still, the drama of this particular legislative battle kept the *Nightline* camera crew on Capitol Hill late into the night. The highly charged debate over reform in the 105th Congress stemmed from the fact that by 1998 the regulatory system governing the financing of federal campaigns had become virtually meaningless. Much of the money raised and spent to influence federal elections was flowing outside of the regulations set in motion by the Federal Election Campaign Act (FECA) of 1971. Political parties, interest groups, nonprofit organizations, corporations, labor unions, and wealthy individuals all had discovered unregulated but technically legal ways to influence federal elections. During the 1996 elections, congressional candidates saw these outside players spend millions of dollars of unregulated and undisclosed money in their elections. This experience and the various campaign finance scandals of those elections motivated many lawmakers to call for comprehensive campaign finance reform.

The leading reform bill, the Bipartisan Campaign Reform Act, is a good vehicle for understanding the contours and intricacies of modern policymaking. Its eventful, dramatic, and somewhat atypical journey through Congress reveals more than just the sequential steps of the policy process. It also clearly illustrates much about contemporary government and politics in the United States, including the often unorthodox nature of modern policymaking; interesting differences between the processes in the House and the Senate; the motivations of lawmakers; the importance of policy entrepreneurs; and the role of political parties, interest groups, and the media.

Campaign Finance Reform and the Legislative Labyrinth

This particular legislative battle is a good case study for learning about the policymaking process precisely because it did not follow the ordinary "textbook" process of how a bill becomes a law. Instead, both supporters and opponents of reform used many unconventional procedures and strategies in their attempts to achieve their desired policy outcome. Thus, we follow recent political science scholarship in rejecting the textbook view of how a bill becomes a law in favor of a view that incorporates the more dynamic process of "unorthodox" lawmaking, whereby legislation travels unconventional routes through Congress.[1]

This book tells the story of the attempt to enact campaign finance reform during the 105th and 106th Congresses, but more important, the focus and organization of the book revolve around the various lessons about policymaking that can be gleaned from this particular policy debate. Thus, it is organized primarily by topic rather than strictly chronologically, and the story unfolds through discussion of these various topics. In Chapters 2 and 3 we chronicle efforts to enact campaign finance reform during the 105th Congress in the Senate and the House, respectively. Then, in each of Chapters 4, 5, and 6, we examine the campaign finance reform effort through the lens of different topics. We believe this combination of chronological and topical analyses offers a comprehensive view of both the subject of campaign finance reform itself and the dynamics of contemporary congressional policymaking.

The story of campaign finance reform in the 105th Congress stimulates many intriguing questions about the nature of lawmaking in the modern Congress. For instance, how did the House reformers overcome a series of seemingly insurmountable obstacles to pass the bill? How did an issue that attracted little public attention make it onto the policy agenda, maintain the attention of the media, and mobilize the interest group community to push for or against this major policy change? Why did the Bipartisan Campaign Reform Act experience such different fates in the House and the Senate? In answering these and other questions we aim to present not just a case study of one bill's journey through Congress, but a template for understanding much of what goes on in the offices and chambers of Capitol Hill.

Both of the authors worked for House members who support reform, one of us for a Republican and the other for a Democrat. Thus, this account naturally draws from our experiences within the proreform camp. It is this insiders' view of the policy process that has given us the understanding to evaluate Congress and campaign finance reform. Therefore, we offer our insight into an interesting, timely, and controversial issue that reveals many important dynamics of the contemporary policymaking process. The book is not designed to advocate reform of the campaign finance system. The case for reform is well articulated by its supporters in the *Congressional Record* and other documents from this legislative battle. Rather, we designed the book so that the processes and politics of the debate over campaign finance reform provide an engaging account of the contemporary "dance of legislation."[2]

Campaign Finance Reform in Historical Context

Campaign finance reform has been a black hole for legislative remedies for almost two decades. This public policy problem is unique in that 535 experts

(435 members of the House of Representatives and 100 senators) each has his or her own ideas about what, if anything, is wrong with the system. Many of them offer remedies for preventing the potentially corrupting influence of money on politics. The policy debate also splits legislators along partisan lines, making it difficult to enact campaign finance reform laws in an era of heightened congressional partisanship and divided government. Sometimes reform is further stifled because of disagreements between the two chambers that may divide members of the same party, in part because senators and House members face different campaign finance challenges. For example, House incumbents rely much more heavily on political action committee (PAC) contributions than do Senate incumbents.

Political action committees are the organizations through which interest groups, corporations, and labor unions must operate to participate in federal elections. They must raise money separately for the express purpose of spending it on federal elections. Because Senate candidates raise less of their money from PACs than their House counterparts, Senate reformers have often proposed severe decreases in PAC contribution limits or a ban on PACs altogether. House reformers, in contrast, generally do not propose serious limits on PACs. Not surprisingly, this jumbled discourse has produced little or no change. If anything, in the time that reformers have attempted to find remedies, the financiers of campaigns have devised more ways to circumvent and short-circuit the campaign finance laws and regulations.

Early Reform Issues

Prior to the 1970s and to the Watergate scandal, which prompted the enactment of many campaign finance reforms in the 1970s, the financing of federal elections in the United States was virtually unregulated and very little campaign finance activity was disclosed to the public. Only a few rules applied to the fund-raising and the spending connected with federal elections. For example, in 1905 President Theodore Roosevelt brought attention to the participation of corporations in campaigns in his annual message to Congress (ironically, several had financed his own 1904 campaign). In response, in 1907, Congress passed the Tillman Act, which banned corporations and national banks from making contributions to candidates for federal office. In 1910 Congress passed the Publicity Act, which required House campaign committees that operated in two or more states to disclose contributors of more than $100 within thirty days after an election. Later, in 1911, Congress extended these filing requirements to Senate candidates. This law also limited the amount candidates could spend to $10,000 for Senate campaigns and $5,000 for House campaigns.

Following the Teapot Dome scandal in 1925, Congress passed the Federal Corrupt Practices Act. The Corrupt Practices Act closed a loophole in the law that allowed contributions given in nonelection years to avoid disclosure. It revised the amount candidates could spend and prohibited offering money to anyone in exchange for a vote. Its scope was limited to general elections and did not apply to campaign committees operating within a single state. The act also did not include any enforcement provisions. In 1939 the Hatch Act was passed. This act barred federal employees from active participation in national politics. Later, in 1940, the Hatch Act was revised to limit the fund-raising and expenditures of party committees operating in two or more states to $3 million and to limit individual contributions to $5,000 a year. This act also sought to regulate primary elections. Finally, in 1947, the Taft-Hartley Act was passed. It aimed to ban political contributions by labor unions.[3]

Then the 1971 Federal Election Campaign Act (FECA), with its amendments of 1974, 1976, and 1979, and the Revenue Act of 1971 and its 1974 amendments dramatically changed the landscape for the financing of congressional and presidential campaigns. The Revenue Act of 1971 provided public funding for presidential elections through a check-off on income tax forms by which taxpayers could divert $1 of their tax liability to the public fund (later raised to $3). Presidential candidates were eligible for the public funds if they agreed to limit their overall spending. The 1971 Federal Election Campaign Act strengthened the existing prohibition against contributions from corporations and labor unions; it also provided the legal basis for business, labor, and other organizations to form political action committees, the entities through which they legally could spend money in federal elections. The 1971 FECA limited personal contributions by candidates and their immediate families, and it tightened campaign finance reporting and disclosure requirements and extended these requirements to primary elections. Finally, the 1971 law placed strict limits on the amount of money candidates could spend on media advertising.

Then the break-in at the Democratic Party headquarters at the Watergate complex in Washington, D.C., on June 17, 1972, began one of the most highly publicized scandals in American political history. The Watergate hearings documented numerous transgressions, including the burglary, millions of dollars in illegal campaign contributions, arm twisting for contributions, money laundering, enemies lists, and a cover-up conspiracy. The scandal brought down President Richard M. Nixon, and Congress responded to the public's demand for change with amendments to the FECA that represent the most comprehensive campaign finance laws ever adopted. The 1974 amendments to the FECA included these major provisions:

1. Limits on contributions from individuals, PACs, and party committees as well as an overall limit for total contributions by individuals.
2. Limits on the amount political party organizations could spend on behalf of federal candidates (called coordinated expenditures).
3. Limits on expenditures by House, Senate, and presidential candidates to replace the media expenditure ceilings in the 1971 FECA.
4. Limits on independent expenditures, or expenditures by individuals or interest groups made independently of a candidate's campaign to advocate the election or defeat of a federal candidate, and a prohibition against cash donations of more than $100.[4]
5. Establishment of the Federal Election Commission (FEC) to implement and enforce the federal campaign finance laws.
6. New disclosure and reporting rules requiring candidates to file quarterly reports on their contributions and expenditures with the FEC, thus making these records available to the public.
7. An amendment to the presidential election public-funding system to allow presidential nominees for the major parties to receive public funds equal to the aggregate spending limit if they agree to refrain from raising additional private money (minor party and independent candidates were to be eligible for a proportional share of this subsidy), and the establishment of a voluntary system of public matching funds for presidential primary campaigns.[5]

These provisions set out a whole new landscape for the financing of federal elections. Then in 1976, the Supreme Court in *Buckley v. Valeo* substantially weakened the efficacy of the FECA by striking down some provisions and letting others stand.[6] The Court upheld the FECA's limitations on direct contributions to candidates from individuals, PACs, and parties as appropriate legislative tools to guard against the reality or appearance of improper influence stemming from candidates' dependence on large campaign contributions. At the same time, however, the Court invalidated the act's spending limits for House and Senate candidates, the spending limit for independent expenditures, and the limits on expenditures by candidates from personal or family resources as violations of the First Amendment right to free speech.[7] The Supreme Court kept in place the spending limits for presidential candidates because these spending limits are voluntary (in exchange for public funding) and, therefore, do not violate the Court's ruling that campaign expenditures are protected political speech and cannot be involuntarily limited.

The Court's ruling in *Buckley v. Valeo* is often criticized by reformers because it deems limits on campaign expenditures and independent expenditures unconstitutional limitations on free speech, suggesting that money equals speech. Given the unequal levels of money that candidates are capable of raising, with incumbents able to raise far more than most challengers, for example, and the unequal levels of resources that individuals and groups control, the Court's ruling potentially implies a very unequal right to free speech. The candidates most successful at fund-raising and the wealthiest individuals and groups, the argument goes, are, in effect, entitled to more speech than most House or Senate challengers and the typical $100 contributor.

Congress passed additional amendments to the FECA in 1976 to comply with the Supreme Court's ruling in the *Buckley* case. In 1979 Congress further revised the law to address some criticisms of the law's effects. For example, candidates and political committees argued that the FECA's reporting requirements were too cumbersome and expensive, and state and local party officials complained that the law reduced spending by their party organizations for traditional party-building activities such as voter registration and get-out-the-vote (GOTV) drives. By restricting party spending on candidates, the FECA made parties choose between spending on grassroots party-building activities or on media advertising, and both parties' presidential campaigns chose to direct their limited resources to media advertising.[8]

With the 1979 amendments, Congress eased the paperwork requirements, and party organizations were granted an exemption from spending limits for select grassroots volunteer activities and party-building programs. Spending for these party-building activities would not count against the party's contribution limits to candidates. This exemption allowed the parties to spend unlimited amounts of federal (or "hard") money on these activities, money that must be raised in relatively small, limited increments from regulated sources such as PACs and individuals. The amounts of hard money raised and spent must be fully reported to the Federal Election Commission. Contrary to common belief, the 1979 party-building exemption did not create "soft" (or nonfederal) money, because the 1979 FECA amendments required that parties spend only hard money for such party-building activities. Soft money is the product of two FEC rulings in which the FECA was interpreted in a way that, in effect, made the amendments avenues for unregulated soft money.[9] Soft money is money collected by parties in unlimited amounts, sometimes from otherwise prohibited sources, such as corporations and labor unions, for party-building activities.[10]

Effects of the 1970s Reforms

These laws, the amendments to them, and the Court's 1976 ruling in the *Buckley* case established a new regulatory regime for the financing of federal campaigns. In Box 1-1 we present a summary of the campaign finance system that resulted from them and that is still in effect today. Candidates, parties, interest groups, and individuals adjusted their activities accordingly and many of the consequences of reform, both intended and unintended, soon became clear. Most results were welcome changes from past practices, as campaign finance expert Anthony Corrado notes:

> the new campaign finance system represented a major advancement over the patchwork of regulations it replaced. The disclosure and reporting requirements dramatically improved public access to financial information and regulators' ability to enforce the law. The contribution ceilings eliminated the large gifts that had tainted the process in 1972. Public financing quickly gained widespread acceptance among the candidates, and small contributions became the staple of presidential campaign financing.[11]

Other consequences of reform were not so desirable, however. For instance, despite the limits on contributions to candidates and parties, the cost of congressional campaigns continued to rise. In Figures 1-1 and 1-2 we show the growth in the average expenditures of House and Senate candidates since 1980. The increasing use of more sophisticated campaign techniques, such as television advertising and polling, greatly added to the cost of running for federal office. This need to raise ever-increasing amounts of money to run for office fueled criticisms that congressional candidates were even more open to the influence of moneyed interests than before the 1970s reform.

These criticisms were aimed squarely at political action committees. One of the rather unexpected consequences of the FECA was the explosive growth in the number of PACs and in the amount of money that flowed from PACs to candidates and political parties. The number of PACs registered with the Federal Election Commission went from 608 in 1974 to 3,835 in 1999.[12] Political action committee contributions to congressional candidates also increased dramatically, going from a total of $55.2 million in 1980 to $206.8 million in 1998.[13] We show this growth in PAC contributions, particularly to House candidates, from 1980 to 1998 in Figure 1-3.

Beginning in the 1980s and through much of the 1990s, these trends led many who were concerned with the inadequacies of the campaign finance regulatory system to focus on two central issues: (1) the rising cost of congressional campaigns (see Figures 1-1 and 1-2) and (2) the substantial reliance on PACs as a source of major funding for campaigns and the resulting

BOX 1-1 Summary of Current Campaign Finance Laws

Contributions by Individuals

- Maximum $1,000 per election to candidates
- Maximum $5,000 per year to state & local parties
- Maximum $20,000 per year to national parties
- Maximum aggregate annual contributions of $25,000

Contributions by Parties

- Maximum $5,000 per election to candidates
- Parties may make coordinated expenditures on behalf of candidates (limit adjusted for inflation each election cycle)

Contributions by PACs

- Maximum $5,000 per election to candidates
- Maximum $15,000 per year to a national party committee
- Maximum $5,000 per year combined limit to state and local party
- No aggregate annual limit

Candidate Spending

- No limits on candidate spending from personal funds
- No personal use of campaign funds

Soft Money

- No limits on national party receipt of soft money, but parties must disclose such receipts
- States parties must follow FEC formula for allocating between hard and soft money for mixed federal-state-local activities
- FECA definition of contribution does not apply to contributions to party committee building funds
- No provision prohibiting candidates from raising soft money

Issue Advocacy

- Based on judicial rulings, disclosure rules, source limits, and FECA prohibitions apply only to spending for express advocacy communications
- FECA defines "expenditure" as money spent to influence a federal election

Independent Expenditures

- Independent expenditures cannot be made in cooperation or coordination with candidates

continued

Box continued

- Parties, groups, and individuals may make unlimited independent expenditures for candidates (based on judicial ruling)
- Requires prompt disclosure in last twenty days before election

Disclosure Requirements

- Candidates must disclose in forty-eight hours any contribution of $1,000 or more made within twenty days before the election
- Candidates must disclose on a calendar-year basis
- Candidates must file postelection reports
- Candidates must use best efforts to obtain donor information for contributions of $200 or more
- FEC may audit only if it has a reason to believe that a violation occurred

FEC Enforcement

- FEC may clarify ambiguities in the law through advisory opinions
- FEC must notify complaint's object
- Statutes prescribe maximum penalties and timetable for enforcement actions

Miscellaneous

- Under *Beck* and other rulings, union-dues-paying nonmembers have right to disallow political use of their funds
- Campaign funds cannot be solicited from federal government buildings
- Bans House franked mass mailings ninety days before an election

Source: Compiled from Joseph E. Cantor, "CRS Report 98-287 GOV: Campaign Finance Reform Bills in the 105th Congress: Comparison of H.R. 3485 (Thomas), S. 25 (McCain-Feingold), and Current Law" (Washington, D.C.: Congressional Research Service, 1998).

influence of wealthy and powerful interest groups (see Figure 1-3). Consistent with these concerns, many political scientists, journalists, public interest groups, and reform-minded legislators also pointed to the incumbency advantage and the lack of electoral competitiveness in congressional elections as detrimental to our system of representative democracy.

Incumbents in the House of Representatives were reelected at rates often well over 90 percent during the 1980s and 1990s (and still are today). Since they already hold the seat being contested, incumbents benefit from many advantages not enjoyed by their challengers. For example, incumbents generally have a higher level of name recognition than those who challenge

Figure 1-1 Average Campaign Expenditures by House Candidates, 1980–1998

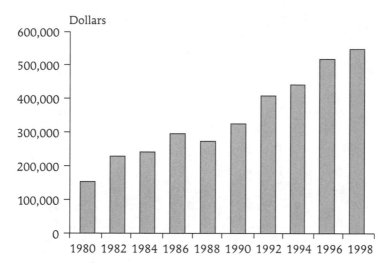

Source: Compiled from data in Norman J. Ornstein, Thomas E. Mann, and Michael J. Malbin, *Vital Statistics on Congress, 1999-2000* (Washington, D.C.: AEI Press, 2000), 80.

Figure 1-2 Average Campaign Expenditures by Senate Candidates, 1980–1998

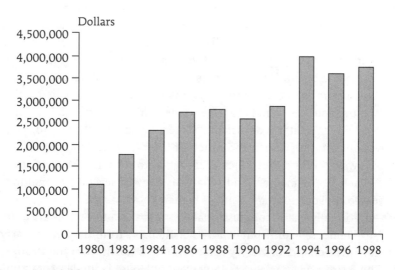

Source: Compiled from data in Norman J. Ornstein, Thomas E. Mann, and Michael J. Malbin, *Vital Statistics on Congress, 1999-2000* (Washington, D.C.: AEI Press, 2000), 86.

Figure 1-3 Total PAC Contributions to House and Senate Candidates,
1980–1998

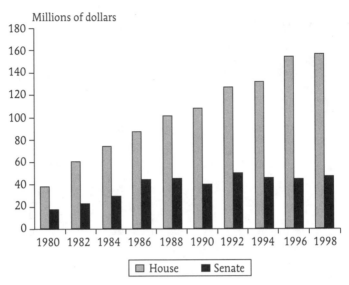

Millions of dollars

House | Senate

Source: Compiled from data in Federal Election Commission, "FEC Releases Information on
PAC Activity for 1997–1998," news release, June 8, 1999.

them, and they find it easier to command media attention as well. As office-
holders, incumbents cater to the needs of their constituents in a way that
generates positive evaluations from the voters back home. House members
and senators also have large staff allowances, and much of that money is
used to hire staff to respond to constituents' inquiries for information, re-
quests for help to obtain federal benefits, or opinions about pending legislation.[14] Lawmakers pay attention to their constituents' opinions when voting
on legislation, and they work hard to get their share of federal funds for special projects in their states or districts (often called pork barrel projects).
Congressional staffers also spend much of their time on publicity efforts
such as newsletters and press releases designed to enhance the legislator's
image.[15] Each House member and senator is allowed several free mailings
every year to constituents back home, a benefit known as the franking privilege.[16] Additionally, many congressional districts and a few states are quite
lopsidedly Democratic or Republican, so challengers from the weaker party
often have little chance of victory against an incumbent from the stronger
party. This helps explain why over 15 percent of House incumbents ran un-
opposed for reelection in 1998.

Figure 1-4 Average Campaign Expenditures by House Incumbents and Challengers, 1980–1998

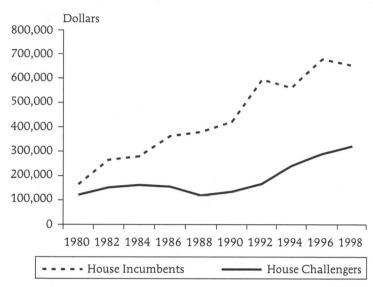

Source: Compiled from data in Norman J. Ornstein, Thomas E. Mann, and Michael J. Malbin, *Vital Statistics on Congress, 1999–2000* (Washington, D.C.: AEI Press, 2000), 80–81.

Perhaps the most significant advantage enjoyed by incumbents is in raising campaign funds. Because incumbents can raise more money from PACs and individuals than their challengers, they have more to spend on campaign activities—such as campaign advertisements, polling, and GOTV efforts—that help them win. In Figures 1-4 and 1-5 we show the average campaign expenditures of House and Senate incumbents and challengers. For House races, the disparity between incumbent and challenger spending has grown significantly over time, as indicated in Figure 1-4. In 1998, House incumbents outspent their challengers by a ratio of four to one. There is less of a spending gap between Senate incumbents and challengers, yet Senate incumbents continue to spend quite a lot more than their challengers.

This disparity is, in part, the result of incumbents' superior ability to attract PAC contributions, particularly incumbents of the majority party. Interest groups ultimately want access to policymakers after the election, so their PACs naturally direct campaign contributions to the candidates who are most likely to win. Because over 90 percent of House incumbents win reelection, PACs see them as a good investment to ensure access to future policymakers. In Figure 1-6 we show the allocation of PAC contributions be-

Figure 1-5   Average Campaign Expenditures by Senate Incumbents and
Challengers, 1980–1998

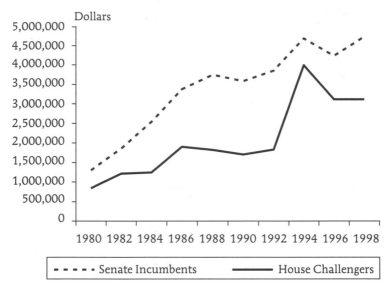

Source: Compiled from data in Norman J. Ornstein, Thomas E. Mann, and Michael J.
Malbin, *Vital Statistics on Congress, 1999–2000* (Washington, D.C.: AEI Press, 2000), 86–87.

tween congressional incumbents and challengers from 1980 to 1998. The
increasing preference for incumbents is quite obvious.

Majority party incumbents are favored because interest groups want access to the lawmakers with the most power to serve their interests, and in
Congress the majority party rules, especially in the House. In fact, the minority party in the House of Representatives during the 1980s, then the Republicans, often argued that the growing cost of campaigns and the financial
and other advantages enjoyed by Democratic incumbents were explanations
for what many believed would be the Republicans' perpetual minority status
in the House.[17] Today, as the majority party, the Republicans raise more PAC
dollars than the Democrats. This switch to the Republicans confirms that
most PACs distribute their campaign contributions in a way that will gain
them access to the most powerful lawmakers—that is, to majority party lawmakers—rather than based on partisanship, ideology, or some other factor.[18]

Contributions from PACs are seen by many as attempts to buy influence.
Therefore, the increase in the amount of PAC money contributed to congressional candidates and congressional candidates' increasing reliance on PAC
funds are viewed by some as evidence of an unseemly relationship between

Figure 1-6 Allocation of PAC Contributions between Congressional Incumbents and Challengers, 1974–1998

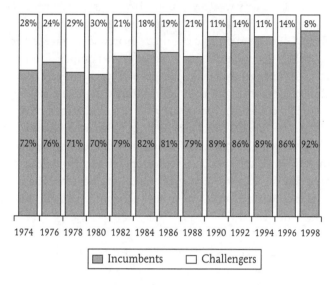

Source: Compiled from Federal Election Commission data.

moneyed interests and congressional lawmakers. Although there is very little evidence to suggest that PAC contributions directly influence how legislators vote, it is fairly clear that contributions do help interest groups gain access to legislators after the election.[19] During the 1980s and early 1990s proreform public interest groups, some proreform lawmakers, and the media all contributed to the perception that political action committees were the evil that should be rooted out of the campaign finance system.[20] Several books written during this period reflect this PAC-bashing view: *The Best Congress Money Can Buy; Money Talks: Corporate PACs and Political Influence; Honest Graft: Big Money and the American Political Process; Gold-Plated Politics: Running for Congress in the 1990s; The Money Chase: Congressional Campaign Finance Reform;* and *Gilded Dome: The U.S. Senate and Campaign Finance Reform.*[21] This view of PACs significantly influenced the reform efforts of the 1980s and early 1990s.

Another criticism of the campaign finance system targeted the high incumbent reelection rate and the apparent lack of competition, particularly in House elections. The rising cost of running for Congress and the many advantages enjoyed by incumbents make it particularly difficult for challengers with modest means or limited financial support to seek election.

One advocate of reform, Sen. Robert C. Byrd, D-W.V., warned that without changes to the campaign finance system, Congress would become the "exclusive domain of the very wealthy," preventing legislators with a "common man's background," such as himself, from seeking public office.[22]

The high cost of campaigns and the incumbency advantage, especially the preference of PACs for incumbents, tend to stifle competition in congressional elections. Elections that lack real competition between candidates call into question the legitimacy of our representative democracy. Competition offers voters a real choice between two or more candidates, a chance, therefore, to hold an officeholder accountable or to judge whether he or she merits continued support. Without a real choice, there may be no effective mechanism of accountability. The reform efforts in the 1980s and early 1990s focused on these criticisms by attempting to decrease the role played by PACs in federal elections and to level the playing field between incumbents and challengers.

Reform Efforts in the 1980s and Early 1990s

The stage set by the Supreme Court with *Buckley v. Valeo* and the issues that emerged out of the new campaign finance regulatory regime characterized campaign finance reform legislation throughout the 1980s and into the 1990s. For instance, in 1985, Sens. David Boren, D-Okla., and Barry Goldwater, R-Ariz., proposed a reform measure that addressed the growing concern about PACs. Their measure limited the amount that congressional candidates could receive from PACs and lowered the PAC contribution limit from $5,000 to $3,000, among other things. The proposal was offered as an amendment to another bill, but the Senate majority leader, Robert Dole, R-Kan., orchestrated the procedures to prevent a vote on the amendment. The proposal surfaced again the next year, once again as an amendment, and it passed in August 1986 by a vote of sixty-nine to thirty, including twenty-six Republican votes in favor of the measure. Yet once again procedural maneuvering ensured that the measure would not pass. The Senate Republican leaders did not allow the bill to which the campaign finance reform amendment was attached to come up for a vote.

Senator Boren persisted. With the 1986 elections, the Democrats took back control of the Senate. As the 100th Congress opened in 1987 the new Senate majority leader, Robert Byrd, worked with Senator Boren and other Senate Democratic leaders to draft a comprehensive campaign finance reform bill. The bill, the Senatorial Election Campaign Act of 1987 (S. 2), included public financing for congressional campaigns in exchange for voluntary spending limits by congressional candidates (much like the presidential public financing system already in place), aggregate PAC limits, limits on PAC "bundling," and on independent expenditures.[23] Despite a record eight cloture votes to try to end the Republican filibuster against S. 2, Senate reformers could not get the necessary sixty votes and the bill was defeated.[24]

In June 1989 the Republican president, George Bush, floated a proposal to abolish corporate, labor union, and membership organization PACs. Meanwhile, reformers in both the House and the Senate tried to forge bipartisan campaign finance reform efforts during the 101st Congress (1989–1991). The House established a bipartisan task force of House members to consider reform. However, the task force could not reach agreement on the major issues, such as PAC contributions, because of what one of its members, Al Swift, D-Wash., called "legitimate partisan differences."[25] In the Senate the two parties' leaders, Majority Leader George Mitchell, D-Me., and Minority Leader Robert Dole appointed an outside bipartisan group of six experts to consider campaign finance reform and propose a reform plan. The group, which became known as the Gang of Six, presented a proposal of modest reforms that gained little support in the Senate.[26] Although these efforts did not produce bipartisan solutions, different campaign finance reform bills did pass the House and the Senate along party lines in August 1990, just months before the midterm congressional elections. However, a conference committee was never appointed to work out the differences between the House and Senate bills. Thus a final bill was never enacted.

During 1991 President Bush repeatedly asserted that he would veto any reform bill that included spending limits, public financing of elections, or separate rules for House and Senate elections. Most Republicans oppose these types of reforms for both ideological and pragmatic reasons. Ideologically, many Republicans argue that spending limits constitute a violation of First Amendment free speech rights, a view they assert is consistent with the Supreme Court ruling in *Buckley v. Valeo*. They oppose voluntary spending limits because they are in exchange for public funding, and public funding of campaigns, they argue, is not a legitimate use of tax dollars. Some Republicans have called public funding of campaigns "welfare for candidates." Republicans also generally favor a smaller government role in most instances, and public funding would significantly increase the government's role in federal campaigns. Pragmatically, many Republicans claim that spending limits would curtail their party's ability to win elections, particularly since the Republicans have historically been able to raise more money than the Democrats. Yet the Democratic majority in Congress did pass a reform bill in 1991 that included some of these provisions as well as severe restrictions on PACs. Passage of this bill was a highly partisan process, which many assert was done for purely political reasons. In the Senate, fifty-one Democrats voted in favor of the bill (S. 3) and five opposed it, whereas only five Republicans supported it and thirty-seven voted against the bill. Many assert that the Democrats passed the bill to appear to be the party of reform, knowing full well that the Republican president would be waiting in the wings to ensure that it would not be enacted, thereby giving the Democrats a "free vote." As expected, President Bush vetoed the bill.[27]

The 103d Congress (1993–1995)—with Democratic majorities in both chambers and a new, proreform, Democratic president—came close to enacting campaign finance reform. But reformers could not overcome Republican delaying tactics and filibusters in the Senate. Thus, no campaign finance reform bill passed. In 1994 the Republicans took control of the House for the first time in four decades, and the GOP took back control of the Senate, which it had lost in 1986.[28] Republican lawmakers, especially the large class of GOP freshman legislators, stormed into office promising reform, but not necessarily campaign finance reform. House Republicans focused on lobbying reform and banning gifts to members of Congress. Yet the issue of campaign finance reform would not go away. On June 11, 1995, at a town meeting in Claremont, New Hampshire, the Democratic president, Bill Clinton, and the Republican Speaker of the House, Newt Gingrich, were asked by a man in the audience to establish a commission to explore changes to the campaign finance system. The commission would be modeled after the base closures commission; this commission, which makes recommendations about which military bases to close, is unique in that Congress must adopt or reject the recommendations without changes. Clinton and Gingrich surprised their own aides by embracing the idea and sealing their agreement with what became a well-publicized handshake.

In 1995, Sens. John McCain, R-Ariz., and Russell Feingold, D-Wis., introduced a bill that would ban PAC donations to Senate candidates, place voluntary limits on spending in congressional campaigns and provide free or reduced-rate television and mailing privileges to candidates who abide by the spending limits, prohibit incumbents from sending franked mail during an election year, and ban soft money. A similar bill was introduced in the House. Neither proposal was considered. In all, more than ninety campaign finance reform bills were introduced in the 104th Congress (1995–1997). None of them passed.

All these efforts to reform the campaign finance system in the 1980s and into the 1990s focused primarily on the influence of PACs and special interests, the growing cost of congressional elections, and the financial advan-

President Bill Clinton (*left*) and House Speaker Newt Gingrich shake hands to agree to create a campaign finance reform commission at a town meeting in June 1995.

tages of incumbents. These reform measures included severe limits on PACs, restrictions on the bundling of contributions by PACs, voluntary spending limits in exchange for public financing or for free or reduced-cost media for candidates, and restrictions on PAC independent expenditures. Although there were some attempts to address other issues, such as soft money, political action committees were the primary target of the reformers and the perceived cause of what was wrong with the campaign finance system. After the 1996 elections, however, the focus of campaign finance reform began to shift toward other issues.

A New Era of Campaign Finance Reform

New developments in campaign financing have shifted the focus of reform efforts toward issues that now appear more menacing than PACs. Critics of the *Buckley* decision complain that the Supreme Court has limited the supply of money for campaigns by limiting contributions, but it has not reduced the demand for campaign funds because it has not upheld spending restrictions as well. This, they argue, eventually encouraged candidates, parties, interest groups, PACs, corporations, labor unions, and wealthy individuals to look for loopholes in the law that would allow them to raise and spend more money. The political scientist Frank Sorauf, an insightful specialist on campaign finance, notes that "the flow of money erodes the regulatory barricades. Political learning—as adept always in avoiding restraints as in honing strategies—finds the new devices of avoidance, the weaknesses in the restraints, the unanticipated avenues of free action. In short, the experts begin to beat the system."[29]

By 1996 the experts had really figured out how to beat the system. Fundraising and spending practices during the 1996 campaign brought allegations that campaign finance laws had been violated or at least skirted. In the final weeks of the presidential election that year, there was an explosion of news stories about illegal foreign contributions to the Democratic National Committee (DNC). For example, the *Washington Post* reported: "Clinton Faces Floodgate of Probes; Campaign Fund-Raising Inquiry Looms"; the *New York Times* announced: "Loopholes Allow Presidential Race to Set a Record"; and the *Los Angeles Times* noted: "GOP Candidate Says President's Failure to Address Democrats' Acceptance of Illegal Donations Is an Admission of Wrongdoing."[30]

The Democrats were also accused of selling overnight stays in the Lincoln Bedroom at the White House and of access to President Clinton in exchange for large contributions to the party. Vice President Al Gore attended a fundraising event at a Buddhist temple and made telephone calls from federal government property to raise soft money. The Democrats ended up returning more than $3 million in large, soft money contributions that may have come from foreign corporations.[31] At least one political observer, the pollster John Zogby, argued that Clinton's failure to get 50 percent of the popular vote in 1996 was due to the campaign finance controversy that surfaced in the last weeks of the campaign.[32]

The Republicans were accused of fund-raising irregularities as well. The Republican presidential nominee, Bob Dole, allegedly accepted illegal corporate contributions, and the Republican Party was accused of selling access to top GOP lawmakers in exchange for $250,000 in soft money contributions.[33] Yet these allegations attracted little media or public attention.

Money from foreign sources was actually only a small portion of the total amount of unregulated soft money raised by the parties during the campaign, but this was the issue that focused public and media attention on campaign finance reform. The campaign finance expert Anthony Corrado commented at the time that "[t]here's a certain xenophobic aspect to it. . . . The real issue is not foreign contributions. It is the entire soft money system which has really gone out of control."[34] The size of soft money contributions to the national political parties in 1996 and the abandon with which both parties raised and spent the controversial money led many to conclude that the wheels had fallen off the campaign finance regulatory system. A key reformer,

Rep. Christopher Shays, commented that the system had begun to "collapse on itself," and one proreform public interest group, Common Cause, accused both parties of "massive violations" of the campaign finance laws.[35]

The 1996 campaign finance transgressions became the most publicized campaign finance scandal since Watergate, and the alleged illegalities revived demands for campaign finance reform. After the elections, in the opening weeks of the 105th Congress, Republican leaders wasted no time in calling attention to the allegations against the Democrats and commenced investigations in both the House and the Senate on the charges. Meanwhile, legislators proposed several campaign finance reform bills. Yet all the reform bills faced strong opposition from the majority-party Republican leaders (but not from all Republicans). Thus, the battle was on.

The Shift in Focus to the "Twin Evils"

After more than a decade of reform efforts that attempted to restrict PACs, limit campaign spending, and provide for public financing of congressional elections, the focus of reform shifted to various perceived loopholes in the campaign finance system that were revealed so starkly during the 1996 election. Political action committees still contribute a good deal of money in federal elections (see Figure 1-3). Their role, however, has been inherently limited because of the PAC contribution limits set by the FECA and because inflation has chipped away at the real value of these limited contributions. The potential for interest groups and their PACs to wield too much influence over who gets elected and what they do once they get to office still exists. Yet the regulated activities of PACs now constitute a much smaller portion of all campaign finance activity than they did in the 1980s as new methods of influencing federal elections, ones that are not nearly as regulated or subject to public disclosure, have come to eclipse PAC spending.

Some of these controversial campaign finance practices were evident by the mid-1980s. Yet concern escalated as more candidates, parties, interest groups, corporations, labor unions, and wealthy individuals began to work through the loopholes in the law to raise and spend significant amounts of money. The most contentious of these campaign finance practices are soft money, first used in the 1980 presidential election by the Republicans, and the use of issue advocacy advertising to influence federal elections. These activities get around the contribution limits imposed by the FECA and allow parties, interest groups, corporations, labor unions, and wealthy individuals to escape the close public scrutiny of regulated campaign finance practices. These campaign finance practices have contributed to the recent growth in the amount of money spent to influence federal elections. They have become the new bad guys of the campaign finance system, the "twin evils" that reformers now aim to root out.[36]

The term *soft money* was coined by the journalist Elizabeth Drew.[37] It refers to political party fund-raising and spending that occur outside of the scope of federal laws that limit contributions and require detailed public disclosure of campaign finance activities.[38] It is called soft money because it is "not subject to the 'hard' limits of the law," and it often is collected from sources that are barred from participation in federal elections, such as corporations and labor unions.[39] As we noted earlier, Congress did not intend soft money to be a loophole for the parties to spend unlimited money from unregulated sources. The 1979 FECA amendments allowed for hard money (federal money that is raised and spent in limited increments from regulated sources) to be used for grassroots, volunteer-based party-building activities, such as voter registration and GOTV drives, and for overhead expenses. The 1979 revisions simply exempted parties from having to count their hard-money spending on these grassroots activities against their limited contributions directly to candidates. The Federal Election Commission, however, issued advisories that allowed political parties to use unregulated and unlimited nonfederal, or soft, money to pay for a portion of these party-building activities (see n. 9). Thus, the national parties were provided with a way to raise unlimited amounts of money from individuals and PACs who may have already given the maximum hard money contribution and to collect unlimited donations from corporations and labor unions, which have long been prohibited from contributing money in federal elections.

What makes soft money so controversial is that it comes in very large amounts from these unregulated sources that were originally barred from participating in federal elections because of the potential for undue influence and corruption. Soft money allows corporations to use their profits, labor unions to use dues collected from their members, and wealthy individuals to use their personal wealth to make huge, unlimited contributions to political party organizations. Soft money thus bypasses the contribution limits for hard money donations and skirts around the intent of the FECA to regulate and make public all federal election campaign finance activities.

The raising and spending of soft money is technically legal. The parties may use soft money to pay for a portion of overhead and grassroots party-building expenses (the FEC has set allocation formulas for this purpose that spell out how the parties must allocate their expenditures for these expenses between hard and soft money). Although soft money may not be spent di-

Figure 1-7   Soft Money Disbursements by National Party Committees from
Nonfederal Accounts, 1992–1998

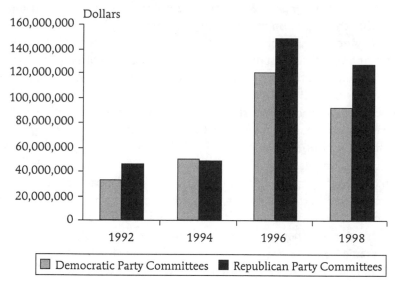

Source: Compiled from data in Norman J. Ornstein, Thomas E. Mann, and Michael J.
Malbin, *Vital Statistics on Congress, 1999–2000* (Washington, D.C.: AEI Press, 2000), 110.

rectly on federal candidates or their races, soft money spending does benefit
federal candidates in three important ways. First, federal candidates benefit
from their party's voter registration and GOTV efforts, because these activities help identify and turn out partisan voters. Second, using soft money to
help pay for voter drives and overhead expenses, such as rent, utilities, and
payroll, frees up the more-difficult-to-raise hard money for giving directly to
candidates and spending on coordinated expenditures (expenditures parties
can make on behalf of candidates). Finally, parties use soft money to produce and run issue advocacy advertisements that indirectly help their candidates win.

Political parties raised and spent record amounts of soft money for the
1996 campaigns. Soft money spending by the national Democratic and Republican party organizations rose from $79 million in 1992 to $271 million
in 1996.[40] In Figure 1-7 we show the growth in the spending of party soft
money from 1992 to 1998. The chart includes the total amounts of soft
money spent by all the parties' national party committees: the Democratic
National Committee, the Democratic Senatorial Campaign Committee, the

Democratic Congressional Campaign Committee, the Republican National Committee, the National Republican Senatorial Committee, and the National Republican Congressional Committee. Campaign finance reformers charge that this explosion of soft money threatens to take "democracy" out of our democratic elections by allowing wealthy interests to play a much greater financial role than ordinary citizens. Thus, it is not surprising that soft money became the primary focus of campaign finance reform efforts in Congress after the 1996 election.

After the 1996 election, reformers turned their attention to another highly controversial campaign finance practice—issue advocacy advertising. The Supreme Court's 1976 ruling in *Buckley v. Valeo* allows interest groups, corporations, labor unions, political parties, and wealthy individuals to avoid regulation by federal campaign finance laws as long as the advertisement does not expressly advocate the election or defeat of a candidate for federal office.[41] They may use unregulated and undisclosed funds to promote their views and issue positions, and they may refer to particular elected officials or candidates. The Supreme Court narrowly defined what is considered a campaign communication, and what, therefore, is subject to regulation, to include only those communications that expressly advocate the election or defeat of a clearly identified candidate by using what have come to be called the "magic words," such as "vote for" or "vote against." The Court held that it was necessary to be precise and clear when specifying what communications would be governed by the FECA, particularly because criminal penalties could be imposed for violating the law. These magic words come from a footnote in the *Buckley* case opinion, in which the Court listed some explicit advocacy terms that satisfy the strict "express advocacy" test: " 'vote for,' 'elect,' 'support,' 'cast your ballot for,' 'Smith for Congress,' 'vote against,' 'defeat,' or 'reject.' "[42]

Communications that use such express advocacy terms are subject to the contribution limits and reporting requirements set out in the FECA and its amendments. Any communication that does not use such terms and, therefore, falls outside of this narrow definition of express advocacy is considered issue advocacy and is not subject to these restrictions. Because issue advocacy ads are not considered to be related to federal elections, the sponsors of such communications are not required to disclose the sources of their funding, or where and how their money was spent. They are free to pay for these issue advocacy advertisements with money that is prohibited or severely restricted when it is used in connection with a federal election. For example, parties use soft money to pay for a portion of issue advocacy communications, and corporations use profits from the corporate treasury. Consequently, interest groups, labor unions, corporations, political parties, and wealthy individuals have come to take advantage of this narrow definition of express advocacy by designing communications that avoid the magic words but are similar to conventional campaign commercials in every other way. The sponsors of issue advocacy advertisements are able to send the same message as the one contained in regulated campaign ads—namely, that some candidate does or does not deserve one's support—while avoiding the contribution limits and reporting requirements stipulated for official campaign communications. When run during the election season, issue advocacy ads cause a great deal of controversy because they potentially influence the outcome of an election without being subject to the campaign finance rules that govern federal elections.

The recent controversy over issue advocacy ads (often called "issue ads") began when the Democratic National Committee used a combination of hard money and soft money to run issue ads in twenty-four states in 1995 and 1996. Since the ads did not use the magic words, the DNC could use soft money to pay for part of them. The DNC transferred the soft money to state party committees so that they could buy the ad time locally. Thus, the DNC was able to conserve its hard money, which is more difficult to raise because it must be raised in small increments and is the only party money that may be spent directly on behalf of candidates.[43] Here is one of the issue advocacy ads run by the DNC early in the 1996 election in which President Clinton was running for reelection against the former senator Bob Dole, (Gingrich was the rather unpopular Republican Speaker of the House at the time):

> *Announcer:* Protect families. For millions of working families, President Clinton cut taxes. The Dole/Gingrich budget tried to raise taxes on eight million. The Dole/Gingrich budget would've slashed Medicare $270 billion, cut college scholarships. The President defended our values, protected Medicare. And now a tax cut of $1,500 a year for the first two years of college, most community colleges [are] free. Help adults go back to school. The President's plan protects our values.[44]

The Republican National Committee ran this issue advocacy ad, titled "Pledge," during the 1996 election:

> *Clinton:* I will not raise taxes on the middle class.
>
> *Announcer:* We heard this a lot.

Clinton: We gotta give middle class tax relief, no matter what else we do.

Announcer: Six months later, he gave us the largest tax increase in history. Higher income taxes, income taxes on Social Security benefits, more payroll taxes. Under Clinton, the typical American family now pays over $1,500 more in federal taxes. A big price to pay for his broken promise. Tell President Clinton: You can't afford higher taxes for more wasteful spending.[45]

Interest groups, corporations, labor unions, and individuals also run issue ads. Here is one that the AFL-CIO, America's largest labor federation, ran in many congressional districts in 1996:

Carolyn: My husband and I both work. And next year, we'll have two children in college. And it will be very hard to put them through, even with the two incomes.

Announcer: Working families are struggling. But Congressman X voted with Newt Gingrich to cut college loans, while giving tax breaks to the wealthy. He even wants to eliminate the Department of Education. Congress will vote again on the budget. Tell Congressman X, don't write off our children's future.

Carolyn: Tell him, his priorities are all wrong.[46]

These television ads are not considered campaign ads because they do not expressly advocate the election or defeat of a candidate by using the magic words. Thus, they can be paid for with unregulated and unrestricted money. Yet it seems clear that they were designed to influence the outcome of an election.

While avoiding the legal tripwire of express advocacy, interest groups and parties were coming uncomfortably close to taking control of the dialogue of candidates' own campaigns, for candidates still had to pay for campaign communications with funds raised in small increments from specified sources. In some 1996 congressional races, spending on issue advocacy broadcasts and mailers exceeded what the candidates spent themselves.[47] Thus, when candidates who had experienced issue advocacy advertisements from outside groups in their own campaigns made it to Congress, many of them were highly motivated to bring these communications under federal regulation, just as their own communications with voters were.

Two other campaign finance practices, bundling and independent expenditures, also concern reformers. Bundling involves an intermediate agent, usually a PAC or interest group, that collects checks made payable to a specific candidate and delivers those checks to the candidate. Both the individuals who write the checks and the PAC or interest group that collects and bundles them get credit for the donations. Bundling allows a PAC to exceed the limits on contributions to candidates because the checks they collect are written by someone else and do not count against the group's limit. Some bundling PACs operate publicly and openly. For example, EMILY's List ("Early Money Is Like Yeast") collects and forwards checks to pro-choice Democratic women candidates. Yet most bundlers' activities and the interests they serve are not known to the public. Reformers, therefore, have become particularly concerned about the growing use of bundling, particularly because most of it occurs behind closed doors. Despite this concern, however, the leading reform bills eventually dropped provisions related to bundling, for the reformers feared that these provisions might impede the bills' passage.

An independent expenditure is money spent by individuals or groups on communications with voters to support or oppose a clearly identified candidate. There can be no coordination or consultation with the candidate or his or her campaign. These expenditures must be paid for with funds that are raised in accordance with the FECA and are reported to the FEC.[48] Yet the Supreme Court held in *Buckley v. Valeo* (1976) that limits on independent expenditures constitute a violation of the First Amendment right to free speech. Thus, a group or individual may now spend unlimited amounts on independent expenditures. In 1996 the Supreme Court ruled that political parties may also make independent expenditures, but that they must use regulated and limited hard money to pay for them.[49] Although this ruling came rather late in the election year, both parties made independent expenditures in 1996. The Republicans started earlier and spent $10 million. The Democrats were waiting for the FEC to issue regulations for party independent expenditures, and when it failed to do so, the Democratic Party went ahead and spent $1.5 million. Independent expenditures in House and Senate elections went from $2.4 million in 1980 to $20.6 million in 1996, and there were charges that some independent expenditures were illegally coordinated with campaigns in 1996.[50] Reformers see these expenditures as excessive and, once again, as something that has the potential of drowning out candidates' own communications with voters.

The terms of the campaign finance reform debate began to shift with the growing acknowledgment that these loopholes posed a more severe threat to the campaign finance system than PACs and high campaign costs. Political action committees, which were once perceived as a source of corruption that threatened to undo the system, were now seen as one of the more legitimate avenues for raising and spending campaign money. After all, at least PACs were regulated and their activities disclosed. Moreover, with their decisive victory in the 1994 congressional elections, the Republicans helped knock the wind out of concerns over issues like competition and incumbency bias.

In the wake of the campaign finance controversies surrounding the 1996 elections, the 105th Congress opened with heightened support for campaign finance reform. Supporters of the Bipartisan Campaign Reform Act, called the McCain-Feingold bill in the Senate (S. 25) and the Shays-Meehan bill in the House (H.R. 3526), understood the changing terms of the debate. In September 1997, the McCain-Feingold bill was pared down to focus primarily on soft money and issue advocacy advertisements. The Shays-Meehan bill also was later altered from its original form to focus on these issues.[51] Attacking these "twin evils" allowed the reformers to take advantage of the media attention focused on these legal loopholes during the 1996 election and to bring together a larger coalition in support of the bill.

Although many reformers preferred the original version of the bill, which included free television time in exchange for voluntary spending limits, sponsors of the Bipartisan Campaign Reform Act in both chambers contended that the updated version still had enough teeth to accomplish meaningful reform of the campaign finance system. The revised version also dealt with foreign money, coordinated independent expenditures, and, to some extent, the advantages enjoyed by wealthy candidates. Perhaps more important, the revised bill actually had a chance of passing. According to Rep. Marty Meehan, "The Shays-Meehan campaign finance reform bill is a scaled back version of our original legislation. It represents a compromise struck between what Chris [Shays] and I wanted to pass and what we believed could pass in the current political climate. It's not the perfect bill. But perfection is too often the enemy of the good."

A Tale of Unorthodox Policymaking

What makes the story of campaign finance reform in the 105th Congress worth telling is the insights that it provides into the contemporary congressional policymaking process. Scholars are accustomed to discussing the flowchart model of "how a bill becomes a law," complete with the predictable journey of introduction, committee and subcommittee action, floor action, conference committee review, final floor consideration, and, finally, presidential approval. Yet this textbook model does not (and perhaps never did) accurately describe the way many bills proceed through Congress. In both chambers, but especially in the House of Representatives, legislation quite often proceeds along a much less predictable path. Modern legislating features a variety of unorthodox or nonstandard strategies for assisting (or hindering) measures in traveling unpredictable and often unique pathways through the legislative process.[52] The journey of campaign finance reform legislation through the Senate and the House during the 105th Congress was characterized by many of these unorthodox procedures and reveals much about how and why they were used as well as the different outcomes that can result in the two chambers.

When the stakes are high and powerful players, such as party leaders, bipartisan groups of legislators, or congressional-presidential coalitions, strongly desire a particular outcome, the inclination toward innovation is also high. Beginning in the 1970s, the regular use of innovative and unorthodox strategies and processes became more common. Now these special procedures and practices have become the norm rather than the exception, particularly in the House. One scholar's survey of the procedures used for major legislation in the House and Senate in the late 1980s and early 1990s revealed that four out of five measures in the House and two out of three measures in the Senate were considered under some unorthodox or unusual process.[53] The textbook model is clearly not the operative model in the modern Congress.

There are many possible unorthodox procedures and practices that might be utilized in the House and Senate. The majority party leaders in the House have perhaps the largest number of unorthodox tools at their disposal and, as a result, a higher likelihood of using these tools to achieve their legislative objectives. For instance, the majority party leadership, and, therefore, quite often the Speaker of the House, controls the schedule of legislation for floor debate. As one might expect, the timing of when a bill is presented for a vote to the entire House can greatly influence its chances of success. Thus, effective floor scheduling requires close attention to a variety of political and policy factors, such as whether there is great public support for the measure or whether the president has threatened to veto the bill.

In the House, bills are generally brought to the floor for consideration either through suspension of the rules or through special rules from the Rules Committee, and both procedures can be used in unorthodox ways to achieve a desired result. These procedures are controlled by the majority party leadership. Noncontroversial bills are often considered under suspension of the rules, which allows for only forty minutes of debate (twenty minutes for each side), no amendments, and a two-thirds vote for passage. The Speaker alone can determine which bills are on the suspension calendar. Use of suspension of the rules is quite common and usually draws little criticism because it tends to move noncontroversial legislation along. Recently, however, Speakers have put controversial legislation on the suspension calendar in an effort to either pass or kill some high-profile measure. Using suspension of the rules in this manner has drawn considerable criticism from within and outside of Congress.

More controversial or significant legislation generally is brought to the House floor by a special rule from the Rules Committee. The special rule allows a bill to be taken up whenever the majority party leadership desires, regardless of when it was introduced or when it emerged from a committee. Majority party members of the Rules Committee are appointed by the Speaker, so he has great influence over the committee's decisions. The special rule establishes the terms for a bill's consideration on the floor. At a minimum, a rule specifies the amount of time that will be allowed for debate and who will control that time, which is usually split between the chairperson and the ranking minority member of the committee that reported the measure or the sponsor and an opponent of the bill. Rules also often specify the number and nature of amendments that will be allowed and provide for other special provisions. In the contemporary House of Representatives, most rules restrict amendments, and, as with campaign finance reform legislation during the 105th Congress, rules are often carefully crafted for specific debates to produce the outcome preferred by the majority party leaders.

In the Senate, legislation makes it to the floor for consideration by all senators via a very different route. The majority party leadership in the Senate has much less control over scheduling bills and the terms for their consideration on the floor primarily because any senator can control the floor indefinitely unless or until sixty senators vote to cut off the debate. That is, any senator can filibuster, or speak for an unlimited amount of time, on a measure, and the debate can be forced to end only when sixty or more senators vote for cloture. Moreover, most bills are brought to the floor for consideration by unanimous consent, whereby any senator can object to a bill's consideration. Thus, the Senate majority leader is compelled to consult with all interested senators, including the minority party leader, before attempting to bring measures to the floor. Clearly, being the majority party in the Senate is not as meaningful as it is in the House.

Other unorthodox procedures include bypassing the committee of jurisdiction altogether, making adjustments to legislation after it leaves committee, and using creative strategies for floor consideration. For example, campaign finance reformers in the House bypassed committee consideration by using a discharge petition to persuade GOP leaders to schedule a vote on campaign finance reform legislation. If a discharge petition is signed by half

(218) of the House members, it will force a measure from a committee to the floor for consideration. As the reformers got closer and closer to the required 218 signatures on the discharge petition, the majority party leaders decided it would be better to bring the issue to the floor on their own terms rather than letting the reformers control the debate, and they created a complex special rule for consideration of a large number of reform bills. GOP leaders hoped that the more comprehensive bill preferred by the reformers would be defeated when it came up against many other options that were less sweeping and, therefore, easier for many lawmakers to vote for.

The political scientist Barbara Sinclair conducted a comprehensive study of the use of unorthodox policymaking procedures in both chambers, and she found that the use of unorthodox procedures tends to make legislating easier in the House but more difficult in the Senate.[54] This was the case with campaign finance reform legislation during the 105th and 106th Congresses, when the issue experienced different fates in the two chambers. The blocking mechanisms available in the Senate, such as the filibuster and unanimous consent requirements, generally serve to hinder passage of legislation, whereas many of the unorthodox procedures used in the House, such as the discharge petition and the power of the Speaker to control the schedule, can ease the way of bills through that chamber.

Contemporary policymaking is further complicated by the regular occurrence of divided government, in which one party holds the White House and the other party controls at least one chamber of Congress, and by the recent increase in partisanship in Congress. If the government is to enact any new laws, Congress and the president generally must agree to it. Divided government makes this much less likely. And when partisan attachments are strong, cooperation between the parties is also unlikely. These conditions encourage lawmakers to try to gain political advantage by blaming the other party for inaction or by using an issue to score political points for the upcoming election rather than actually acting on it.

The battle for campaign finance reform in the House and the Senate featured numerous examples of unorthodox methods under the conditions of divided government and heightened partisanship that help bring the dynamics of contemporary congressional policymaking into clear focus. The following chapters chronicle these strategies, as well as more traditional procedures, as they were used by both reformers and those opposed to reform in attempts to influence the outcome of this intense policy debate. By calling attention to these insights about the process, we can better understand the changing roles that party leaders, interest groups, the media, and individual legislators might assume.

Plan of the Book

In the chapters that follow we examine the roles of various players in the legislative journey of campaign finance reform during the 105th and 106th Congresses, the strategies they employed, the unusual nature of this issue, and the story itself. Chapter 2 covers the campaign finance reform process in the Senate and the complex constitutional issues that surround campaign finance reform. Congress is a bicameral institution within a system of separate government institutions, and no policy proposal will succeed without positive consideration by both chambers. Although this book is primarily about the journey of the Shays-Meehan Bipartisan Campaign Reform Act through the House of Representatives, the Senate process is important to understand, for the fate of the issue was ultimately determined there. Moreover, the different nature of policymaking in the two chambers can be grasped only with a clear understanding of how things work in both.

In Chapter 3 we describe the campaign finance reform debate in the House of Representatives, paying particular attention to the many unconventional policymaking tools and strategies that were used by both sides to advance or halt the progress of reform. We chronicle the convoluted journey of a bill that just would not die despite the best efforts of the majority party leadership to kill it. This examination of these unorthodox methods gives the reader familiarity with the various strategies pursued during the process, and in other chapters we draw on these methods in analyzing the role of different players and factors in the policymaking process (for example, the Senate, political parties, interest groups, and the media).

In Chapter 4 we examine the reformers and their opponents themselves and how campaign finance reform is an unusual policy area because it is an issue with little or no direct "electoral connection" for most members of Congress.[55] That is, giving one's time and energy to this issue is generally thought to have no real individual payoff at the next election as other issues do, such as obtaining federal funds for highway construction or securing tax cuts for one's constituents. Thus, campaign finance reform attracts an unusual group of issue leaders and policy entrepreneurs willing to devote their time to the issue and able to grasp the complexities of the laws, regulations, and court decisions they aim to reform. We discuss the leaders on both sides of the campaign finance reform debate within the context of theories about policy entrepreneurship, constituency and electoral influences, interest group influence, and other hypotheses that aim to explain why and how legislators become leaders on policy issues.

The role of the political parties in the debate over campaign finance reform is the focus of Chapter 5. Many scholars and journalists have argued that the election of the Republican majority in 1994 signaled a return to strong party government in the House. But the battle over campaign finance reform points to the impact that the manifestation of factions within the new Republican majority has had in the context of an institution that lends credibility to issue leaders and "cover" to majority party members who defy their party's leaders on this issue. The campaign finance reform debate is a perfect illustration of the development of a modern cross-partisan coalition, one that is primarily made up of legislators from one party with a small but significant number of legislators from the other party. A cross-partisan coalition involves numerous trade-offs and constraints in order to maintain such a disparate group in pursuit of a common policy goal. Within this unstable context, where the moorings of party are loosened, we further explore the importance of strong issue leaders on both sides of the issue for whom expertise and intense interest concerns become strong motivators for behavior.

In Chapter 6 we discuss the importance of the external issue network of interest groups and the media. These external players can have a great effect on the course and outcome of legislative debates. We examine how a number of organized interest groups have long worked to enact campaign finance reform legislation and sought to have a voice in its development, and how other groups mobilized to counter their efforts. The reform effort also hatched some unusual partnerships or alliances of "strange bed fellows," such as the one between the Christian Coalition and the American Civil Liberties Union (ACLU). The "strange bed fellow" alliances that emerged during the course of the campaign finance reform debate are colorful and intriguing examples of how and why interest groups form coalitions to achieve their policy goals. The strategies employed by groups on both sides of the reform debate nicely illustrate the many ways that interest groups attempt to influence the policymaking process.

We also consider the media in Chapter 6. The political power of the media has long been recognized. Yet, most congressional scholars argue that the media play at most a marginal role in congressional policymaking as regards agenda setting and influence.[56] Indeed, most textbooks on Congress do not include a chapter on the media. We saw firsthand, however, that the media can and did have a great impact on the fate of legislation in Congress.

Chapter 7 chronicles the effort to pass campaign finance reform in 1999 during the 106th Congress. It is a tale of history repeating itself, as reform went down to defeat in the Senate as before. Once again the use of many unorthodox policymaking procedures characterized the debate over reform, and this second round of campaign finance reform drives home the particularly obstructive nature of these unorthodox methods in the Senate. We also consider the role of campaign finance reform as an issue in the 2000 presi-dential election, particularly the focus put on reform by Senator McCain, a GOP presidential candidate and one of the leading sponsors of the Biparti-san Campaign Reform Act in the Senate.

In Chapter 8 we discuss what this unusual process of policymaking has taught us. The effort to enact campaign finance reform allows us to draw some general conclusions about Congress, politics, and policymaking, as well as about congressional leaders, political parties, interest groups, and the media. For example, we draw on some of the classic and more contemporary policymaking models to assess what can be learned about legislating in today's complex environment.[57] We also explore what the process illustrates for each of the actors involved, and we consider what can be learned about reform politics in general.

2

ENTERING THE LABYRINTH
Considering Campaign Finance Reform in the Senate and Debating the Constitution

The self-proclaimed "Darth Vader" of the campaign finance reform debate stood on one side and the prisoner-of-war-turned-crusader on the other. Both from the same party, they were definitely not on the same side of this issue. It seemed like a match-up destined for headlines, but this legislative battle played out under very little media scrutiny. Arch reform opponent Sen. Mitch McConnell, R-Ky., confidently announced that "[n]o one in the history of American politics has ever won or lost a campaign on the subject of campaign finance reform."[1] Winning elections was a primary concern for McConnell—not only winning his own election but also securing victory for other Republican Senate candidates. During the 1997–1998 election cycle, McConnell chaired the National Republican Senatorial Committee (NRSC), which is responsible for electing Republicans to the Senate.

As we saw in Chapter 1, most Republicans oppose campaign finance reform. Most GOP legislators are ideologically opposed to further government regulation in this and other areas, but the practical reality is that the current campaign finance system gives the Republicans the financial advantage. Thus, Senator McConnell was hardly motivated to change the laws, for the current system allowed him to raise record amounts of money, much of it soft money, for Republican Senate candidates. For example, in the 1998 election cycle, McConnell's NRSC raised $80 million for GOP candidates. Yet

McConnell also vehemently believed that many of the campaign finance reform proposals would impinge on fundamental First Amendment free
speech rights. McConnell is consistent in his beliefs regarding the First
Amendment, even if it means that at times he must defy his party's position.
For example, McConnell voted against a constitutional amendment that
would have prohibited flag burning, a measure that most of his Republican
Senate colleagues supported. McConnell has become a relentless crusader
against attempts to reform the campaign finance laws and has led more than
one filibuster to kill the measures in the Senate. The various renditions of
McConnell as the "black knight" or the "Darth Vader" of campaign finance
reform capture his determination to defeat reform that he considers to be an
"evil" that threatens the First Amendment to the Constitution.[2]

In the 105th Congress, that "evil" was the McCain-Feingold Bipartisan
Campaign Reform Act, a bill championed by two mavericks, Sen. John Mc-
Cain, R-Ariz., and Sen. Russell Feingold, D-Wis. Although the bill was the
product of a bipartisan effort between the two senators, Senator McCain
clearly was the more identifiable of the two. Perhaps it was because of his status as a war hero. McCain spent five and a half years as a prisoner of war in
Viet Nam, where he endured torture and solitary confinement after his Navy
fighter plane was shot down. Like other public figures who have fought for
their country or a great cause, McCain enjoys a special kind of respect because of his POW experience.[3] Or maybe McCain received more attention
because he was willing to take such a prominent position on an issue his
party did not support. He has a reputation for independence and has defied
his party's leaders on other issues as well, such as the tobacco settlement legislation he sponsored in 1998.

Or perhaps McCain's notoriety as a reformer stemmed from the fact that
he himself was caught in the Keating Five scandal a decade earlier. He was
one of five senators who in 1987 intervened in a federal investigation of a
failed savings and loan company operated by a wealthy contributor, Charles
Keating. McCain's own ethics were called into question, and in 1991 the
protracted Ethics Committee investigation of the Keating Five affair resulted
in a rebuke from his Senate colleagues. More than one commentator has
speculated that McCain's drive for campaign finance reform might be to reform his own image. Yet McCain seems quite sincere in his advocacy of reform issues. His reform efforts are not confined to campaign finance reform.
McCain's disgust with corruption and waste in government has earned him
the respect of many of his Senate colleagues and a large number of good-
government groups and journalists. For example, each year Senator McCain

releases a report of the most offensive pork barrel projects contained in the proposed federal budget.[4] His report highlights both Democratic and Republican projects, much to the discomfort of his own Republican colleagues. On another reform issue, McCain brokered the compromise that led to passage in 1995 of new Senate rules that restricted the value of gifts and meals senators may accept from lobbyists to $50 and eliminated vacations for legislators paid for by lobbyists and their interest groups. During that debate, McCain said, "We do not need tickets to lavish balls to do our jobs. We do not need $100 gift baskets to do our jobs. And we do not need unlimited, expensive free meals to do our jobs."[5]

McCain was the perfect GOP advocate for campaign finance reform. He is a conservative, and being out front on this contentious issue sent a signal to other legislators that it was legitimate for a conservative to support campaign finance reform. His tell-it-like-it-is, no-nonsense style also helped keep reporters interested, just as he did with his virtually continuous press conference aboard his campaign bus, the "Straight Talk Express," during his bid for the Republican presidential nomination in 2000. For all these reasons Senator McCain was known as a reformer, and by the time the 105th Congress opened in 1997 he was seen as that body's most prominent proponent of campaign finance reform.

Although the legislative battle on campaign finance reform promised to be a fascinating policy debate, its execution was grounded in constitutional debates, case law summaries, and legislative rule manipulation. In the Senate, where a minority of senators may prevent action on a measure, this match between the reformers and their opponents is key to understanding why campaign finance reform would not become law despite the fact that a majority of senators supported it. This match-up in the Senate would prove to be the opening act for the House process, and one that lent important insights to the rounds that lay ahead.

An Impetus for Reform? Congress Addresses the 1996 Scandals

Many thought that campaign finance reform stood a chance of passage in the 105th Congress. The alleged campaign finance scandals of the 1996 election involving the Democrats and President Bill Clinton had led to an increased demand for change. That election left a bad taste in many lawmakers' mouths. Numerous charges flew between the two major parties in the wake of the election: illegal foreign contributions; attempts by the Chinese government to influence U.S. elections; nights in the White House Lincoln

Bedroom in exchange for campaign contributions; the laundering of campaign money through conduit groups; the huge sums of soft money collected by both political parties from corporations, labor unions, and wealthy individuals; and the uncontrolled use of issue advocacy ads by outside groups and parties. Congressional Republicans wasted no time calling attention to the allegations against the Democrats, and as the majority party in Congress they had the tools at their disposal to do so. In the opening weeks of the 105th Congress, GOP leaders commenced investigations and scheduled hearings in both the House and the Senate on the campaign finance scandals of 1996. These investigations focused almost exclusively on allegations against Democratic president Bill Clinton and his vice president, Al Gore.

Yet in this charged atmosphere, campaign finance reform was not necessarily the goal of congressional Republican leaders. The Senate investigation was led by Sen. Fred Thompson, R-Tenn., an advocate of reform, and the House probe was headed by Rep. Dan Burton, R-Ind., who was no great fan of campaign finance reform. Their hearings did not feature discussions of remedies to avoid such scandals in the future, for the proceedings were designed to highlight wrongdoings by the Democrats, not to avoid such improprieties in the future. The two chairmen's personalities, however, had as much to do with the tone of their panels' investigations as these other considerations. Representative Burton conducted his panel's investigation in the House as an exposé of Democratic campaign finance transgressions with fiery speeches, much grandstanding about alleged violations of the law, and dramatic visuals on videotape and poster boards. The House proceedings were made-for-television political theater. Yet they received very little news coverage, perhaps *because* of the high-pitched rhetoric that characterized them.

Chairman Thompson was more reserved, and although the Senate investigation he led certainly was characterized by its partisan focus, the proceedings were conducted in a less sensational manner. Senator Thompson was chosen because of his tough but fair approach and because of the significant role he had played in the Watergate hearings more than twenty years earlier. As a young lawyer, Thompson was the top staff attorney to Sen. Howard Baker Jr., R-Tenn., and received praise for his adept handling of the Watergate questioning. The chance to use his notoriety to legitimize the current investigation was not lost on the Republican leaders. The GOP leaders, however, did not expect Senator Thompson to make the hearings bipartisan by allowing discussion of alleged Republican improprieties or to attempt to extend the investigation to congressional campaigns. They had no intention of using the hearings as a forum to craft campaign finance reform proposals and designed the proceedings accordingly. Thompson himself underestimated the partisan pressures that would come not only from the Democrats and the White House but from his own leadership. The hearings did raise many of the campaign finance indiscretions of the 1996 campaigns, but the proceedings never really captured the attention of the public. No "smoking gun" was uncovered, and although the Senate hearings received more news coverage than the House proceedings, the news media generally ignored much of what transpired. Reporters really took note only of the partisan bickering and possible foreign involvement in the 1996 election. As a strong advocate of campaign finance reform, Thompson was probably frustrated that the hearings did not lead to more constructive action, and eventually he acted to bring the hearings to an end. Later he would agree that the investigative hearings fell well short of promoting solutions for serious campaign finance problems.

Charges of campaign finance violations also were levied against Republicans, but these allegations received little attention.[6] When the media did cover the hearings they focused primarily on the allegations against the Democratic president and vice president during and immediately after the election. Republican wrongdoings were largely ignored also because the Democrats were the minority party in both chambers of Congress and had little ability to control the hearings' schedules and proceedings. After all, the House and Senate hearings were devised to cast aspersions on the Democrats. The Senate majority leader, Trent Lott, R-Miss., hoped that the hearings would expose the Democrats' wrongdoings while he worked behind the scenes to ensure that the proceedings would not contribute to the call for campaign finance reform. It was a risky political strategy, because exposing the Democrats' campaign finance improprieties also exposed the significant weaknesses of the campaign finance regulations, which might lead to a greater demand for reform.

Debating Reform in the Senate

To many, the Senate was the first and last best hope for passage of campaign finance reform legislation. With generally more flexible rules in the Senate than in the House and the support of a majority of senators, reform proponents hoped that it was only a matter of time before the legislation would receive Senate approval. The opponents of reform, however, had powerful weapons of their own, the First Amendment of the Bill of Rights and the filibuster, that they ultimately used to defeat campaign finance reform in the Senate.

Reformers in the Senate and House agreed that the Senate should take the lead with the McCain-Feingold bill, a measure with both Democratic and Republican support (but mostly Democratic) that offered a comprehensive package of reforms. In the early stages of the reform effort at the beginning of the 105th Congress, Senate and House reformers met with allied interest groups to discuss bill language, possible conflicts, ways to achieve consensus, and methods to assist and ensure passage first in the Senate and then in the House. Opponents of reform, led by the Republicans Mitch McConnell in the Senate and Tom DeLay of Texas in the House, also met at this point to devise strategies to defeat reform.

The McCain-Feingold bill, S. 25, the Bipartisan Campaign Reform Act of 1997, was introduced in the Senate on January 21, 1997, and referred to the Committee on Rules and Administration.[7] Senator McConnell was a senior member of the committee then and went on to become the committee's chairman in the 106th Congress. As discussed in Chapter 1, the bill started out as a comprehensive reform measure that contained provisions such as free television and radio time for candidates in exchange for campaign spending limits, reduced political action committee (PAC) contribution limits, and prohibitions on bundling. Yet many issues made these provisions controversial. For example, providing candidates with free television and radio airtime was opposed by one of the most powerful interest groups in the country, the National Association of Broadcasters. The NAB lobbyists did not hesitate to point out that their local affiliates in every congressional district in the nation controlled not only the scheduling of paid advertising, but local news programs as well. These local news affiliates covered the activities of every House member and senator in the country. Television stations raise a good deal of revenue selling airtime to candidates, and their owners were not going to forgo that income without putting up a fight. Republican leaders also opposed free airtime despite much positive editorial press in favor of the proposal.[8]

In addition, the Republicans challenged the proposed limits on PAC contributions as violating First Amendment free speech rights. Some were even concerned that the bill tried to accomplish too much. Consequently, a campaign finance system such as the one proposed in the original McCain-Feingold bill seemed unable to attract the support of a majority of senators, necessary for passage, much less the sixty votes needed to overcome the expected filibuster. Senators McCain and Feingold realized that they had to build a larger and more bipartisan coalition; a larger coalition of supporters to get enough votes to pass the bill and a more bipartisan—that is, more Republican—coalition to lend symbolic legitimacy to their effort and to help them beat down a GOP filibuster.

Lead sponsors of the Bipartisan Campaign Finance Reform Act in the Senate, Sens. John McCain, R-Ariz. (*left*), and Russell D. Feingold, D-Wis.

Herein lies one of the major problems lawmakers face in trying to craft a bill that will lead to a winning coalition of bipartisan support. One group of legislators might insist that a certain provision be included in the bill if they are to support it. If the sponsors of a bill include that provision, however, they may risk alienating other legislators who might otherwise support the bill if it were not for that provision. When dealing with groups on different sides of the partisan aisle, these differences sometimes can be quite fundamental. As a result, the debate surrounding a bill may center on ancillary provisions as opposed to the core issues that the bill addresses. Thus, legislators often must make strategic decisions as to what provisions will and will not be included in their legislation when they offer it on the floor. Political realities often dictate that lawmakers significantly alter their proposals to accommodate the need for a larger and broader coalition of supporters.

This problem led McCain and Feingold to modify their original bill in order to attract more supporters and improve the bill's prospects. The modifications limited the bill to these provisions:

1. Prohibit all soft money contributions to the national political parties from corporations, labor unions, and wealthy individuals, and prohibit state parties from spending unregulated soft money on activities in connection with a federal election.

2. Modify the statutory definition of "express advocacy" to provide a clear distinction between expenditures for communications used to advocate candidates, including those that do not use the magic words, and those used to advocate issues. Candidate-related expenditures would be subject to federal election laws regarding public disclosure and contribution limits; true issue advocacy expenditures would not.

3. Strengthen election laws by requiring greater disclosure of candidate fund-raising and expenditures to the Federal Election Commission.

4. Provide a strict codification of the Supreme Court's 1988 decision in *Communications Workers of America v. Beck,* in which the Court ruled that nonunion employees who are obligated to pay to a labor union their share of the cost of collective bargaining (that is, agency agreement fees) cannot be required to fund union political spending.[9] Labor unions must notify nonunion employees that they are entitled to have their agency fees reduced by an amount equal to the proportion of fees used for political purposes if they file an objection.

5. Bar the political parties from making "coordinated expenditures" on behalf of Senate candidates who do not agree to limit the spending of their own personal money for their campaigns.

6. Strengthen current law to prohibit foreign nationals from making any contributions or expenditures in federal, state, or local elections.

See Box 2-1 for a more detailed summary of the provisions in the McCain-Feingold bill.

Later, McCain and Feingold announced that they would make some additional modifications to the bill. Their press release on September 29, 1997, said they planned to offer an amendment to "level the playing field." The amendment would create a voluntary system to provide Senate candidates with a 50 percent discount on television costs if they agreed to raise a majority of their campaign funds from their home states, to accept no more than 25 percent of their campaign funds in aggregate PAC contributions, and to limit their personal spending to $50,000 per election.[10] This amendment, however, was never offered, probably because these controversial provisions were likely to drive away potential supporters rather than attract them.

Thus, with the controversial provisions removed, the McCain-Feingold bill focused primarily on efforts to regulate *sources* of funding outside the control of candidates themselves. The bill aimed to limit the raising and spending of soft money by political parties and to bring the spending on issue advocacy communications by interest groups, parties, corporations,

BOX 2-1 Summary of the McCain-Feingold Bill (S.25)

Contributions by Individuals
- Raises maximum contribution to state and local parties to $10,000 per year
- Raises maximum aggregate annual contributions to $30,000

Contributions by Parties
- No provision to change current law

Candidate Spending
- Prohibits party-coordinated expenditures when candidate spends more than $50,000 of personal funds
- Codifies regulations regarding personal use of campaign funds

Soft Money
- Bans national parties from raising or receiving soft money
- Bans state/local parties from spending soft money for certain activities
- Increases disclosure requirements
- Prohibits federal candidates from raising soft money for any federal election activity

Issue Advocacy
- Defines express advocacy to cover contexts in which the "magic words" are not used; exempts voter guides
- Amends FECA definition of *expenditure* to include payment for message with express advocacy, or refers to clearly identified candidate, to influence federal election

Independent Expenditures
- Tightens definition of coordination and cooperation
- Prohibits parties from making both coordinated and independent expenditures for general election candidates
- Strengthens disclosure requirements for large expenditures near election

Disclosure Requirements
- Requires electronic filing for large committees, and Internet posting within twenty-four hours
- Prohibits candidates from depositing contributions over $200 without required ID
- Lowers itemization threshold to $50 for contributions

continued

Box continued

- Allows random audits of campaigns within twelve months after election

FEC Enforcement
- Changes enforcement initiation criteria to "reason to investigate" standard
- Increases penalties for knowing and willful violations and establishes automatic penalties for late filing
- Expedites FEC enforcement actions late in election

Miscellaneous
- Codifies *Beck* decision and requires unions to notify nonunion workers of right to disallow political use of their dues
- Bans franked mass mailings in election year
- Strengthens law that prohibits foreign nationals from participating in any election.

Source: Compiled from Joseph E. Cantor, "CRS Report 98-287 GOV: Campaign Finance Reform Bills in the 105th Congress: Comparison of H.R. 3485 (Thomas), S. 25 (McCain-Feingold), and Current Law" (Washington, D.C.: Congressional Research Service, 1998).

---

labor unions, and wealthy individuals in the last sixty days of an election under the Federal Election Campaign Act (FECA) regulations. Many candidates, as well as those who advocate campaign finance reform, had come to view the use of soft money and campaign-like issue advocacy ads as threatening to take control of the campaign dialogue away from the candidates themselves, in part because soft money and issue advocacy activities are not subject to the contribution limits or to many of the disclosure requirements of the Federal Election Campaign Act. As we saw in Chapter 1, soft money and issue advocacy have become known as the "twin evils" of the campaign finance system, replacing PACs as the target of reform efforts. Compared with these new legal loopholes, PAC spending and potential influence now seem tame and controllable, particularly since inflation has diminished the value of PAC contributions.

The revised McCain-Feingold bill began making its way through the Senate in an atmosphere charged by the ongoing House and Senate investigations of just such campaign finance abuses during the 1996 election. This was an environment that reformers hoped would favor the adoption of changes to the nation's campaign finance laws. However, they did not count on the heightened partisanship that would steer the process. The Senate Republican leaders were using the investigative process in an unusual manner. Normally, the committee holding the hearings would investigate the allegations of wrongdoing, issue findings, and offer legislative remedies for addressing the problem. In this case, the GOP leaders did not want the Thompson committee hearings to be a forum for consideration of reform. Thus, they narrowed the scope of the committee's deliberations to the investigation of illegal activities only, ensuring that proposals for reform would not be considered. This put the Thompson committee's activities and findings on a separate track from the reform efforts of McCain, Feingold, and others. The committee's narrowed scope demonstrates how legislative leaders can use unorthodox procedures to inhibit (or advance) the progress of legislation.

Reform proponents had much working against them from the beginning of the debate. For instance, as the end of the first session of the 105th Congress grew near, Senate majority leader Trent Lott was not moving to bring campaign finance reform up for a vote before the chamber adjourned for the year. It was not until President Clinton threatened to use his authority to reconvene Congress if it adjourned without considering campaign finance reform that Senate leaders agreed to bring the revised McCain-Feingold bill up for a vote.[11] Presidents rarely use this power or even threaten to do so. Some might view this as evidence that President Clinton helped keep campaign finance reform alive at a key moment, but many on the Hill dismissed the action as a mere political show.

Yet, although the GOP Senate leaders had agreed to consider reform, they certainly had not agreed to support it. In fact, they did all they could to kill the McCain-Feingold bill. For example, Majority Leader Lott used a parliamentary tactic known in legislative parlance as "filling the amendment tree" with his own amendment, thus preventing anyone else from offering another amendment.[12] An amendment tree is the name given to the structure of a pending bill and its attached amendments.[13] The base bill represents the tree's trunk, and the proposed amendments are the branches stemming off from the trunk. The Senate's rules allow only two degrees of amendments (or to continue the tree analogy, two types of branches): first-degree amendments that would modify the base bill and second-degree amendments that would change a first-degree amendment.

When all the positions on the amendment tree (the pending bill, the first-degree amendments, and the second-degree amendments) are occupied, the amendment tree is filled.[14] As one scholar has noted, senators make tactical use of the amendment tree in three ways.[15] First, senators attempt to fill the amendment tree in such a way that their particular amendment is

voted upon first. Second, they try to use the amendment tree to preclude
their amendment from itself being amended. Finally, "perhaps the most
common amendment tree maneuver is to attempt to prevent any further
amending at all."[16]

It was this last maneuver that Majority Leader Lott used to block campaign finance reform. Although filling the amendment tree is a fairly common tactic among rank-and-file senators, Senate leaders rarely use this maneuver. When they do use it, it is to defeat legislation.[17] Lott's amendment
was the so-called Paycheck Equity Act (also known as the paycheck protection measure), originally sponsored by the majority whip, Sen. Don Nickles,
R-Okla. The amendment required that labor unions receive authorization
from both union members and nonmembers before using any dues, fees, or
payments for any political purposes. Such a requirement would place a
rather heavy and costly administrative burden on the unions and would significantly impair their ability to conduct political activities, which overwhelmingly favor Democratic candidates. Not surprisingly, the paycheck
protection measure was "vehemently opposed by Democrats as a 'poison
pill' " amendment that was designed to split the fragile coalition of reform
supporters.[18] House Democrats came to call the paycheck protection provision the "worker gag rule," a reference to their belief that the provision
would deny American workers (that is, union members) a voice in election
campaigns. Moreover, many Democrats viewed the Paycheck Equity Act as
retribution for the approximately $35 million that organized labor had spent
on issue advocacy ads against GOP candidates in 1996.[19] Senator Lott hoped
that bringing this amendment forward would force the Democrats to filibuster the proposal. Thus, in the eyes of the public, the Democrats would be
responsible for killing campaign finance reform.

The Senate minority leader, Tom Daschle, D-S.D., tried working with Sen.
Olympia Snowe, R-Me., to reach a compromise that would defeat the paycheck protection amendment and "re-open the amendment tree."[20] Senator
Snowe then worked with Sen. James Jeffords, R-Vt., to offer this compromise
in the form of the Snowe-Jeffords amendment to the McCain-Feingold bill.
In an attempt to soften the McCain-Feingold bill's restrictions on issue
advocacy ads in order to gain more support for the measure, the Snowe-
Jeffords amendment proposed to narrow the type of communications that
would be considered express advocacy and therefore subject to new, more restrictive regulation. The amendment replaced the broad definition of express
advocacy in the McCain-Feingold bill with the term *electioneering communications* and narrowly defined such communications as those that refer to a
candidate for federal office and are broadcast in the last sixty days of a gen-

eral election or the last thirty days of a primary election. The Snowe-Jeffords amendment further required that once a group spent $10,000 in a year on such electioneering messages, it must disclose these activities to the Federal Election Commission.

More controversially, however, Senators Snowe and Jeffords sought with their amendment to find a compromise between the Republican leadership's antiunion paycheck protection language and the reformers' position. To this end, the Snowe-Jeffords amendment would require all membership organizations, including labor unions, corporations, and interest groups such as the National Rifle Association and the Sierra Club, to get the consent of their members or stockholders before spending dues or profits on political activities.[21] Senator Nickles summed up the Republican response to the Snowe-Jeffords amendment by indicating that he would "vigorously oppose attempts to require prior written consent of shareholders before corporations can fund political activities."[22] Most GOP senators wanted to curb union political activity but not corporate political activity, which generally favored Republican candidates. Many accused the Republicans of being less interested in reform than in punishing labor for its 1996 issue ads and crippling an important supporter of Democratic candidates.

This high-stakes bargaining over campaign finance reform illustrates how much each side potentially had to gain or lose depending on whether and how the rules of the game changed. As one might expect, no compromise on union and corporate political activity was reached, and the Senate debate on the pared-down McCain-Feingold bill led to three failed attempts on October 7, 8, and 9, 1997, to get the sixty votes necessary to invoke cloture and stop the GOP filibuster. On October 7 the vote was fifty-three for and forty-seven against cloture; on October 8 and 9 it was fifty-two for and forty-seven against. With these votes, reform opponents sustained their filibuster and blocked passage of the McCain-Feingold bill.

Despite this defeat, however, Senate reformers saw some hope for the future. Even though the reformers repeatedly fell short of the sixty votes needed to end the filibuster, they still garnered support from a majority of the senators. This implied that if campaign finance reform ever were to be voted on directly in the Senate, it likely would pass. Additionally, even though the votes generally split along partisan lines, seven Republicans crossed the aisle to vote with the Democrats for cloture. Given these promising numbers, reformers continued to press for a vote on the McCain-Feingold bill itself.

As a result, Majority Leader Lott and Minority Leader Daschle agreed to a unanimous consent agreement, a procedural method used in the Senate to move business along by setting the terms for consideration of a bill. Al-

though any one senator potentially can block a unanimous consent agreement (UCA), such agreements serve as the primary means by which the
Senate structures proceedings on certain bills. The UCA provides the Senate
leadership with "a tool for scripting proceedings" by, for example, setting
time limits on each component of debate, deciding which senators will control debate time, and establishing certain voting procedures. The UCA also
has a greater effect than simply deciding procedural issues; negotiations over
the content of the unanimous consent agreement sometimes can affect the
substantive outcome of legislation.[23] The Lott-Daschle UCA called for a vote
on the McCain-Feingold bill sometime before March 6, 1998. According to
the agreement, after the vote on the McCain-Feingold bill, Senator Lott
"would be permitted to hold a vote on an alternative bill to his liking."[24]
Many expected this bill to be the controversial Paycheck Equity Act.

Prior to the opening of the second session of the 105th Congress in January 1998, Majority Leader Lott was rumored to be planning to spring a vote
on the reform bill before the reformers could get ready, but Lott called the
idea of a "surprise" vote "humorous."[25] Also around this time, excerpts from
the Senate Governmental Affairs Committee's 1,500-page draft report on
the alleged campaign finance violations during the 1996 election were released. The report was prepared by the Republican staff, and it chronicled
primarily alleged Democratic campaign finance violations. As is customary,
the final report included only a small section written by the minority party.
The Democrats' section highlighted questionable Republican campaign finance activities.[26] Meanwhile, Senators Snowe, Jeffords, and John Chafee,
R-R.I., had continued working on a compromise on labor union and corporate political activity since the October filibuster. According to Senator
Snowe, they were "trying to bridge the gap between [supporters of campaign
finance legislation] and the concerns on the Republican side about leveling
the playing field in terms of the role unions play."[27]

On February 25, 1998, the Snowe-Jeffords language was added to the
McCain-Feingold bill by voice vote. But the very next day, reformers failed
to end a GOP filibuster of the amended bill, securing only fifty-one of the
sixty votes needed for the cloture vote to cut off debate. Immediately after,
the Senate considered Senator Lott's Paycheck Equity Act, and it too was defeated when only forty-five senators voted for cloture to end a Democratic-
led filibuster. This left the Senate in a stalemate, so Lott pulled the bills from
the floor and moved on to consideration of "popular pork barrel legislation
to allot transportation projects to the states, [and] no one objected."[28]

On the Senate floor the Republican leaders and key Republican senators,
such as Mitch McConnell of Kentucky, were able to turn the debate over

campaign finance reform into one about the First Amendment and freedom of speech. Faced with this barrage of First Amendment attacks, the McCain-Feingold legislation was hopelessly filibustered. During the debate supporters of the McCain-Feingold bill and the Snowe-Jeffords amendment tried to fend off the constitutional attacks hurled by the opponents, but reform opponents found ways to call each proposal into question by portraying campaign finance reform as an attack on the First Amendment.

Calling on the Constitution and the Courts

Ever since Congress passed the original Federal Election Campaign Act of 1971 and its subsequent sweeping amendments in 1974, courts have had to address a variety of challenges to these laws. Most of the current debate over campaign finance reform can be traced back to the seminal decision in the 1976 Supreme Court case *Buckley v. Valeo*. Stemming from this case, the main arguments raised by opponents of the McCain-Feingold bill centered on the issue of whether reforms that attempt to restrict communications that advocate a candidate's election or defeat and reforms that limit campaign expenditures are unconstitutional limits on First Amendment freedom of speech rights. Additionally, other constitutional issues raised in the debate included the codification of the Supreme Court's decision in *Communications Workers of America v. Beck* regarding the use of money collected by labor unions and certain Tenth Amendment issues arising from attempts to ban soft money transfers to the party committees in the states.

Constitutional Issues Involving Campaign Finance Reform

In the *Buckley* case, the Supreme Court addressed First Amendment issues related to the regulation of campaign finances for the first time.[29] The Court ruled that expenditures made by candidates and others in relation to a federal campaign, as opposed to contributions to a candidate or party, are a form of political expression protected by the First Amendment. As a result, the Court found most of the 1974 amendments to the FECA to be unconstitutional, including the provisions establishing spending limits (except those for political parties). Furthermore, while upholding limits on contributions to political campaigns generally, the Court distinguished between an expenditure that expressly advocates the election or defeat of a candidate and an expenditure that advocates a position on an issue. The FECA's limitations on expenditures for express advocacy, in which someone expressly promotes the election or defeat of a candidate by using what have come to be called the "magic words" such as "vote for" or "vote against," were deemed constitutional.[30]

The Court ruled that the First Amendment, however, protected expenditures made by noncandidates that do not use the magic words expressly to advocate the election or defeat of a federal candidate. As a result, the Court rejected the FECA's restrictions on expenditures for issue advocacy communications—that is, television, radio, or printed communications that advocate some position on an issue—even if they mention a candidate for federal office. But some reformers argued that even though many of these so-called issue advocacy advertisements do not use the magic words to expressly advocate the election or defeat of a candidate, they still make it clear that particular candidates should be supported or opposed because of their position on some issue. Moreover, since many of these advertisements are run in the final days before an election, voters often perceive the message as advocating one candidate over another. Yet the Supreme Court ruled in *Buckley* that spending for these issue advocacy communications could not be limited and did not have to be reported to the FEC for public disclosure, because they constituted speech protected by the First Amendment.

Thus, for example, an interest group, corporation, labor union, party, or individual could spend an unlimited amount of money that did not have to be disclosed publicly to the FEC to run an issue advocacy ad such as this one ten days before the election: "Congress recently raised taxes for senior citizens on Social Security, and Senator Scrooge voted for this tax increase. Call Senator Scrooge and tell him he is wrong to raise taxes on senior citizens." Yet the same organization or person could spend only limited amounts that were collected in small increments and have to report that fund-raising and spending to the FEC if the ad were a campaign ad such as this: "Congress recently raised taxes for senior citizens on Social Security, and Senator Scrooge voted for this tax increase. Vote against Senator Scrooge on November 8."

One would have to listen very carefully to detect much of a difference between the two ads. One very politically involved observer, the executive director of the National Rifle Association's Institute for Legislative Action, put it this way: "It is foolish to believe there is any practical difference between issue advocacy and advocacy of a political candidate. What separates issue advocacy is a line in the sand drawn on a windy day."[31]

Finally, as a result of the *Buckley* decision, individuals were not restricted in spending their own funds on their own campaigns or as independent expenditures, for such expenditures were deemed by the Court to be protected speech. Thus, wealthy candidates such as Ross Perot and Steve Forbes may spend as much of their own money on their own campaigns as they wish. Moreover, any individual (or PAC) may spend an unlimited amount of his or her own money on independent expenditures to advocate the election or defeat of a candidate other than themselves, as long as those expenditures are not coordinated with the candidate they are intended to help. Critics see these rulings as establishing an unfair advantage for the wealthy.

The Supreme Court has addressed campaign finance issues in two other key cases in which the Court extended its distinction between express and issue advocacy. In *Federal Election Commission v. Massachusetts Citizens for Life, Inc.* (1986), the Court concluded that only express advocacy expenditures (that is, only those that use the magic words) violated the FECA's prohibition against the use of corporate funds in connection with a federal election.[32] Therefore, corporate funds *could* be used for issue advocacy communications (such as the first ad above), even in the last days before an election. Ten years later, in *Colorado Republican Federal Campaign Committee v. Federal Election Commission* (1996), the Court permitted political parties, in addition to PACs and individuals, to make unlimited independent expenditures as long as the political party's expenditures were truly independent of candidates and their agents and were paid for with regulated and disclosed funds.[33] This ruling split the justices and has been criticized by some observers who argue that it is impossible for a party to act independently of its own candidates, particularly when some party spending is coordinated (for example, coordinated expenditures).

The *Buckley* decision and these other cases narrowed the extent to which campaign financing is regulated. Some U.S. courts of appeals, however, have interpreted the *Buckley* case differently, with the most notable difference of opinion arising between the Ninth Circuit Court on one side and the First and Fourth Circuits on the other. In *Federal Election Commission v. Furgatch* (1987), the Ninth Circuit Court concluded that the distinction between express advocacy and issue advocacy is not as clear-cut as the *Buckley* decision would imply.[34] The Ninth Circuit argued that an advertisement could promote the election or defeat of a candidate without using the so-called magic words. In the *Furgatch* case, the Court insisted that the context in which the communication is made must be taken into account. It developed a three-pronged test that centered on whether a reasonable person would determine that an advertisement is express advocacy that conclusively calls for the election or defeat of a candidate and therefore should be subject to regulation:

First, even if it is not presented in the clearest, most explicit language, speech is "express advocacy" for the present purposes if its message is unmistakable and unambiguous, suggestive of only one plausible meaning. Second, speech may only be termed "advocacy" if it presents a clear plea for action, and thus speech that is merely informative is not covered by the Act.

Finally, it must be clear what action is advocated. Speech cannot be "express advocacy of the election or defeat of a candidate" when reasonable minds could differ as to whether it encourages a vote for or against a candidate or encourages the reader to take some other kind of action.[35]

The Federal Election Commission made the *Furgatch* test part of its regulations. The First Circuit Court, however, in *Maine Right to Life Committee, Inc. v. Federal Election Commission* (1996) rejected the FEC's use of this reasonable person standard.[36] In the *Maine Right to Life Committee* (MRLC) case, the court interpreted *Buckley* as providing a "bright-line test"—that is, a rigid and easy-to-apply test in which a communication is considered express advocacy only if the magic words are used.

This decision followed the First Circuit's decision in *Faucher v. Federal Election Commission* (1991).[37] The issue in *Faucher* was whether voter guides prepared by the Maine Right to Life Committee constituted express advocacy. The voter guides indicated whether or not members of Congress had voted for positions supported by the National Right to Life Committee. But they also included this statement: "The publication of the MRLC November Election Candidate Survey does not represent an endorsement of any candidate(s) by MRLC." Finding that the voter guides constituted issue advocacy rather than express advocacy, the court held in the *Faucher* case that "trying to discern when issue advocacy in a voter guide crosses the threshold and becomes express advocacy invites just the sort of constitutional questions the Court sought to avoid in adopting the bright-line express advocacy test in *Buckley.*"[38]

The Fourth Circuit supported the First Circuit's interpretation in *Federal Election Commission v. Christian Action Network* (1997).[39] Noting that the magic words were necessary to establish express advocacy (or as stated in the decision, the "Constitutional minima"), the Fourth Circuit Court believed that the *Buckley* decision "unambiguously" stood for the proposition that the Constitution "forbids the regulation of our political speech under . . . indeterminate standards."[40] The differing interpretations of express advocacy by these courts meant that both sides of the reform debate had the support of case law for their arguments.

The Senate directly and extensively debated the First Amendment issues raised by campaign finance reform generally and by the McCain-Feingold bill specifically. We will consider how senators invoked these issues in more detail below. In the House of Representatives, the debate regarding First Amendment freedom of speech focused on the issue of voter guides such as those discussed in the *Faucher* case (see Chapter 3). The First Amendment arguments posed during the Senate debate seemed to catch some of the reform proponents off guard. The task force of reformers from the House and Senate, however, worked to fortify their position against these constitutional arguments so that the House reformers were more prepared to respond to them than their Senate colleagues had been.

Although the First Amendment issues discussed above were the primary constitutional focus during the campaign finance reform debate, other legal and constitutional issues arose as well. For example, many opponents of the McCain-Feingold and Shays-Meehan bills questioned the section of the measures that purported to "codify" the Supreme Court's 1988 decision in *Communications Workers of America v. Beck.*[41] The *Beck* case involved the agency fees collected by unions from nonunion employees who enjoy the benefits of the union's collective bargaining agreements. The *Beck* decision and the corresponding provision in the McCain-Feingold and Shays-Meehan bills ensured the right of nonunion members to get back that portion of their agency fees used for political purposes. Campaign finance reform proponents contended that in combination with the ban on soft money and treating issue ads that featured the name or likeness of a candidate as campaign ads to bring them under FECA regulations, the *Beck*-derived provision would greatly limit the usage of union dues—even if voluntarily designated—for political purposes.[42]

For reform opponents, the *Beck* codification in the McCain-Feingold bill (and Shays-Meehan bill in the House) did not go far enough. For them the concept of campaign finance reform and union money meant the implementation of the so-called paycheck protection measure. This would have the effect of extending the *Beck* decision to union members as well, thus severely hampering unions' ability to expend *any* of their funds on political activities. Although derived from a legal argument, the effort to implement the paycheck protection measure was strongly motivated by partisan politics, for the proposal sought to impair the ability of labor unions, a core Democratic constituency, to participate in politics. Moreover, Republican leaders in both chambers of Congress knew that attaching the paycheck protection provision to any campaign finance reform bill would be a poison pill amendment that would drive away Democratic support and therefore ensure defeat of that measure. It should not be surprising then that many GOP lawmakers opposed to reform tried to amend reform bills by adding the paycheck protection provision.

A final constitutional issue arose in the House and involved the Tenth Amendment, which reserves to the states those powers "not delegated to the United States by the Constitution, nor prohibited by it to the States." Campaign finance reform opponents and even some supporters expressed concern that the McCain-Feingold and Shays-Meehan bills' ban on soft money at both the federal and state levels would have the effect of federalizing state campaigns, thus violating the Tenth Amendment. They argued that only the states themselves, not the federal government, have the authority to ban the use of soft money on the state level. This was a fundamental question of federalism for them, for the provision aimed to change the balance of power between the states and the federal government. The reform proponents countered that state parties would still be able to raise soft money permissible under state law, provided that they did not spend the money in connection with federal elections. Neither side, however, was convinced by the other.

In each of these areas—free speech, union dues, and federalism—both proponents and opponents of campaign finance reform sought to base their positions squarely on constitutional principles. Yet, for each the use of constitutional arguments served a decidedly political purpose, namely, the passage or defeat of campaign finance reform legislation. Although issues related to the *Beck* decision and the Tenth Amendment played important roles in the legislative process, the fundamental constitutional debate centered on the First Amendment freedom of speech issue. And nowhere was the connection between constitutional analysis and political goals more explicit than in the Senate's second debate over the McCain-Feingold bill in February 1998.

Invoking the Constitution on the Senate Floor

In early February 1998, the Senate debated campaign finance reform for the second time in the 105th Congress. By this time, reform opponents had shaped the Senate debate successfully by making campaign finance reform a First Amendment issue. As a result, they continued characterizing the McCain-Feingold bill as a measure that violated the freedom of speech. Reform supporters, faced with having to debate their bill on terms established by their opponents, argued in support of their bill along several different lines. In the end, however, even with only a minority of senators on their side, the reform opponents who set the tone of the debate won it.

Senators infused the debate with references to court cases and constitutional controversies. Reform opponents tried to portray the restrictions that the McCain-Feingold bill would place on the issue advocacy ads under question as violations of the First Amendment. Sen. Mitch McConnell mocked the reformers' definition of issue ads as campaign ads: "[s]ham issue advocacy is the reformer's favorite pejorative term of art for First Amendment

Source: Congressional Quarterly

Sen. Mitch McConnell, R-Ky., the leading opponent of campaign finance reform in the Senate.

protected speech. . . . They say it is sham speech because—brace yourself—it might actually affect an election. Well by all means." Contending that interested voters and organizations should be able to express their viewpoints on issues, McConnell continued, "And there could be some citizen group with all their 'sham' issue advocacy spoiling the election, messing the election up, fussing the election up with issues, for goodness sake—with issues."[43]

With this last point, Senator McConnell highlighted the difference between what he saw as the political ramifications of issue advocacy and its constitutional implications. McConnell conceded that candidates (himself included) do not like independent issue advocacy ads, particularly those ads run against them, but, he argued, campaigns are not for candidates to control. McConnell noted, "the Supreme Court has given no indication that the political candidates are entitled to control all of the discourse in the course of a campaign."[44] By framing the debate in these terms—that is, who should be allowed to participate in the electoral discourse—McConnell put reform proponents on the defensive. They had to show that the McCain-Feingold bill with the Snowe-Jeffords amendment, which narrowed the type of communications that would be considered express advocacy, would not exclude any dialogue from electoral debates.

Faced with the daunting task of having to defend the constitutionality of their bill on terms established by their opponents, reform proponents used several approaches. One approach was to counter that reform opponents did not, in fact, have the Constitution on their side and to imply that their opposition was perhaps more strategic than sincere. For example, Senator Jeffords used this argument during the February 1998 debate, noting that "there is an adage in the legal debate that when the facts and law are not in your favor you tend to shout loudly and improperly about irrelevant principles of free speech. The opposition has done a masterful job on that."[45]

The reformers' main approach, however, did not challenge their opponents head on. Instead, reformers accepted the primary assertion that the *Buckley* decision generally protected campaign-related expenditures as speech, and they sought to place their bill within the limited restrictions that the *Buckley* decision allowed. Senator Snowe, in defending the constitutionality of her amendment, argued that "it would meet the *Buckley* standards handed down in that Supreme Court decision of not being invasive. . . . [T]his would pass constitutional muster."[46] Senator Snowe placed her amendment within the standards that the judiciary had established for regulating campaign finance:

> [T]he Supreme Court has made clear that, for constitutional purposes, electioneering is different from other speech. . . . Congress has the power to enact a statute that defines "electioneering" in a more nuanced manner, as long as its definition adequately addresses the vagueness and overbreadth concerns expressed by the Court. This amendment carves out, in a clear and narrow way, a new category of electioneering that meets the Court's criteria.[47]

Snowe's language reflects the difficult situation that reform proponents faced in defending their legislation on their opponents' terms. Whereas Senator McConnell argued in terms of fundamental tenets underlying American democracy, reform supporters such as Senator Snowe talked about nuances and narrowly drawn legislation. The tenor of such a debate lacks the type of drama that draws the interest of the media, the attention of the constituents back home, or the support of other legislators. It also lacked the drama found in other parts of the campaign finance reform debate.

Despite the disadvantage of arguing on unfavorable terms, Senator Snowe continued to attempt to address the reform opponents, specifically Senator McConnell, by arguing that Supreme Court doctrine supported reform. She cited a 1954 Supreme Court case in which "the Court upheld disclosure requirements for lobbyists, despite the alleged chilling effect that those requirements might have on the right to petition the Government." In direct response to McConnell, Senator Snowe noted that "[o]f course, the *Buckley* Court itself, which the Senator from Kentucky [McConnell] frequently refers to, upheld disclosure requirements for groups who make independent expenditures," a suggestion that there is really no reason to exempt those who run issue advocacy ads from disclosure requirements.[48] She also listed the names of fourteen highly prominent constitutional and political scholars, including Norman Ornstein of the American Enterprise Institute, E. Joshua Rosenkranz of the Brennan Center for Justice, and Professor (and former member of Congress) Abner Mikva, of the University of Chicago, who all agreed that the reformers' approach indeed was constitutional.

Many outside groups used this last tactic as well in mobilizing to assist the reformers. For example, the Brennan Center for Justice recruited more than a hundred constitutional scholars to sign a letter that affirmed the constitutionality of the reforms proposed in the McCain-Feingold bill. In addition, the Aspen Institute Campaign Finance Project, led by former vice president and senator Walter Mondale, D-Minn., and former senator Nancy Kassenbaum Baker, R-Kan., organized a coalition of former House members and senators from both parties who favored campaign finance reform.

Finally, other reform proponents used a third line of argument to highlight the perceived need for change to the current campaign finance system. Instead of relying on judicial doctrine to support their position, these proponents contended either explicitly or implicitly that the courts were part of the problem. Specifically, judicial decisions helped create the rules, loopholes, and limitations on campaign finance regulations that allowed many of the abuses in the system. Senator Jeffords argued that "issue ads [permitted under *Buckley*] have turned into blatant electioneering" and are one of the primary reasons for the extreme growth in campaign spending and an area of great concern.[49] Sen. Byron Dorgan, D-N.D., asserted this viewpoint more directly on the Senate floor:

> We passed a piece of campaign finance reform legislation in 1974, and the rules since 1974 have been bent and twisted and people have gone under them and over them, and the result now, not only because of what has happened with those rules but *also because of some court decisions,* is that we have a campaign finance system in total chaos.[50]

Reform opponents, however, rejected these assertions. Once again, they couched their arguments in a call to protect the fundamental First Amendment right to free speech. Sen. Pat Roberts, R-Kan., asserted that "[a]dvocates of this resolution want us to believe the need for Congress to limit campaign spending is so great that First Amendment rights are secondary." Roberts also drew on *Buckley* and noted what he saw as the negative effects of the proposed reform legislation: "A restriction on the amount of money a person or groups can spend on a political communication during a campaign necessarily reduces the quantity of expression by restricting the number of issues discussed, the depth of their exploration, and the size of the audience reached."[51]

Of course, Senator McConnell entered the debate on the Snowe-Jeffords amendment as well. Confident that the force of the First Amendment was on his side, the self-proclaimed Darth Vader of campaign finance reform set out to destroy the proponents' arguments. He started by taking apart the judicial underpinnings of the reform effort: "Now, those who advocate McCain-Feingold and the Snowe-Jeffords proposal . . . have precious few court cases upon which to base their arguments. Most prominent among these is the Ninth Circuit's *Furgatch* decision. . . . The *Furgatch* limb upon which their issue advocacy regulation case rests is a pretty weak limb."[52]

McConnell also countered Senator Snowe's claim that scholars considered her amendment to be consistent with the First Amendment. Rejecting this claim, McConnell emphasized that the "American Civil Liberties Union [ACLU], America's experts on the First Amendment, say that it falls short of the free speech requirements of the U.S. Supreme Court in the First Amendment." Having the leaders of this traditionally liberal free speech advocacy organization on his side was a bit of a coup for Senator McConnell and one in which he took great pride. In addition to citing the ACLU, McConnell noted on more than one occasion that his view also had been articulated by "the great conservative Thurgood Marshall . . . that money is essential for effective communication in a political campaign."[53] Here McConnell was ironically referring to one of the most liberal justices to have served on the Supreme Court to lend legitimacy to his position.

Finally, McConnell invoked the nature of American democracy to question whose views should be presented in the context of an election: "The proponents of this proposal seem to me to be dismayed at all of this speech out there polluting our democracy and our campaigns. The presumption underlying that, of course, is that we as candidates somehow ought to be able to control elections, as if only our voice should be heard."[54] These were difficult arguments to counter.

In the end, although the reform proponents hoped that the Snowe-Jeffords amendment would be a sufficient enough compromise to attract additional support for reform, the odds were stacked against them entering the February 1998 debate. Even though a majority of senators apparently supported reform, reform opponents knew that they could defeat any cloture vote on their filibuster. Additionally, reformers were unable to counter effectively the fact that their opponents had defined the terms of the debate by presenting campaign finance reform as a First Amendment issue. Perhaps the statement made during the debate on the Senate floor that best characterizes the nature of the debate was offered by Senator McConnell: "We are not quietly killing [the McCain-Feingold bill], we are proudly killing it. We are not apologizing for killing this unconstitutional bill. We are grateful for the opportunity to defend the First Amendment."[55]

Reform Dies in the Senate—Again

Although the reform opponents' constitutional arguments indeed had caught some of the reformers off guard, in the end, reform was stymied by a filibuster, not by the force of convincing constitutional arguments. The McCain-Feingold bill did have the support of a majority of senators, but not the supermajority of sixty votes needed to invoke cloture to end the GOP's filibuster. Additionally, campaign finance reform opponents had the majority party leadership on their side, ensuring that the rules for considering reform would favor them. Senator McConnell acknowledged this support upon defeat of the McCain-Feingold bill with his filibuster:

> I want to thank the distinguished majority leader [Senator Lott] for his superb leadership and for helping us pick our way through the mine field of campaign finance one more time. He has truly been outstanding. I just wanted to tell him how much I and the rest of the 48 of his party who believe deeply in the First Amendment appreciate this, and for his leadership on this subject.[56]

With the majority party leaders and their procedural tools on their side and with the ability to filibuster, campaign finance reform opponents were virtually ensured victory in the Senate.

Despite the defeat by filibuster in the Senate once again, the House moved to take up reform. This too was a winding and difficult road. But after a long, hard fight the Shays-Meehan bill passed in the House in August 1998. Reformers were ecstatic and hopeful that the measure might pass the Senate in a third round of consideration. As might be expected, however, GOP Senate leaders were reluctant to consider the issue at all, having already done so twice before in the 105th Congress, and they hoped that it would go away without further consideration by the Senate. Moreover, the Senate reform effort lost a good deal of steam as Senator McCain seemed to withdraw his active support of the McCain-Feingold bill. Some reformers suspected that McCain was not up for another bruising battle after losing the last two rounds to a filibuster and also failing to gain Senate passage of his significant anti-tobacco legislation.[57] Indeed, a third and final attempt to pass the McCain-Feingold bill in the Senate, prompted by House passage of its companion bill, the Shays-Meehan bill, ended in much the same way as prior efforts. The bill was offered as an amendment (S. Amdt. 3554) to the Department of the Interior appropriations bill on September 8, 1998, but the amendment was withdrawn on September 10 after a 52–48 cloture vote failed to end yet another filibuster.

In the contemporary Senate, as in the House, more and more bills are handled in unorthodox ways that do not conform to the traditional model of how a bill becomes a law. Campaign finance reform is a good example, for it has been repeatedly subject to filibusters, a parliamentary tool used more frequently in this era of unorthodox policymaking. In general, the use of such unconventional procedures makes legislating more difficult in the Senate but facilitates lawmaking in the House. As the political scientist Barbara Sinclair notes:

> Given senators' willingness to exploit their prerogatives [for example, their right to talk as long as they wish, to filibuster, to offer multitudes of amendments, and to propose nongermane amendments] and the lack of any cost to them within the chamber of doing so repeatedly, successful lawmaking requires accommodating individual senators and most controversial legislation requires sixty votes for Senate passage [that is, the sixty votes required to invoke cloture and end a filibuster].[58]

In the struggle over campaign finance reform, such unusual procedures as the frequent use of the filibuster did make legislating more difficult in the Senate and in this case gave the Senate opposition the tools necessary to block the legislation. In contrast, unorthodox methods often smooth the path of legislation in the House.

Conclusion: At a Crossroads in the Labyrinth

The battle for campaign finance reform in the Senate laid the groundwork for understanding the political dynamics of the debate. The debate raised issues of constitutionality and law and highlighted for the House reformers the arguments that opponents would use to drive wedges in coalitions and holes in the initiative. The First Amendment arguments that opponents made against reform were particularly difficult to counter. The same First Amendment assertions emerged during the debate over reform in the House of Representatives. The Senate process provided valuable insight for the House Republican leaders to use in opposing reform and for proreformers in advocating it. The House GOP leaders used whatever legislative tactics they could to try to stop campaign finance reform, and the reformers were better prepared to counter the First Amendment attacks and the Republicans' many tactical strategies.

In the Senate, however, the ability of a small number of individuals to prevent action through filibusters provides a unique barrier to pursuing reform in the future. A majority is not good enough to pass a bill in the Senate, for a supermajority of sixty out of a hundred senators is necessary to overcome a filibuster. Thus, until there are sixty senators who all favor the same reform measure, comprehensive campaign finance reform is unlikely to make it to the president's desk.

3

CAMPAIGN FINANCE REFORM IN THE HOUSE
An Issue Whose Time Had Come?

The headline of the *Washington Post* op-ed piece read "Guinea Pigs in California."[1] The column was about the special election to pick a successor to the late Democratic representative Walter Capps from the central coast area of California. This House race had become the latest illustration of the inadequacies of the campaign finance regulatory system: "It could mark the beginning of a new era in American politics when outside groups with money to throw around seize control of campaigns from the parties, from local people and even from the candidates they are purportedly trying to help."[2] National political groups had spent at least $325,000 on independent expenditures, issue advocacy ads, phone banks, direct mail, and voter guides for the January 13, 1998, all-party special primary election.[3] The election pitted two GOP California assemblymen against one another and gave Democrat Lois Capps, Walter Capps's widow, 45 percent of the vote. Falling short of an outright majority, Capps would face Republican state assemblyman Tom Bordonaro in the March 10 special general election.

The barrage of noncandidate "independent" ads continued through the special general election, even though both candidates urged the outside groups to stay out of their race. But there was nothing the candidates could do about it. While the outside groups focused on late-term abortion and term limits, the candidates tried to talk about education, immigration, health care, and Social Security. These outside groups can raise unlimited amounts of unrestricted money to broadcast their messages as issue advocacy ads, whereas the candidates must raise money in small increments from restricted sources. Thus, the candidates themselves are at a financial disadvantage, which diminishes their ability to compete with the outside groups for airtime to deliver their campaign messages. This California special election, coming just as campaign finance reform was going down to defeat for a second time in the Senate, reenergized campaign finance reformers in the House, and the victor, Lois Capps, became for some the new "poster child" for campaign finance reform. She was the candidate who had made it through the battleground of issue ads and independent expenditures and was determined to do something about the unbridled influence of these unregulated messages.

Yet the McCain-Feingold campaign finance reform bill had fallen victim in the Senate to attacks that it violated First Amendment free speech rights. These attacks allowed those who opposed campaign finance reform, including the Senate Republican leadership, to wrap their arguments in the shield of the Bill of Rights, a powerful means of calling any legislative action into question. Thus, it is not surprising that the McCain-Feingold bill was hopelessly filibustered and died in the Senate for a second time on February 26, 1998. Still, the ability of a minority of senators to defeat a bill with a filibuster is a potent tool not available to House members.

Defeat of campaign finance reform in the Senate did not temper the drive for reform in the House. Instead, reform leaders in the House believed that their passage of a reform bill might encourage the Senate to revisit the issue and mobilize political pressure to gain the additional eight senators needed to defeat a likely filibuster. The Senate's inaction also seemed to stimulate the development of creative and unusual strategies to push for passage of a House campaign finance reform bill. An unusually high number and variety of unorthodox procedures were used in the House, demonstrating the inclination of contemporary congressional lawmakers to find nontraditional ways to pursue their goals when the stakes are high and the drive to succeed is strong. In this chapter we chronicle the campaign finance reform battle in the House during the 105th Congress, and we demonstrate the significance of such unorthodox processes in contemporary congressional policymaking.

In the Other Chamber: Addressing the 1996 Scandals

Like the Republicans in the Senate, House Republicans undertook an investigation into President Clinton's alleged campaign finance improprieties during the 1996 election. As in the Senate, the focus of the House investigation itself, led by GOP representative Dan Burton of Indiana, chair of the House Government Reform and Oversight Committee, was not on reforming the campaign finance system. Yet the constant attention to the excesses and irregularities of the 1996 elections ignited the interest of many of those more inclined to think that the legal loopholes in the system were the root of much of the trouble. Ironically, those opposed to reform often drew attention to the scandals, as this litany of charges contained in an amendment offered by the House majority whip, Tom DeLay, R-Texas, illustrates:

> Numerous published reports describe circumstances that suggest that President Clinton may have received campaign contributions in return for official government actions he took on behalf of the contributors. . . . On February 13, 1997, the *Washington Post* reported that the Department of Justice had obtained intelligence information that the government of the People's Republic of China had sought to direct contributions from foreign sources to the Democratic National Committee ("DNC") before the 1996 presidential campaign. . . . President Clinton also entertained 938 overnight guests in the White House during his first term. This, too, became a means of fundraising. . . . Documents that the White House has only recently released revealed that Vice President Gore made 86 fundraising calls from his White House Office. More disturbingly, these new records reveal that Vice President Gore made twenty of these calls at taxpayers' expense. The use of taxpayer resources for private political uses may violate . . . United States Code.[4]

The amendment went on for more than three small-print pages of the *Congressional Record,* the verbatim record of proceedings of the U.S. Congress. In his effort to accuse and embarrass the White House and the Democratic Party publicly, Representative DeLay reminded Democratic and Republican reformers, as well as the media and the public, why there was a need for campaign finance reform.

The 1996 scandals also provided those opposed to the type of reforms proposed in the McCain-Feingold and Shays-Meehan bills (a ban on soft money and restrictions on campaign-like issue ads) with ideas for alternative reform bills that might help defeat the reformers' bills. For instance, conservative Republicans argued that current laws needed to be enforced before enacting new ones. Rep. John Doolittle, R-Calif., offered a popular yet much less comprehensive bill to beef up disclosure of campaign finance activity with the intent of trying to trump the Shays-Meehan bill.

The First Standoff in the House: Unorthodox Methods Prevail

By early 1998 the climate for campaign finance reform in the House was more favorable than it had been in the recent past. Yet important and powerful opponents, including the GOP leadership, guaranteed that the battle would be a tough one. House reformers had been working on campaign finance reform for some time but had agreed that the Senate should take the lead. Most in the reform community believed that the upper chamber offered a more fertile forum for debate on the issue. In early 1997 most reformers were convinced that little or no action would take place in the House and that the House Republican leadership would never allow discussion, let alone a vote, on campaign finance reform. By the time the McCain-Feingold bill was filibustered for the second time in the Senate in late February 1998, many campaign finance reform bills had already been introduced in the House, including the Bipartisan Campaign Reform Act sponsored by Christopher Shays, R-Conn., and Martin T. Meehan, D-Mass.

This measure was similar to the original McCain-Feingold bill. The Shays-Meehan bill would eventually emerge as the leading campaign finance reform bill in the House, with forty-five cosponsors by mid-summer. Even though its companion bill in the Senate, the McCain-Feingold bill, was filibustered, a majority of senators had supported it. This gave many reformers

Source: Douglas Graham, Congressional Quarterly

Reps. Christopher Shays, R-Conn. (*left*), and Martin T. Meehan, D-Mass., sponsors of the Bipartisan Campaign Reform Act.

hope that if the House passed the Shays-Meehan bill and returned it to the Senate, it might be able to attract enough additional support to overcome the likely GOP filibuster and pass there as well. Yet, as expected, the House Speaker, Newt Gingrich, R-Ga., and the Republican House leaders would not schedule debate or votes on campaign finance reform legislation, so House reformers had to find ways to push the issue if they expected any reform legislation to see the light of day in the 105th Congress.

Long before the McCain-Feingold bill met defeat in the Senate in February 1998, House reformers had acted to overcome the GOP leadership's blockade of campaign finance reform legislation. On October 7, 1997, thirty House Republicans sent a letter to Speaker of the House Gingrich requesting an

> opportunity for a full and fair debate on all aspects of campaign finance reform. . . . As Republicans, we did not like the Democrats refusing to let us vote on the Synar-Livingston bipartisan proposal in 1993. We now are the majority party and we hope that we will not conduct ourselves as the Democrats did. We urge you and every member of our leadership to provide a framework for full and open debate when this matter comes to the floor.

Later that month, the Blue Dog Coalition, a group of moderate and conservative House Democrats, primarily from the South, circulated a discharge petition to force campaign finance reform legislation out of committee and to the floor for consideration by the full House. Discharge petitions are rarely used in the House. Indeed, since 1910, when the rule allowing discharge petitions was adopted, only two discharged bills have become law.[5] Yet, in recent years, discharge petitions have been used more frequently, not so much actually to dislodge a bill from a committee, but as a threat or for leverage to get a committee or the majority party leadership to move on a bill.[6]

If 218 or more House members (one-half of the membership of the House) sign a discharge petition, the measure immediately proceeds to the floor under the rule specified in the petition and the majority party leadership loses control of the process. Clearly, this was contrary to the GOP leadership's wishes. The petition's rule would, in effect, bypass the Rules Committee, which under normal circumstances writes a rule for consideration of each bill brought before the House. Rules stipulate such things as the time allowed for debate, how that time will be split between opposing and supporting sides, who will control the debate, whether amendments will be allowed, how many and sometimes which amendments will be allowed, and other procedural matters. The Rules Committee is generally considered to be an agent of the majority party leadership. In fact, under Gingrich, one GOP member of the Rules Committee dubbed the panel "the handmaiden of the Speaker."[7]

The campaign finance reform discharge petition, which became House Resolution (H.R.) 259, was introduced by a leader of the Blue Dog Coalition, Rep. Scotty Baesler, D-Ky. The petition created a special rule under which campaign finance reform would be considered.[8] Ironically, the Blue Dog discharge petition did not call for consideration of the Shays-Meehan bill, the measure that was emerging as the leading campaign finance reform bill. Yet many in the press and the Republican leadership mistook the petition as one designed to bring the Shays-Meehan bill to the floor. This perception became reality, and, fortunately for supporters of the Shays-Meehan bill, this misperception drove many reform interest groups and newspaper editorial boards to push for the petition. Moreover, it encouraged more members to sign the petition. It may seem odd that some House members were not aware of the true content of the petition. Yet, with so many issues and projects on members' agendas, and lacking the time to focus on each item closely, they often must rely on secondhand sources for information. Those in the know, therefore, control a powerful commodity on Capitol Hill—information. Moreover, a rule change forced by the Republicans in 1993 gave the reform groups and supporters in Congress the ability to know who had signed a discharge petition and who had not. This knowledge provided the necessary information to obtain more signatures. The information also was helpful in holding members accountable—that is, if they wanted to be a reform member they had to act like one.

During the week of October 24, 1997, 172 House members signed the discharge petition, including five Republicans: Chris Shays, Marge Roukema of New Jersey, Nancy L. Johnson of Connecticut, Tom Campbell of California, and Constance A. Morella of Maryland. Reformers were getting closer to the 218 signatures needed to force consideration of campaign finance reform. This swift gain in support for the petition clearly worried Republican leaders, and Speaker Gingrich held a press conference on November 13, 1997, announcing that campaign finance reform would be brought to the floor some time in February or March of 1998. At the press conference, Gingrich promised that there would be a "fair, bipartisan process of voting" on campaign finance reform.[9]

After the Speaker's promise to take up campaign finance reform, active efforts to get the 218 signatures on the discharge petition were dropped. The GOP leaders had managed to head off this attempt by reformers to force a vote on campaign finance reform, but many more challenges were ahead. House reformers continued to meet to be ready to address the issues raised during the Senate debate, especially the First Amendment issues, and to discuss strategies for ensuring passage of a comprehensive reform bill. The Shays-Meehan bill was emerging as the primary vehicle for reform. In part this was because it mirrored the McCain-Feingold bill considered in the Senate and because it had the support of the many public interest groups pushing for campaign finance reform, such as Common Cause, the League of Women Voters, the Public Interest Research Group, and Public Citizen. Lobbyists from these groups, especially Common Cause, had been involved in crafting and advocating for campaign finance reform legislation for many years, and this round of reform was no different. Interest groups opposed to reform did not mobilize until later when it began to appear as if the Shays-Meehan bill actually might pass. In Chapter 6 we discuss the substantial role played by these interest groups throughout the campaign finance reform debates of the 105th Congress and the significant influence interest groups can have on the content and the fate of legislation in Congress.

The Freshman Bill

While support for the Shays-Meehan bill was solidifying, many representatives were offering their own reform bills. In all, more than 134 campaign finance reform bills were introduced in the House of Representatives during the 105th Congress.[10] One, in particular, was attracting a good deal of attention. A major reform proposal was introduced by a diverse group of Republican and Democratic House freshmen headed by Republican Asa Hutchinson of Arkansas and Democrat Tom Allen of Maine. Their comprehensive campaign finance reform bill, H.R. 2183, became known as the Freshman bill. This particular group of legislators enjoyed a certain level of legitimacy in part because they were first-term House members who perhaps could offer an untainted perspective on the campaign finance system and who were generally not expected to jump right into crafting legislation. This quick action by the new legislators earned them some measure of respect from their more senior colleagues. The process by which their bill emerged was, like many aspects of modern legislating, quite unconventional. The bipartisan group formed outside of the party or committee structures and without the support of party leaders. The freshmen established their own bipartisan task force, bypassing the normal committee process. They studied the issue and held their own hearings to craft a reform measure that could gain support from both parties. Upon its introduction, the freshmen's proposal had more Republican support than the Shays-Meehan bill did. A summary of the Freshman bill, prepared by the Office of Asa Hutchinson, can be found in Box 3-1.

Because many of these freshman lawmakers had recently been through tough campaigns featuring some of the most obvious examples of the soft money and issue advocacy loopholes, they were seen as effective advocates for reform. In fact, those in Congress who were the "victims" of soft money spending and issue ad attacks were some of the most ardent reform advocates. Even some who may have benefited from soft money spending and issue ads favored campaign finance reform because they did not want to see candidates lose control over their own campaign messages. For example, Rep. Lois Capps was both helped and hindered by issue ads, yet she was just as angry about the ads run by a term limits organization that were meant to help her get elected as she was about the ones that were designed to defeat her, for these outside groups had drowned out the candidates' own messages.

Like the Shays-Meehan bill, the Freshman bill focused on the "twin evils" of soft money and issue advocacy. However, the Freshman bill was seen as a less palatable option by some reformers, primarily because, although it banned soft money at the national level, the bill allowed state political party organizations to raise and spend soft money in ways that could potentially benefit federal candidates. The Freshman bill did not include a ban on state party soft money because the bill's sponsors believed that such a ban might violate the Tenth Amendment of the Constitution, which provides that all powers not delegated to the federal government or prohibited to the states are reserved to the states or the people. Critics of the Freshman bill pointed out that soft money would still be directed to and spent in the states to benefit federal candidates, thus the bill did not close the soft money loophole in federal law.

The Freshman bill also removed the cap on the amount parties could spend on behalf of candidates.[11] Further, it replaced the $25,000 aggregate annual limit on hard money individual contributions to parties, candidates, and PACs with a limit of $25,000 to parties plus $25,000 to candidates and PACs.[12] This potentially doubled the amount an individual could contribute each year. These provisions struck many reformers as contrary to the goals of campaign finance reform. For example, Ann McBride, president of Common Cause, one of the leading proreform public interest groups, noted, "doubling the amount that wealthy contributors can give in hard money . . . will significantly increase the influence that can be bought by the wealthiest citizens." Finally, the Freshman bill had a weaker issue advocacy provision than the Shays-Meehan bill, calling only for disclosure of expenditures for

BOX 3-1 The Bipartisan Campaign Integrity Act of 1997 (The Freshman Bill)

H.R. 2183 Summary

Soft Money Ban

■ National parties could not accept soft money, raise it on behalf of state parties, or direct it to state parties. Individuals, corporations, labor unions, and other organizations would be prohibited from giving soft money to the national parties. Federal candidates and office holders would also be barred from raising soft money on behalf of or directing soft money to state parties. Transfers of soft money between state parties would be prohibited.

■ Increase individual contributor limits to all candidates from $25,000 per election cycle to $25,000 per year. Maintain individual contribution limit of $1,000 to any single candidate per election and the PAC limit of $5,000 per candidate per election.

■ Increase individual contributor limits to parties from $20,000 to $25,000 per calendar year. The party contribution limit would be in addition to the $25,000 annual limit for federal candidate giving.

■ Increase PAC contributor limits to national parties from $15,000 to $20,000 per calendar year.

■ Remove party/candidate coordination limits.

Indexing Contribution Limits to Federal Parties and Candidates

■ Index with inflation the federal individual, PAC, and party contribution limits. The index would be assessed every presidential election year and increased by $100 increments. The total adjustment would be rounded to the nearest $100.

Issue Advocacy

■ Disclosure would be required for third party groups, including nonprofit organizations and labor unions, who run issue television or radio advertisements. The disclosure requirement would be triggered by an expenditure of $25,000 in a single district or $100,000 nationally on advertisements that bear the name or likeness of a candidate for the purpose of influencing public opinion.

■ Disclosure entails reporting the identity of an organization and amount of the expenditure. The identity consists of the name of the group, name of the principal officer, address, and phone number.

Candidate Disclosure

■ Candidate monthly disclosure during election year. Federal candidates would file electronically once $50,000 was raised. The Federal Elections Commission (FEC) would be required to provide a standardized software package to facilitate electronic filing.

■ Elimination of the "best efforts made" loophole in reporting donor occupation and employer. For donations over $200, or an aggregate thereof, an occupation must be included in the campaign finance report. Without the occupation, these donations cannot be legally reported and must be returned.

continued

Box *continued*

BACKGROUNDER ON THE FRESHMAN BILL: (H.R. 2183)

The Bipartisan Campaign Integrity Act
Prepared by Congressmen Asa Hutchinson and Tom Allen

1) Does the Freshman Bill, the "Bi-Partisan Campaign Integrity Act," ban "soft money" to the national political parties?
Yes.

2) Does the Freshman Bill ban interstate transfers of "soft money" between the parties?
Yes. Unlike other proposals being debated in the House, the Freshman bill prohibits state parties from laundering soft money by raising it and transferring it to other state parties.

3) Does the Freshman Bill prohibit Dick Gephardt and Newt Gingrich from raising "soft money" for state parties?
Yes. This is the major difference on "soft money" between the Freshman proposal and the other competing proposals.

Other bills would leave the loophole of allowing national party leaders to crisscross the country raising soft money for state parties. State parties could then transfer those funds, or they could exchange that soft money for hard money with other state parties. This is a significant loophole that should be blocked now.

The Freshman bill only allows federal officeholders and candidates to attend fund-raisers in the state which they represent.

4) Don't some of the other proposals ban state parties from raising "soft money?"
No. None of the competing bipartisan proposals ban the state from raising "soft money." And only the Freshman bill prohibits state parties from transferring those funds.

Other proposals place restrictions on how "soft money" is spent. These restrictions may raise constitutional objections as discussed below.

5) What other differences are there between the Freshman Bill and the other proposals?
The Freshman proposal avoids the 10th Amendment constitutional question of prohibiting state parties from spending money legally raised within their own states—it avoids an attempt to federalize local elections. The U.S. Supreme Court has in recent years struck down a number of federal statutes on the basis of encroachment on the sovereign rights of states in state matters, particularly the *Lopez* case. For instance, other proposals would prohibit the Maryland State Republican party from spending money legally raised within the state for Get-Out-the-Vote phone calls for their gubernatorial nominee. Many believe that this provision would cause the Court to strike down this provision in other bills and imperil the entire effort.

Source: Adapted from backgrounder prepared by Office of Rep. Asa Hutchinson, spring 1998.

issue ads and not of the sources of these funds. The Shays-Meehan bill, in contrast, completely redefined express advocacy to bring so-called sham issue ads under all federal limits and disclosure requirements.[13] Many thought the freshmen's approach would not curb the use of these unregulated communications by outside groups, parties, and wealthy individuals.

Although supporters of both the Shays-Meehan bill and the Freshman bill sought to enact comprehensive and somewhat similar reform of the campaign finance system, the two camps competed for support from their fellow members. There was, of course, some pride of authorship, but more important, there were real differences between the two bills. On February 26, 1998, Shays and Meehan met with the Freshman bill sponsors—Republicans Asa Hutchinson and Steve Horn, R-Calif., and Democrats Tom Allen and Jim Turner, D-Texas—in an attempt to merge the Shays-Meehan and Freshman bills. Negotiations broke down over the state party soft money language. The intricacies of policymaking do not always lend themselves to singular solutions to major policy problems. And in this case the problem was complicated by the bipartisan nature of each of the coalitions, whereby it was difficult enough to keep Democrats and Republicans together on one bill and not very likely that some compromise bill would maintain the same level of support. Many observers criticized the reformers for not presenting a united front against the GOP leaders and others opposed to reform, and they warned that this in-fighting among the reformers might dash all hopes of enacting any comprehensive campaign finance reform legislation. Indeed, the Republican leadership would later use this split among reformers to try to kill the reform effort altogether.

Promises, Promises

House Speaker Gingrich's pledge for a "fair, bipartisan process of voting" on campaign finance reform in February or March of 1998 was the first in a series of promises broken by the GOP leadership during the 105th Congress. Even though the rescheduling of debates and votes on legislation is commonplace in Congress, the Republican leaders had established a record of not honoring their promises regarding campaign finance reform during the previous Congress (1995–1997). For example, President Clinton had taken some initial steps to establish the campaign finance reform commission that he and Speaker Gingrich had agreed to with a handshake in 1995, but Gingrich did not follow up in the House. Additionally, on May 7, 1996, the House majority leader, Dick Armey, R-Texas, announced that the week of

Speaker of the House Newt Gingrich.

July 8, 1996, would be "Reform Week" and promised to bring up campaign finance reform legislation then. The week of July 8 passed with no consideration of campaign finance reform, and two weeks later, on what was reduced to "Reform Afternoon," the GOP leadership brought up H.R. 3820, a bill opposed by every major public interest group as "sham reform" and "a fraud."[14] The measure was defeated.

Thus, when Speaker Gingrich promised in November 1997 to bring up campaign finance reform in February or March of 1998, most reformers were skeptical at best. Some thought, however, that the bad press and increased public attention that would come from yet another broken promise on reform would motivate GOP leaders to make good on their promise this time. Gingrich and the other Republican leaders were well aware that support for comprehensive campaign finance reform legislation was growing in the House, and pressure to consider meaningful reform proposals was coming from some key members of the Republican Conference, not just from the Democrats. Of course, as one of the lead sponsors of the Shays-Meehan bill, Christopher Shays had long urged his party's leaders to give campaign finance reform a fair vote on the House floor. But other GOP legislators, such as Tom Campbell and Nancy Johnson, also were pressuring the Speaker to live up to his promise to bring campaign finance reform to the whole House for a vote under a fair and bipartisan process.

On February 4, 1998, thirty-four Republicans, including Chris Shays, Asa Hutchinson, Zach Wamp of Tennessee, William Goodling of Pennsylvania, Mark Sanford of South Carolina, and Porter Goss of Florida, sent a letter to Speaker Gingrich urging that he not only keep this promise of a vote in February or March, but that "during the floor debate, there be an opportunity for a vote on one or more bipartisan alternatives that include a ban on soft money." One hundred ten Democrats, under the direction of House Oversight Committee ranking minority member Sam Gejdenson of Connecticut, sent a similar letter on February 12, 1998. In this letter the Democrats promised to "renew and redouble our efforts to secure the final 31 signatures needed to complete the discharge petition for House Resolution 259, a rule which makes all of the leading campaign finance reform bills" if the Speaker would not allow a vote on bipartisan campaign finance reform.

February passed with no vote on campaign finance reform. The House Oversight Committee did, however, hold hearings on February 5, 1998, to allow those who had not testified yet on campaign finance reform to do so. The House Republican Conference *Legislative Digest* of February 27, 1998, entitled "Anticipated Legislation for the 105th Congress (Second Session)" and sent to all Republican members, stated under the House Oversight Committee section that "[t]he committee plans to hold hearings on several campaign reform measures. The leadership in both the House and the Senate have indicated that the issue will be addressed this spring."[15]

In early March the Senate Committee on Governmental Affairs under the leadership of Chairman Fred Thompson, R-Tenn., released its report on the Senate's investigation into the "illegal and improper activities in connection with the 1996 federal election campaigns."[16] In a letter to his House colleagues about the report, Senator Thompson stated:

> I regret that we were unable to pursue these matters to a more complete and final conclusion. However, I am confident that the work of your committee [the House Government Reform and Oversight Committee under GOP representative Dan Burton of Indiana] in the future will pick up where we left off, and will provide the American public with a more complete insight into the serious illegal and improper activities undertaken during the last federal election.[17]

This letter and the release of the Senate report signaled that more inquiries would follow and that solutions were definitely needed. Yet Senate GOP leaders had ensured that the Thompson committee would not be a forum for consideration of reform, and House GOP leaders were similarly opposed to campaign finance reform that addressed soft money and issue advocacy.

During the week of March 13, 1998, Rep. Bill Thomas, R-Calif., chairman of the House Oversight Committee, spoke to the Tuesday Group about campaign finance reform. The Tuesday Group, previously known as the Tuesday Lunch Bunch, is a group of moderate Republican House members that meets weekly over lunch to discuss strategies regarding their party's positions on key issues. Thomas outlined the Republican leadership's framework for reform that would include at its base the paycheck protection measure. This controversial measure to limit the ability of labor unions to collect and use union dues for political activities was clearly designed to weaken one of the Democratic Party's most powerful supporters. No agreement was reached during this discussion, which quickly broke down over the issue of how to restrict the use of corporate shareholders' funds, as well as union members' funds, in an effort to bring some partisan balance to the GOP leaders' reform effort.

By mid-March there was still no sign from the Republican leadership that the issue would be scheduled for a vote. Shays and Meehan used the time to solidify further support for their bill. On March 17, Meehan met with Minority Leader Richard Gephardt, D-Mo., and Minority Whip David Bonior, D-Mich., to secure the House Democrats' endorsement of the Shays-Meehan bill. The Democratic leaders were sensitive to the fact that many Democrats had introduced campaign finance reform bills, and they were particularly cautious not to slight supporters of the Freshman bill. They agreed to recommend endorsing the Shays-Meehan bill to the full Democratic Caucus, but would not rule out support of the Freshman bill.[18] The issue was sent first to the Democrats' Task Force on Campaign Finance Reform, chaired by caucus chairman Vic Fazio, D-Calif. On March 18, after much discussion of various reform proposals and without completely ruling out the Freshman bill as an option, the Task Force decided to back the Shays-Meehan bill. Task forces such as this one and the one the freshmen used to develop their bill are another unorthodox method used by lawmakers to try to influence the outcome of legislative debates, for they bypass the traditional committee process.

The Democratic Party endorsement was an important turning point for campaign finance reform in the House. The Democratic Caucus and its leaders were now committed to the issue as one of its priorities, which meant that the party would devote resources to the effort. One of the most important resources that a party can offer is whipping, whereby the party's whip and his or her deputy whips encourage party discipline and mobilize the party's members on behalf of the party leadership's legislative priorities. Votes are counted and recounted as the whips work to persuade their colleagues to vote with the party. Many Democratic whip meetings were held between March and July to secure votes for campaign finance reform. Deputy whips and Democratic reform members gathered often in Minority Whip Bonior's office in the Capitol building, a small but elegant room with a spectacular view of the city, to look over the list of all Democratic House members. Any member whose position was not known would be assigned to one of the whips, who became responsible for persuading the undecided member to vote with the party. Quite often staff would make the whip phone calls, but if the undecided member might not be so easily persuaded, member-to-member contact was necessary. Members responsible for whipping might call the targeted member or speak with him or her on the House floor between votes, at a committee meeting, or even at the House gym during a workout. Whipping is a vital function of party strategy, for it is clearly helpful to know whether there are enough votes to achieve the desired legislative outcome before moving on a measure. Whipping also involves more of the party's members in leadership decision making. This builds party loyalty and gives members a stake in the party's success.

In the case of campaign finance reform, the Democrats had little to lose. It was an issue that set them apart from the increasingly unpopular Republican leadership, yet one that had not attracted much public attention. Very few constituents in members' home districts had focused on the issue, yet campaign finance reform in general was viewed as a positive policy goal.[19] Moreover, the Democratic Party had become increasingly worried about its financial situation in comparison with that of the Republicans. Since losing majority control of Congress to the Republicans in 1994, the Democrats had fallen even further behind in fund-raising than they normally were, particularly in soft money fund-raising. Although both parties and their allied interest groups ran issue advocacy advertisements, the GOP and its groups had more money to run these ads. Thus it was even more difficult for Democratic candidates and their party to counter the growing number of negative messages broadcast in their districts. Clearly, the party had a pragmatic interest in closing the soft money and issue advocacy loopholes.

With the Democrats set to push for reform, the Republican leaders canceled their plans to bring campaign finance reform to the floor during the week of March 23. Many speculated that the GOP leaders canceled floor consideration after discovering they were likely to lose a key procedural vote on the issue to the Democrats, and losing control of the House floor was not a desirable option.[20] Reform interest groups, the media, and congressional reformers publicly scolded the GOP leaders and accused them of breaking yet another promise. This *New York Times* editorial denouncing Republican leaders for changing the schedule on campaign finance reform ran on March 27, 1998:

> In a brazen repudiation of his own promises, Newt Gingrich has yanked campaign finance reform from the House agenda. The Speaker's action yesterday came after a frantic but fruitless effort by his aides to round up the votes to block genuine reform legislation on the House floor. Mr. Gingrich's allies are now reportedly plotting to reschedule consideration of reform bills next month, but only under rules requiring a two-thirds vote for approval. These desperation tactics are an abuse of power reminiscent of conduct Mr. Gingrich himself deplored for years.[21]

Perhaps in reaction to this kind of portrayal by a large number of newspapers and remarks by the *New York Times* in support of Shays's standing up to his party's leadership, GOP leaders announced on March 27 that they would not wait until April or May to bring up campaign finance reform after all. Instead, campaign finance bills were scheduled for votes the following Monday, March 30, the day of Republican representative Steven H. Schiff's funeral in New Mexico. Usually, votes are canceled on the day of a fellow member's funeral to allow members to attend the services. Many speculated that the schedule was designed to keep proreform members from returning from the funeral in time to vote on the measures.

Four bills of the GOP leaders' choosing, some of which had not even been introduced yet, would be considered under suspension of the rules, a procedure usually reserved for noncontroversial measures. Bills on the suspension calendar are limited to forty minutes of debate, no amendments are allowed, and a two-thirds vote is required for their passage. Although the suspension-of-the-rules procedure is used much more frequently today than in past years, it is still meant for noncontroversial measures and not for rushing through major bills.[22] Thus, members often complain when the procedure is used in this way. Campaign finance reform clearly was not a noncontroversial issue, and reformers were quick to note the disingenuousness of the leadership's plan. In a terse exchange on the House floor the evening of March 27, Representative Shays questioned Majority Leader Armey on the soundness of bringing campaign finance reform to the floor in this manner. Here is a sampling of that exchange:

Shays: I am trying to understand that we began this session last year, we waited all year long for a debate on campaign finance reform, at the end of that year of our legislative session, we asked the leadership if and when we would be having a debate on campaign finance reform. Our leadership, my leadership, said we would have a fair and open debate in February or March, and I am interested to know if this meets the leadership's definition of a fair and open debate on campaign finance reform.

Armey: As the gentleman knows, we have worked diligently on this whole issue in committee and in leadership, and with a great deal of commitment and conviction to the purposes at hand, that of securing honest elections, with great integrity on behalf of the American people. We believe that we are bringing to the floor next week, under suspension, all opportunities of merit that could not be available to the American people to provide them that assurance, and we are very excited and proud of the opportunity for all of our Members to have the opportunity to express their commitment to that by a yes vote.

Shays: Will you tell me who has decided that we brought all bills of merit? Who has made that decision?

Armey: This has been a decision that has been made through the entire leadership team in consultation with the committee of jurisdiction, and I appreciate my colleague's interest.

Shays: Were any Democrats consulted on whether there would be bills that they think deserve debate and discussion? Was anyone on the other side of the aisle considered before the leadership made the determination to come out with these bills?

Armey: I should, of course, feel assured, and as it should be, we have bipartisan activity in the committee of jurisdiction, and we are very proud of the work that the committee reported out.

Shays: Mr. Leader, I asked a sincere question, and I would appreciate a sincere answer. And the question was: Was anyone in leadership on the other side of the aisle consulted before it was decided to bring out four Republican bills?

Armey: . . . the answer is no.[23]

Shays's concern for whether Democrats were consulted was not because he really expected the GOP leaders to run the plan by the Democrats. Rather, by pointing out the lack of bipartisanship in the GOP leaders' process, Shays exposed their cynical strategy, which was designed to avoid debate on comprehensive campaign finance reform.

Following this exchange, a series of press conferences took place in which supporters of reform denounced the suspension process for consideration of campaign finance reform. While Dick Armey continued to tell reporters and others that his announcement was routine, "privately sources said the leaders were fed up with Shays and his brigade. If they demanded a vote, then, here, they would get one."[24] Ironically, this announcement lit a fire under reform activists from both sides of the aisle. The media added fuel to the fire, as is clear from this *New York Times* editorial published on March 30, 1998:

> Republicans are ready to defy the speaker by joining with most Democrats to vote for legislation sponsored by Representatives Christopher Shays of Connecticut and Marty Meehan of Massachusetts. . . . The bills that Gingrich is sponsoring are either anemic, irrelevant or tied to an anti-union provision repugnant to most Democrats. With a two-thirds approval requirement, they cannot pass. Of course, Gingrich does not care if his own fraudulent legislation wins or loses. All he seeks is the chance to say the House considered campaign finance reform and was unable to pass a bill. It is a cynical maneuver that will come back to haunt Gingrich and any House member who supports it.[25]

On March 28, the *Hartford Courant,* a leading newspaper in Shays's home state of Connecticut, noted that "[t]he chief hope of Shays and his backers is that so much public outrage will surface in April, when Congress takes a two week recess, that House leaders will be forced to allow a vote on their bill later this year."[26]

Debate on the Republican bills began in the early evening of March 30. The main bill, the Campaign Reform and Election Integrity Act of 1998 (H.R. 3485), sponsored by Bill Thomas, was soundly defeated in a 74-337 vote, despite a last minute attempt to make the bill more appealing to reformers by making it appear that its provision on soft money would be a complete ban.[27] The Paycheck Protection Act (H.R. 2608), the controversial measure to limit the ability of labor unions to collect and use union dues, which the Democratic leadership had dubbed the "worker gag rule," also was defeated with a mostly party-line vote of 166 for and 246 against. Although

Republican leaders and some GOP reformers called this measure "paycheck protection," the GOP leaders knew that the labor union measure was a deal breaker, a "poison pill" that would force the bipartisan reform coalition apart. The two other bills, the Campaign Reporting and Disclosure Act (H.R. 3582) and the Illegal Foreign Contributions Act (H.R. 34), were politically potent measures that did not really address what reformers viewed as the main issues of campaign finance reform, and they passed by large margins. Members from both parties saw no reason to vote against these measures, particularly since a "no" vote might be perceived as a vote against reform regardless of how inadequate the bills really were. In the end, it was clear that meaningful campaign finance reform had not been considered in the four bills brought up under suspension of the rules. After more than four and a half hours of debate and voting on these measures, reform members left the House chamber about 11:00 P.M. furious but fired up to continue the fight.

GOP leaders had hoped to put the issue to rest and claim that campaign finance reform had been considered. They tried to bypass conventional procedures for considering bills on the floor by bringing the four pseudo-reform measures up under suspension of the rules. Again, we see lawmakers using unorthodox methods in an attempt to achieve legislative goals, but this time it did not have the desired effect. The Republican leaders had hoped that campaign finance reform was behind them. Instead, the *Washington Post* and others accused them of hypocrisy:

> Republicans have spent a year and a half claiming to be indignant about the fund-raising abuses in the last campaign. . . . But given the chance to change the law to ban the principal abuse, having to do with the raising and spending of so-called soft money, they flinch. They like the money even more than they like delivering the sermons deploring its influence over the system. . . . The tactic has been to offer up mock reform bills that they could be pretty sure (a) wouldn't pass, in part because they were written to be offensive to Democrats, and (b) wouldn't achieve reform if they did pass. Republicans who wanted could safely vote aye and provide themselves with cover, secure in the knowledge that nothing would be enacted. . . . Fake votes were staged Monday night on mostly fake bills; no one was fooled.[28]

The editorial was accompanied by a cartoon of Gingrich hanging campaign finance reform, a graphic illustration of yet another promise on campaign finance reform broken by the GOP leaders. The public interest group Public Citizen dubbed the episode the "Monday Night Massacre of Re-

"I KEPT MY PROMISE TO TAKE IT UP"

from Herblock: A Cartoonist's Life (Times Books, 1998) ©1998 HERBLOCK

Source: Herblock: A Cartoonist's Life, Times Books, 1998.

form."[29] According to one newspaper in Texas (a state from which many in the GOP leadership hail), "The size of the vote [against the Thomas Bill] . . . can only be taken as a denunciation of the leadership."[30] And quoting the actor Woody Allen in a line from the movie *Bananas,* Representative Meehan called the process "a travesty of a mockery of a sham."[31] Clearly, GOP leaders had not avoided public criticism and bad press in their effort to put campaign finance reform to rest. In fact, many agreed with a statement made by the *New York Times:* "It has been fashionable in Washington to say there is no public groundswell for a campaign cleanup. But the maneuvers by Mr. Gingrich and his obstructionist crew showed that only undemocratic measures can now block sound legislation."[32] Although some publications did not attack the GOP leaders quite so severely, most of the mainstream press expressed their disapproval of the process.

Scramble for Control: Campaign Finance Reformers Fight Back

In the wake of this failed attempt by GOP leaders to preempt the reform effort with their self-crafted bills, the House Blue Dog Coalition revived the

discharge petition effort to force to the floor bipartisan campaign finance reform alternatives. As of March 31, the petition had 191 of the 218 signatures
needed to force a vote on their preferred campaign finance reform bills. In
conjunction with this effort, the proreform interest groups, especially Common Cause, worked to raise the profile of the campaign finance reform issue
in members' home districts. The groups put many legislators on the spot in
community meetings back home, and they spoke with editorial boards of
local newspapers to urge editors to cover the issue, particularly in the districts
of undecided legislators and of those who had not signed the discharge petition. Many lawmakers scrambled when accused of not being supporters of
reform by their own constituents. Members also received phone calls in their
Washington offices urging them to support the reform effort. One House
member, Tom Davis, R-Va., noted that his decision to sign the discharge petition had been influenced by a Common Cause volunteer at a district meeting.[33] A 1993 House rules change requiring that the names of those who had
signed a discharge petition be made public also helped reformers put pressure
on uncommitted members.[34] In fact, on April 18, 1998, in an unusually
forceful editorial the *New York Times* published a list of who was on and who
was off the discharge petition. Other newspapers across the country also
urged their local House members to sign the petition and support reform.

By late April a critical mass of twelve Republicans had signed onto the discharge petition.[35] This alarmed the Republican leaders, who did not want to
lose control of the floor to the Democrats. The GOP leaders knew they could
not stop the momentum of the reformers to force consideration of campaign finance reform, and they were in no mood for more bad press on the
issue. When the number of Republicans signing the petition grew to twelve
and previously unlikely signers such as Zach Wamp of Tennessee and Frank
Wolf of Virginia signed on, the leaders looked for a way out. The *New York
Times* pointed out that "[s]ome Republicans and Democrats are reluctant to
sign petitions to bring bills to the floor in deference to House Leaders. But
Mr. Gingrich, with his crude blocking tactics, has forfeited any respect."[36]

In an effort to move beyond the issue, the Speaker and key GOP leaders
offered Shays and other Republican reformers yet another commitment to
bring campaign finance reform to the floor by mid-May in exchange for Republican members removing their names from the discharge petition.[37] The
Republican reformers and GOP leaders agreed that several bills would be
considered in an "open" process (as opposed to the suspension-of-the-rules
process of the last round) and that the base bill would be the Freshman bill
with consideration of other bills, including the Shays-Meehan bill. In a writ-

ten statement, the GOP leaders said, "These requirements clearly highlight the Leadership's intention that this process be open, flexible, and bipartisan. . . . Members are choosing an approach that is more open, more bipartisan, and allows a fuller debate on the issue."[38] On April 22 nine of the twelve Republicans, including Shays, removed their names from the petition. The next day, two more Republicans removed their names, leaving Connie Morella as the only Republican on the petition.

Shays himself suggested the Freshman bill as the base bill for consideration, knowing it would be more palatable to the Republican leadership, who saw it as a means to defeat the Shays-Meehan bill. The agreement, however, would at least give Shays the opportunity to bring his bill to the House floor. The Republican leaders, for their part, were willing to accept this agreement, since the Freshman bill was untested in the Senate and was not acceptable to key reformers there. The Shays-Meehan bill would be far riskier because its companion bill, the McCain-Feingold bill, had already gained the support of a majority of senators. Despite these strategic decisions, Republican leaders held out hope that if the laborious process in the House did not kill reform, the Senate would. Many would suggest that because of the "promise" of another Senate filibuster, the House process and subsequent votes became *free votes*. In other words, House members would be able to vote for reform knowing it would eventually be defeated in the other chamber.

The deal angered many Democrats, for they felt the reform coalition was close to getting what it wanted—an up or down vote on the Shays-Meehan bill with no amendments to water it down or alter it in ways that would cause the fragile reform coalition to fall apart. Moreover, making the Freshman bill the base bill, that is, the first bill to be considered with all other bills considered as substitutes for it, reinvigorated the freshman reformers to push for their bill over the Shays-Meehan bill. This, of course, reinforced the split between the two camps of bipartisan reformers. The GOP leaders' use of this "divide-and-conquer" strategy proved somewhat effective, for reformers were kept busy trying to persuade one another to support each others' bills. Representative Meehan met with the Freshman Democratic Task Force on Campaign Finance Reform on April 28 to try to persuade the first-term legislators to back the Shays-Meehan bill and offered to give the freshmen the lion's share of the credit for passing campaign finance reform. The freshmen, however, were not persuaded and they continued to try to gain more support for their own bill. Opponents of reform used the time and the prospect of a "more open debate" to craft amendments that would have the potential of dividing the reform coalition.[39] All sides were preparing for the big showdown.

Securing support from the White House was another important goal for both the Shays-Meehan and the Freshman bill supporters. President Clinton had helped keep the campaign finance reform issue on the political agenda by, for example, mentioning it as one of his legislative priorities in the State of the Union address in January 1998. The president had also publicly supported the McCain-Feingold bill in the Senate, which was almost identical to the Shays-Meehan bill in the House. At a meeting with White House staff on April 29 to discuss strategy for a tobacco settlement bill, Meehan used the opportunity to express his concern about the president's plan to meet with the primary sponsors of the Freshman bill, the Democrat Tom Allen and the Republican Asa Hutchinson. High-level White House staffers, including Clinton's chief of staff, John Podesta, agreed with Meehan that the president should endorse only one bill and that his meetings with members should reflect that decision.

With the help of Common Cause, which lobbied the White House to endorse the Shays-Meehan bill, the president decided to meet only with Shays and Meehan. On May 12, they met with both President Clinton and Vice President Al Gore, and the president offered to help pass the bill. He stated, "I strongly support the bipartisan legislation offered by Representatives Christopher Shays and Marty Meehan, which is the best chance in a generation for real reform. . . . Now every Member of the House of Representatives has a responsibility to vote for this measure to ban large soft money contributions, improve disclosure, and restrict backdoor campaign spending."[40] This was another important step for the Shays-Meehan bill in solidifying support for the measure and raising the public profile of the issue; it was clearly a blow to the freshman reformers, who had hoped to get a hearing at the White House.

Yet President Clinton's efforts on this and other issues were becoming increasingly overshadowed by the charges that he had an affair with White House intern Monica Lewinsky in the Oval Office. The story broke in January 1998, and through the rest of that year the allegations against the president, his public denials, and his eventual confession that he had lied about the affair seriously reduced Clinton's credibility and effectiveness. The House voted to impeach President Clinton on December 19, 1998, for lying under oath about his relationship with Lewinsky, but the Senate acquitted him on February 12, 1999, and Clinton remained in office to serve out his term. These events clearly had an effect on his ability to influence policymaking in Congress.

By the time the Shays-Meehan bill received the White House's endorsement, Representatives Shays and Meehan had introduced another measure,

Source: The White House

President Bill Clinton in the Oval Office with Reps. Martin T. Meehan, D-Mass. (*left*), and Christopher Shays, R-Conn. (*right*), on May 12, 1998.

less sweeping than their original bill. The new bill, H.R. 3526, closely mirrored the pared-down final version of the McCain-Feingold bill that was defeated in the Senate in February (see Box 3-2). As with the Senate bill, controversial provisions were removed to build bipartisan support for the bill. There was growing consensus among reformers from both parties, the interest group community, and many newspaper editorial boards that this revised Shays-Meehan bill was the best vehicle for meaningful campaign finance reform, especially because removal of controversial provisions made the bill more likely to pass. Moreover, since the McCain-Feingold bill had garnered majority support in the Senate, but not the sixty votes needed to overcome a Republican filibuster, there was increasing optimism that House passage might force the Senate to consider the bill again.

The Republican Leadership's "Death by Amendment" Strategy

After GOP leaders struck the deal with the Republican reformers for an "open" process, the matter was handed over to the House Rules Committee to come up with a procedure to consider campaign finance reform legislation. Thirty-eight members testified at the meeting of the Rules Committee on May 20, 1998, and thirteen substitute bills (substitutes to the Freshman bill) and more than three hundred amendments were submitted to the committee for possible consideration. On the same day, President Clinton sent a

BOX 3-2 Summary of the Shays-Meehan Amendment in the Nature of a Substitute to H.R. 2183

1. **Soft Money Ban.** Completely eliminates federal soft money, as well as state soft money that influences a federal election. Increases the aggregate hard dollar contribution limit from $25,000 to $30,000.

2. **Recognition of sham issue ads for what they truly are: campaign ads.** Strengthens the definition of "express advocacy" to include those radio and TV advertisements that:

   - refer to a clearly identified federal candidate, run within 60 days of an election, or
   - include unambiguous/unmistakable support for or opposition to a clearly identified federal candidate, run at any time.

   Ads falling under this definition could only be run using legal, "hard" dollars.

3. **Codification of *Beck*.** Codifies Supreme Court decision stating workers cannot be forced to fund political activities. Nonunion employees who pay for union representation do not have to finance union political activities.

4. **Improved FEC Disclosure and Enforcement.** Requires FEC reports to be filed electronically, and provides for Internet posting of this and other disclosure data. Also provides for expedited and more effective FEC procedures.

5. **Wealthy Candidates.** Bans coordinated party contributions to candidates who do not agree to limit the amount of personal money spent on their campaigns to $50,000.

6. **Franking.** Expands ban on unsolicited franked mass mailings from the current three months before a general election to six months.

7. **Foreign Money and Fund-raising on Government Property.** Clarifies that it is illegal to raise not only hard money—but soft money as well—from foreigners or on government property.

Source: Office of Rep. Christopher Shays, May 1998.

letter to each member of the Democratic Caucus asking that they support the Shays-Meehan bill:

> Of all the campaign finance bills under consideration by the House, only Shays-Meehan represents real, comprehensive, bipartisan reform. . . . Talking about reform is easy; this week the House of Representatives has a rare and fleeting opportunity to act. Each and every member of the House must decide whether to take that step—and the American people are watching. I urge you to make this year the year that Congress confounds public cynicism, and passes bipartisan, comprehensive campaign finance reform.[41]

The Rules Committee promised to make some sense out of the process, but in the end the committee made in order the Freshman bill as the base bill, eleven substitute bills, including the Shays-Meehan bill, hundreds of germane amendments (a germane amendment is one that is relevant to the section of the bill that it seeks to modify), and an unprecedented 258 nongermane amendments (amendments that are not related to what they seek to modify).[42] Allowing this extraordinary number of amendments meant that debate over campaign finance reform legislation could drag on for a very long time. Rep. Rick White, R-Wash., sponsor of one of the other substitute bills that would form an independent commission to consider reform proposals, said he expected the process to be as "open as you can possibly imagine . . . maybe too open. It might just go on forever."[43]

The process was indeed "open," as promised, so open that it invited many possible lines of attack on reform bills such as the Shays-Meehan and Freshman bills. Indeed, many of the amendments were considered poison pill amendments. Democratic leaders, reform House members, many of the proreform public interest groups, and some editorial boards accused GOP leaders of devising a process of "death by amendment" in order to kill the Shays-Meehan bill, the Freshman bill, and other comprehensive reform measures.

The process the GOP leadership established for consideration of the Freshman bill and the eleven substitute bills was a "Queen-of-the-hill" rule. Under this scenario, the base bill and each of the substitute bills gets a vote and whichever bill receives the most votes, as long as it receives a majority, wins. Special rules like this are powerful tools of the majority party, for they allow the majority to structure the options from which legislators must choose. Such special rules are among the parliamentary devices used more frequently in recent years by the majority party members in the House to improve the chances of achieving their desired legislative outcome. In this case, the Queen-of-the-hill rule is yet another example demonstrating that contemporary congressional leaders are more apt to use unorthodox procedures to achieve important legislative goals than to rely on the standard procedures for consideration of legislation.

The Republican leaders no doubt hoped that this process would bring about the defeat of comprehensive campaign finance reform, since both the Shays-Meehan and the Freshman bills were to be subject to many poison pill amendments and were up against other reform bills that might trump them. Indeed, some of the substitute bills presented a real challenge to the Shays-Meehan bill under this Queen-of-the-hill process. In particular, a bill known as the Commission bill had a good chance of gaining more votes than the Shays-Meehan bill. The Commission bill was a bipartisan measure to establish an independent campaign finance reform commission that would study the issue and propose reform legislation to Congress. The Commission bill was sponsored by, among others, John Dingell, D-Mich., the powerful former chairman of the Energy and Commerce Committee known as the Dean of the House. Dingell actively sought support for the bill among his fellow Democrats, thus potentially draining support away from the Shays-Meehan bill.

Commission bill supporters from both parties argued that the partisan and contentious process of reform was not likely to result in enacting new campaign finance laws. They believed that a commission that operated outside of the political arena, much like the independent commission on military base closings, stood a better chance of suggesting reforms able to garner significant bipartisan support in both chambers. Moreover, the Commission bill offered a way for Republicans in particular to cast a vote for reform without supporting the Shays-Meehan bill. This would allow them to claim to support reform and, therefore, avoid criticism back home as well as escape the wrath of their party leaders. Thus, the Commission bill was a great threat to the Shays-Meehan bill, and Shays-Meehan supporters quickly went into action to try to ensure that the Commission bill did not trump the bill they favored.

The substitute bills were only part of the puzzle. The hundreds of amendments made in order by the special rule presented a tremendous challenge as well. The purpose of the GOP's death-by-amendment strategy was to weigh down the Shays-Meehan bill with poison pill amendments to prevent a clean vote on it and cause supporters to peel off. For example, many amendments proposed attaching some version of the so-called paycheck protection measure to the Shays-Meehan bill. Others were attempts to weaken the "motor-voter" law by, for example, requiring extraordinary procedures for verifying the citizenship of prospective voters.[44] Both types of poison pill amendments were designed to make the Shays-Meehan bill unpalatable to Democrats and therefore to destroy the bipartisan coalition in support of the bill.

Other amendments included ones that would have weakened the issue advocacy provision in the Shays-Meehan bill, gutted the restrictions on soft money, and created giant loopholes in the name of protecting the First Amendment right to free speech. In early May, GOP antireformers, led by Majority Whip Tom DeLay, formed what they called the Free Speech Coalition, a team of Republican members organized solely to kill campaign finance reform. The Capitol Hill newspaper *Roll Call* reported that DeLay's Free Speech Coalition was created "to bury the various reform proposals with a pile of partisan amendments designed to shift the debate to the First Amendment and the fundraising allegations swirling around President Clinton."[45] Recall that the McCain-Feingold bill in the Senate also was battered with attacks based on charges that it violated First Amendment free speech rights, and debates in the Senate often featured GOP senators reciting a litany of charges of illegal fund-raising by the president and vice president. The Free Speech Coalition assailed the reform proposals with floor speeches, talk radio appearances, op-ed pieces, and a series of "Dear Colleague" letters distributed to all House members.[46] These letters had titles such as "Oppose the 'Bipartisan' Gag Order, Protect Your Constituents' Right to Speak," "Protect Free Speech, Oppose Unconstitutional Campaign 'Reform,' " "The Shays-Meehan Bill's Year-Round Restrictions on First Amendment Rights," and "Unconstitutional 'Campaign Reform' Means 'Government Control.' " One Dear Colleague letter from DeLay featured the cartoon shown here with this message from DeLay:

> Dear Colleague: Don't be seduced by so-called campaign finance 'reforms.' Stand true to the principles which have guided our country for more than two hundred years—free speech. Oppose Shays/Meehan (H.R. 3526) and the Freshman Bill (H.R. 2183) which betray our constitutional rights.

By mid-May, the Free Speech Coalition was poised to offer a barrage of amendments designed to weigh down and eventually kill the Shays-Meehan bill. For example, its members planned to introduce an "Air Force One" amendment to outlaw the use of the president's official jet for rewarding fund-raisers and another to prohibit fund-raising in a place of worship. These were thinly veiled references to the Democratic fund-raising scandals of 1996 as well as practices already addressed in existing law. These measures were designed not only to weigh down the Shays-Meehan bill but also to em-

barrass the White House and the Democratic Party. Politics is never very far removed from policymaking in the debates over campaign finance reform.

The Shays-Meehan reformers had originally said that they would accept no amendments at all, but the sheer number of cleverly crafted amendments made it politically impossible to insist on no amendments.[47] Staffers quickly mobilized to evaluate all the amendments to determine which ones were poison pills, and therefore would endanger passage of the Shays-Meehan bill, and which ones did not threaten to weaken the bipartisan reform coalition and thus would not be opposed. The great number of possible amendments made this a difficult and time-consuming task. Moreover, the staff members had to conduct this work in secret so as to avoid leaks about the reformers' strategy to those trying to bring down the Shays-Meehan bill.

In a flurry of activity reformers and their staffs attempted to shore up support for the Shays-Meehan bill and ensure that killer amendments would not hit their mark. Various staff members met almost constantly to stay on top of the latest developments. The large group of all members who supported the Shays-Meehan bill met regularly as well, as did the smaller core group of reformers. Additionally, core Shays-Meehan supporters met separately with their party caucuses to gain more support from their fellow partisans. For instance, each party's reform members circulated a letter among their party's colleagues asking them to sign it in an attempt to show mounting support for their cause. The Republican working group focused on handling the more powerful arguments against the Shays-Meehan bill, especially the charges that the measure violated the First Amendment. These Republicans also had face-to-face meetings with other GOP members to explain the bill and answer any concerns. Several GOP members, such as Tom Campbell and Zach Wamp, were vital in fending off conservative groups that attacked the Shays-Meehan bill on First Amendment grounds. Gaining more Republican votes was definitely a priority, for virtually the entire Democratic Caucus already supported the Shays-Meehan bill, whereas fewer than 40 of the 227 Republicans were on board at this time.

The Democrats had the support of their leadership as well, which greatly enhanced their ability to shore up and maintain Democratic support for the bill. Minority Leader Gephardt committed staff resources and vocal public support to the effort. Campaign finance reform member and staff meetings were held in his conference room in the Capitol. Additionally, he included campaign finance reform on the agenda of many "leadership meetings" held during this period. Democratic leadership meetings are intimate and informal meetings chaired by Gephardt; they are held regularly at about 5:30 P.M. to discuss strategy. Only key Democratic lawmakers, such as committee chairpersons, senior members, important issue leaders, and a handful of staff people are invited to these meetings. Minority Whip Bonior conducted whips on many of the amendments and substitute bills. The Democratic Caucus chairman, Vic Fazio, worked closely with important Democratic reformers such as Marty Meehan, Sander Levin of Michigan, and Sam Gejdenson of Connecticut, and he called regular meetings of the Democratic Caucus Campaign Finance Reform Task Force to build and maintain support for reform.

Only a few Democrats opposed the Shays-Meehan bill, among them some members of the Congressional Black Caucus who were pressured by religious organizations and pro-life groups to oppose the Shays-Meehan bill. These groups guarded their membership lists closely and had avoided disclosing them thus far by conducting only activities that technically would not be considered campaigning, such as running issue advocacy advertisements and distributing ostensibly nonpartisan voter guides. Under the Shays-Meehan bill some of these activities would be considered campaigning if they were conducted in the last sixty days before an election.

The chairman of the Democratic Congressional Campaign Committee (DCCC), Martin Frost, D-Texas, also expressed opposition to the Shays-Meehan bill, because it contained a severability clause that would allow sections of the law to remain intact even if the courts struck down other sections.[48] Frost argued that such selective enforcement of the bill could put the Democratic Party at an even greater financial disadvantage in relation to the Republican Party, particularly if the issue advocacy provision were struck down but the soft money ban was implemented. Democrats raise quite a lot of soft money, but not as much as the Republicans; most of the issue advocacy communications come from the Republican Party and interest groups affiliated with the GOP. Thus, a soft money ban alone would hurt the Democrats more than the Republicans, or at least Frost and others thought it would.

The Republican reformers faced a tough battle within their own party's caucus. Only thirty or forty GOP members supported reform. Not only was it imperative that Republicans raise the number of GOP supporters to ensure passage, but it was also vital that they deal with the lobbying by the GOP leadership and the Conservative Action Team (CAT) members, who were making support of the Shays-Meehan bill a difficult proposition. The Conservative Action Team was formed by a group of Republican House members to push for more conservative policies such as tax cuts and deregulation. Many of the key members of the CAT, such as Tom DeLay, took it upon themselves to lobby against the Shays-Meehan effort. For example, in early June, DeLay invited

> a few dozen leaders of political action committees to join him at a June 18, 1998 meeting. His goal: concocting a strategy to defeat 'liberal' campaign finance reform proposals pending in the House, measures that the tough-talking lawmaker dubbed an 'election-law power grab.' The so-called reformers, [he said], were creating a bureaucracy that tramples our electoral system and certainly tramples on the First Amendment to the Constitution.[49]

Staffs prepared a great deal of research and background material for all Shays-Meehan supporters. Members were armed with far more information and strategic material than is usual for legislative battles. For example, extensive briefing books were put together for all the Shays-Meehan core group members.[50] The books contained various materials, including a thorough section on the many proposed amendments to the Shays-Meehan bill. An appropriate response to each amendment was given, as well as a detailed explanation of why the reformers did or did not support such an item. The briefing books also included arguments against the other substitute bills as well as the Freshman bill. These materials were made available to anyone who desired to speak on the issue to the press or on the House floor. Additional materials were prepared by Democratic staff to counter the expected attacks on President Clinton and the Democratic Party regarding the fundraising scandals of the 1996 election. Each possible attack was matched with similar charges of Republican campaign finance irregularities.

At this crucial stage of the process, once again the public interest groups were extremely helpful in securing positive news coverage. This positive coverage emboldened some members to defy more easily those interest groups that were opposed to the reform effort. The reform groups also worked with congressional staff to help lobby other members and other groups for support. As always they provided valuable expertise and knowledge. Indeed, many of the public interest group lobbyists were veterans of other campaign finance reform battles. These efforts bolstered Shays's comment that "people outside of Washington do care about campaign finance."

In Spite of It All, the Bill Passes the House

Consideration of campaign finance reform, especially further consideration of the paycheck protection issue, was delayed again until after the June 2 primary election in California, where a proposition that would limit union political activity (that is, a paycheck protection measure) was on the statewide ballot. Many in the GOP, including Pete Wilson, then the governor of California, did not want the outcome of the initiative to be affected by potential House action. Furthermore, many speculated that the GOP wanted to use a potential California win as a way to reraise this issue in this round of debate.[51] In the end, the paycheck protection measure was defeated at the polls in California, but the prospect of an antiunion outcome had many reformers holding their breath and many antireformers hoping to achieve such a victory on the national level.

By early June, as campaign finance reform, under the unorthodox and complex process set out for it, approached consideration on the House floor, the Commission bill continued to worry the Shays-Meehan reformers. The Commission bill was sure to attract many votes, perhaps enough to trump the Shays-Meehan bill. In the final days before floor consideration, however, Democratic Shays-Meehan supporters struck a deal with John Dingell and Carolyn Maloney, D-N.Y., the key Democratic sponsors of the Commission bill. Dingell and Maloney agreed to vote "present" on their Commission bill and to support its attachment to the Shays-Meehan bill as an amendment.[52] Dingell and Maloney distributed a Dear Colleague letter outlining the agreement and asking others to follow their lead, and they appeared at a June 4 press conference to announce the merger of the Commission bill with the Shays-Meehan bill. The Commission bill would be accepted by all Shays-

Meehan supporters as a friendly amendment. This move pleased many supporters of the Commission bill, but it enraged several Republican backers,
such as Commission bill cosponsor Rick White, who had wanted the Commission bill to replace the Shays-Meehan bill.

Nevertheless, adding the reform commission to the Shays-Meehan bill
actually improved the proposal somewhat, for it allowed a commission to
consider issues that were not covered by the bill, such as millionaire candidates and contribution limits. More important, the deal ensured that the
Commission bill would not trump the Shays-Meehan bill. Without the support of its original Democratic sponsors, the Commission bill failed on June
17 with 156 yeas, 201 nays, and 68 (including Dingell and Maloney) voting
present.

With the Commission bill out of the way and the Republican leadership unable to stop the mounting support for the Shays-Meehan bill, the
challenge that remained for the reformers was the barrage of potentially
coalition-destroying amendments that were to be offered to the Shays-
Meehan bill. On June 18 Shays secured a commitment from Majority Leader
Dick Armey that the debate on campaign finance reform would be concluded by the August recess. Many supporters of the Shays-Meehan bill were
pleased at this promise, but Shays had to smooth over Democratic anger that
the promise was not more specific about the exact timing and procedures for
the debate. And, of course, many did not take promises regarding campaign
finance reform from GOP leaders very seriously.

General debate on the Shays-Meehan substitute bill began on June 18,
1998. One of the first challenges faced was an amendment offered by Republican Bill Thomas that would have made each of the parts of the Shays-
Meehan bill "non-severable." The amendment would have required that if
part of the act were struck down by the courts, then the entire law would fall
with it. Martin Frost, the DCCC chairman, spoke in favor of the amendment on the House floor, but other Democrats and GOP reformers saw it as
a poison pill amendment. This was the first poison pill amendment faced by
the reformers. If passed, the amendment would have led to a division in support for the Shays-Meehan bill. This amendment, however, failed on June 19
by a 155–224 vote. The first challenge had been met, but the death-by-
amendment special rule ensured that many more amendments were waiting
in the wings. Some of the amendments attempted to alter the Shays-Meehan
bill substantively, and others merely tried to break up the coalition of support for its passage.

Throughout this time the reform staffers met regularly to develop strategies regarding responses to upcoming amendments. They worked on poten-

tial responses to critiques and how to use the rules of debate, such as the five-minute rule, to their advantage. The House limits debate on an amendment offered in the Committee of the Whole to five minutes for its sponsor and five minutes for an opponent.[53] With unanimous consent more time can be granted. The staff and members also were versed in using a pro forma amendment entitled, "Strike the last word." A member gains recognition to speak from the chair by asking to "strike the last word" spoken by the last speaker and therefore to pick up where he or she left off. When a member uses this amendment, he or she does not intend to offer any changes to the measure under discussion but, rather, seeks to have five minutes of further debate. However, a member may use "Strike the last word" only once. Using these parliamentary procedures strategically allowed both sides to exercise more control over the debate.

On another front, fourteen Republican reform members met with the Campaign Reform Project's Business Advisory Committee on June 24.[54] Many key business executives were in attendance: Jerry Kohlberg of Kohlberg & Company; Warren Buffett, chairman of Berkshire Hathaway; Thomas Murphy, former chairman and CEO of Capital Cities/ABC; Raymond Plank, chairman and CEO of Apache Corporation; and Robert Stuart, chairman emeritus of Quaker Oats. These corporate executives favored reform, in part because they were tired of being asked by both parties for huge soft money contributions and of fearing that they would be shut out of the legislative process if they did not comply. During the gathering, Majority Leader Dick Armey was invited in to meet the Advisory Committee members.[55] This meeting sent a message to the Republicans that leaders in the business community, perhaps the most important GOP constituency, strongly supported campaign finance reform. Later these businessmen would place a key advertisement in major newspapers in support of the reform effort, an action clearly contrary to the wishes of the GOP leaders.

The reform effort was assisted once again by the Clinton administration in the form of a letter sent to Speaker Newt Gingrich from the Department of Justice indicating that several of the amendments to be offered to the Shays-Meehan substitute were legally unacceptable.[56] This was another clear message to Republican leaders that momentum was building for campaign finance reform. Additionally, the reformers were emboldened by a statement from nine leaders of the American Civil Liberties Union (ACLU), who "rejected the group's long-standing basic argument that campaign spending is a form of free speech."[57] The reform opponents' best ace-in-the-hole had been the ACLU, because this traditionally liberal organization was the most well-known advocate of free speech rights. Thus, this statement by some high-profile ACLU members that limits on campaign spending are not a violation of free speech rights weakened one of the reform opponents' most powerful advocates.

Yet many Dear Colleague letters were beginning to surface, attacking various provisions of the Shays-Meehan bill. One in particular drew a good deal of attention—a July 13, 1998, letter entitled, "Vote NO on the Shays-Meehan 'Campaign Finance Reform' Bill," signed by fifty-three nonprofit, issue-oriented citizen advocacy groups. These groups claimed that they could end up violating several provisions in the Shays-Meehan bill if they publicly commented on the views held by members of Congress or candidates, regardless of what time of year (that is, during an election season or otherwise) they made their comments. This was an argument that just might defeat the Shays-Meehan bill, so Shays-Meehan supporters knew they needed to work hard to address this and other concerns. It became clear that educating people about the bill's contents was going to be vital in this game where the unknown and misunderstood might contribute to the bill's demise. The battle for control of information began with each side releasing Dear Colleague letters to make key points or counter the other side. A war of paper ensued, as a continual stream of these letters clogged House members' fax machines and mailboxes.

The number of amendments to be offered to the Shays-Meehan substitute alone made it clear to everyone that this process might never end, an outcome neither side desired. In an effort to avoid this, Republican Bill Thomas helped broker a deal between Shays-Meehan supporters and the Republican leadership in early July for a unanimous consent agreement that would whittle down to fifty-five the number of amendments offered to the Shays-Meehan substitute.[58] Even though unanimous consent agreements are common in the Senate, they rarely are used in the House. The agreement that Thomas helped craft was an important part of the Shays-Meehan bill's unorthodox legislative journey. Although the Shays-Meehan bill still faced many potential pitfalls, this agreement not only decreased the number of amendments that would be considered but clearly listed what the amendments would be and in what order they would be considered. This made preparation for both sides much easier. The unanimous consent agreement also made it clear that if a particular amendment was not offered when it came up for consideration on the floor it could not be brought up again. This was an option that would prove helpful to the reformers as the debate waged on. However, while the unanimous consent agreement improved the process, it did not shield the Shays-Meehan bill from poison pill amendments intended to kill it.

The GOP leaders were probably anxious to get the debate on campaign finance reform over with. Consideration of the hundreds of possible amendments would have dragged on for quite some time and given the reform interest groups and the press more and more reasons to beat up on the Republican leaders. They did not need any more bad press as they approached the August recess, when members would have to face their constituents back home. They also began to think about the potential impact of campaign finance reform as an issue in the midterm elections just four months away.

Chief among the potential killer amendments was one offered by the Republicans Tom DeLay and John Doolittle. This amendment aimed to gut the issue advocacy provisions of the Shays-Meehan bill in the name of protecting First Amendment free speech rights. DeLay and Doolittle argued that the Shays-Meehan bill would ban the use of voter guides, a favored tool of the Christian Coalition and other conservative groups. A voter guide specifies candidates' positions on various issues important to the guide's sponsor. The Christian Coalition distributes its voter guides in churches across the nation on the Sunday before election day. Reformers pointed out that the Shays-Meehan bill already contained a provision to allow for printed voter guides, and that the DeLay-Doolittle amendment would continue to allow outside groups to spend unlimited and unreported amounts of money anonymously to broadcast campaign ads (masquerading as issue advocacy ads) in federal elections. This was indeed a poison pill amendment. For many members, reining in the uncontrolled use of issue advocacy ads was the primary purpose of the reform effort, and they would not support the Shays-Meehan bill if it did not do that.

The reformers were well prepared to fight this and other amendments. The Senate battles had familiarized them with the possible constitutional attacks the opposition would level against their bill, and the Senate reformers' mistakes had taught them much. Many times the debate dragged on well toward midnight, and as one might expect, these late-night debates made it difficult to keep members focused on the issue and motivated to debate it on the floor of the House. Part of the GOP leadership's strategy, it seemed, was to wear down the reformers. Thus, a great effort was made to ensure that there would always be reform members available to speak on the floor, especially for the late-night sessions. For example, members were asked to sign up to be available for certain time slots and prepared to speak on campaign finance reform. Such extensive planning was rarely seen for debates on other issues. The opposition appeared to be less organized, offering the same speakers and arguments over and over again.

Reps. Tom DeLay, R-Texas (*left*), and John T. Doolittle, R-Calif. (*right*), who were against the campaign finance reform legislation.

The DeLay-Doolittle amendment was defeated, effectively neutralizing the First Amendment issue. After each defeat of a killer amendment by the Shays-Meehan reform coalition, outside public interest groups, as well as Shays and Meehan themselves, made positive statements to the press about key members' support. Additionally, Shays and Meehan sent personal thank-you notes to everyone who helped defeat these key amendments.

During the course of June and July, the Shays-Meehan bill encountered a series of amendments on the floor of the House, with most of the debate coming on July 20 and July 30, 1998. Shays and Meehan provided vote cards containing descriptions of these amendments as well as their positions to all representatives on the House floor who desired them for use in voting. Of the forty-one amendments voted upon, twenty-three passed, including eight by voice vote. One important amendment was a compromise crafted out of the six individual amendments offered by Rep. Linda Smith, R-Wash., regarding voter guides. This compromise was achieved through long negotiations between Shays, Smith, and their respective staffs. With the support of the reformers, this amendment passed 343 to 84. Passage of the Smith amendment essentially slammed the door on other amendments about voter guides. The reform coalition successfully defended its legislation from all fourteen poison pill amendments it faced. The sponsors of five other poison pill amendments chose not to offer their amendments for the House's consideration.[59] Box 3-3 (p. 102) provides a more thorough listing of each amendment the bill faced, as seen from the eyes of the Shays-Meehan reformers.

The Shays-Meehan reformers successfully defended their reform bill against the destructive poison pill amendments and had the momentum to persuade sponsors of some of the other substitute bills to withdraw their bills. Reps. David Obey, D-Wis.; John Tierney, D-Mass.; Sam Farr, D-Calif.; and Tom Campbell, R-Calif., withdrew their substitute bills. On August 3, the Shays-Meehan substitute bill passed the House by a margin of 237 to 186. The remaining substitutes, the Doolittle and Freshman bills, were defeated on August 6 by votes of 131–299 and 147–222, respectively.[60] In a symbolic gesture of appreciation for the efforts of the freshmen, Shays and Meehan allowed their bill to amend in whole (and replace) the Freshman bill, thus passing the Shays-Meehan bill as H.R. 2183, under the original Freshman bill number. The final vote for the Shays-Meehan bill was on August 6, 1998, with 252 members voting for its passage and 179 against it, far more than the 218 needed for passage.

In all, sixty-one Republicans voted for final passage of the Shays-Meehan bill, a blow to House Republican leaders who were seen as the "big losers" of the day.[61] Ironically, the GOP leadership may have contributed to the final passage of the bill they sought to prevent. Republican Marge Roukema, who previously had signed the discharge petition, noted, "The odd thing is that the House Republican leadership improved the bill's chances by trying so hard to kill it. This prolonged the debate, made the issue more prominent and put more members on the spot."[62] However, at the end of the day, credit properly was given to the reformers, most notably to Chris Shays and Marty Meehan, for not giving up on what had been seen by many as a "no-hope issue."[63]

After the long, hard fight, reformers were ecstatic and hopeful that the measure might pass the Senate this time around. As might be expected, however, GOP Senate leaders were reluctant to consider the issue at all, having already done so twice before in the 105th Congress and hoping that it would go away without further consideration by their chamber. As we saw in Chapter 2, the reform effort failed to attract enough votes to thwart a filibuster for a third time in the Senate.

Conclusion: Successfully Negotiating the Labyrinth

The journey of the Shays-Meehan campaign finance reform bill through the House of Representatives was indeed unusual, and it illustrates many important characteristics of contemporary congressional policymaking. The unique character of the issue itself forces lawmakers to consider their personal ambitions and motivations as well as the issue's impact on important constituencies, their districts, and the country. The structure of campaign finance regulations affects each legislator's professional life, and the political parties potentially have much to gain or lose if changes are made to the campaign finance system. Few issues bring into focus both a pressing public problem and the motivations and ambitions of political actors.

The experience of the Shays-Meehan bill also illustrates many of the unorthodox procedures used in contemporary policymaking. It is indeed unusual for one bill to be subject to so many unconventional procedures, and the ability to examine them in the context of one policy battle is particularly instructive. Both sides used various tools to try to either promote or kill the issue. The reformers twice successfully used a discharge petition to force the Republican leaders to put campaign finance reform on the schedule. They formed both bipartisan and partisan task forces to help keep the issue alive. The GOP leaders used a variety of unusual methods to try to deny the Shays-Meehan bill a clean vote on the floor of the House. For example, they tried to make the issue go away altogether by putting their own campaign finance bills on the suspension calendar. They tried to kill the bill by subjecting it to hundreds of amendments and making it compete with other campaign finance reform bills that offered members political cover. As the political scientist Barbara Sinclair points out, a hostile political climate often forces innovation in the legislative process, and the story of campaign finance reform in the 105th Congress confirms her theory.[64]

Campaign finance reform had been on the policy agenda for years and even passed Congress in 1992 only to be vetoed.[65] What the political scientist John Kingdon has called the policy window had been open before, and once again the circumstances and attitudes that seemed ripe for success were present.[66] Campaign finance reform offers an interesting case study for Kingdon's policymaking model. Why has the issue made it on to the agenda many times but not actually been enacted into law? The nature of the issue itself is undoubtedly part of the explanation. The stakes are high for lawmakers and parties when changes are made to the system for financing their campaigns. Indeed, campaign finance changes are notorious for resulting in many unintended consequences (for example, the rise of thousands of political action committees in the wake of passage of the Federal Election Campaign Act and its amendments in the 1970s). Thus, resistance to change is understandable. Moreover, despite a new crop of campaign finance scandals from the 1996 election, the public was not focused on campaign finance reform as a top policy priority. Although the policy window may have been partially open, perhaps the idea's time had not fully come.

BOX 3-3 Proposed Amendments to the Shays-Meehan Bill

Date	Action	Shays-Meehan Position	Shays-Meehan Assessment
6/19/98	Thomas amendment fails, 155–254	No: poison pill	Provides that if any portion of the bill is found to be unconstitutional, the entire measure would be invalid. This type of non-severability provision is extraordinarily rare.
6/19/98	C. Maloney amendment passes, 325–78	Yes	Strengthens the legislation, by establishing a commission to further study campaign finance reform.
6/19/98	Gillmor amendment passes, 395–0	Yes	Expresses the sense of the House that all Americans should be treated equally in their ability to make campaign contributions.
7/14/98	Doolittle voter guide amendment fails, 201–219	No: poison pill	Guts bill's provision that treats sham "issue ads" as campaign ads, by exempting from the definition of "express advocacy" any printed or electronically posted communication that discusses the voting record of a candidate, unless it uses the magic words.
7/14/98	Fossella amendment passes, 282–126	No	Undermines the ability of legal permanent residents to participate in the campaign system by prohibiting anyone who is not a U.S. citizen from making campaign contributions.
7/20/98	Wicker White House accommodations amendment passes, 391–4	Yes	Prevents the quid pro quo exchange of campaign contributions for White House accommodations.

7/20/98	Stearns amendment (similar to Fossella) passes, 267–131	No	Undermines the ability of legal permanent residents to participate in the campaign system, by prohibiting anyone who is not a U.S. citizen from making campaign contributions—to parties as well as candidates.
7/20/98	Pickering amendment passes, 344–56	Yes	Strengthens the foreign money ban by prohibiting the use of willful blindness as a defense against charge of violating the ban.
7/20/98	Nick Smith foreign money ban amendment passed by voice vote	Yes	Strengthens the foreign money ban by increasing the penalties for violating the ban.
7/20/98	DeLay "controlling legal authority" amendment passes, 360–36	Yes	Helps ensure federal property is not used for fund-raising, by expressing the sense of Congress that controlling legal authority prohibits fund-raising on federal property.
7/20/98	McInnis amendment passes, 391–7	Yes	Prohibits solicitation of funds in return for obtaining access to government property.
7/20/98	Paxon union disclosure amendment fails, 150–248	No: poison pill	Requires additional reporting and disclosure of union financial activities. The Shays-Meehan bill already greatly increased disclosures of union campaign activity, but this amendment is very broad, going far beyond the scope of campaign finance reform.

continued

BOX 3-3 Proposed Amendments to the Shays-Meehan Bill *continued*

Date	Action	Shays-Meehan Position	Shays-Meehan Assessment
7/20/98	Hefley Air Force One reimbursement amendment passes, 222–177	Neutral	Requires reimbursement to the federal government any time Air Force One is used for campaign activity.
7/20/98	Hefley Air Force One prohibition amendment is withdrawn	Withdrawn	Prohibits the use of Air Force One for political fund-raising.
7/20/98	Northup walking around money amendment passes, 284–114	No	Imposes an over-broad prohibition of any cash payments by parties on election day.
7/30/98	Goodlatte motor-voter amendment fails, 165–260	No: poison pill	Rolls back Motor Voter Law (thus breaking apart coalition of support for Shays-Meehan) by requiring proof of citizenship and Social Security numbers to register to vote, allowing photo ID requirements without anti-discrimination safeguards, and eliminating mail-in registration. Goes far beyond the scope of campaign finance reform.
7/30/98	Wicker photo ID amendment fails, 192–231	No: poison pill	Rolls back Motor Voter Law (thus breaking apart coalition of support for Shays-Meehan) by allowing states to require photo IDs to vote, without safeguards to protect against

Date	Amendment	Position	Description
7/20/98	Snowbarger amendment passes by voice vote	Neutral	discrimination, particularly against minorities, older women, and the poor. Goes far beyond the scope of campaign finance reform.
7/20/98	Whitfield presidential soft money amendment passes by voice vote	Accept	Ban on coordinated soft money activities by presidential candidates.
7/30/98	Calvert in-district amendment fails, 147–278	No: poison pill	Opposed by many candidates in minority and low-income districts because of concerns it harms their ability to run an effective campaign (thus breaking apart coalition of support for Shays-Meehan). The amendment, which requires all candidates to raise at least 50 percent of their contributions from within their home districts, is unconstitutional, according to Congressional Research Service experts.
7/30/98	Salmon amendment passes by voice vote	Was expected to be withdrawn	Requires post of names of certain Air Force One passengers on the Internet.
7/20/98	Stearns foreign nationals amendment is withdrawn	Withdrawn	Prohibits soft money from foreign nationals.

continued

BOX 3-3 Proposed Amendments to the Shays-Meehan Bill *continued*

Date	Action	Shays-Meehan Position	Shays-Meehan Assessment
7/30/98	Linda Smith amendment passes, 343–84	Yes	Strengthens the Shays-Meehan substitute by clarifying the bill's protections of voter guides. Six Smith amendments were modified and combined into one.
7/30/98	Rohrabacher "independently wealthy" amendment fails, 155–272	No: poison pill	Eliminates the individual contribution limit (currently $1,000) for candidates whose opponents use personal funds in excess of $1,000. Would allow candidates whose opponents spend more than $1,000 of personal money to raise unlimited amounts from individuals, up to the amount of the opponent's personal contribution. This would allow a candidate to raise hundreds of thousands in hard money from a single contributor.
7/30/98	Paul signature requirements amendment fails, 62–363	Lean no	Undermines ability of states to structure their elections by preempting state laws on signature requirements for ballot access.
7/30/98	Paul debates amendment fails, 88–337	Lean no	Prohibits publicly funded presidential candidates from participating in debates where certain third-party candidates are excluded.

Date	Amendment	Pass?	Description
7/30/98	DeLay "legislative alert" amendment fails, 185–241	No: poison pill	Guts bill's provision that treats sham "issue ads" as campaign ads, in the name of protecting "legislative alerts." Legislative alerts are already protected by the bill, but this amendment goes too far by creating a broad exemption for any communication that deals with any issue that may be the subject of a vote, and urges people to call their Representative. This would permit sham issue ads to continue.
7/30/98	DeLay independent counsel amendment is withdrawn	No	Expresses the sense of Congress that the attorney general should appoint an independent counsel to investigate the Clinton White House. This lengthy, partisan amendment reads like an indictment, is far beyond the scope of Shays-Meehan, and could undermine support for the bill.
7/30/98	J. Peterson "motor voter" amendment fails, 165–260	No: poison pill	Rolls back Motor Voter Law (thus breaking apart coalition of support for Shays-Meehan) by establishing an unworkable voter eligibility confirmation program through the Social Security Administration and INS. Overrides anti-discrimination safeguards. Goes far beyond the scope of campaign finance reform.
7/30/98	Barr "motor voter" amendment is withdrawn	No: poison pill	Rolls back Motor Voter Law (thus breaking apart coalition of support for Shays-Meehan) by allowing states to require proof of citizenship to vote, overriding anti-discrimination safeguards. Goes far beyond the scope of campaign finance reform.

continued

BOX 3-3　Proposed Amendments to the Shays-Meehan Bill continued

Date	Action	Shays-Meehan Position	Shays-Meehan Assessment
7/30/98	Barr Voting Rights Act amendment fails, 142–261	No: poison pill	Rolls back Voting Rights Act (thus breaking apart coalition of support for Shays-Meehan) by prohibiting bilingual voting material. Overrides anti-discrimination safeguards. Goes far beyond the scope of campaign finance reform.
7/30/98	Traficant amendment passes by voice vote	Lean no	Overrides House ethics process by establishing expulsion procedures for House members who violate the foreign contribution ban.
7/30/98	Delay background music amendment passes by voice vote	Neutral (if modified)	Exempts background music in campaign ads in determining whether an ad constitutes "express advocacy."
7/30/98	Delay "anything of value" amendment is withdrawn	No	Weakens the anti-coordination provisions in the bill by allowing coordination with candidates on anything of value, including any ad, unless it contains express advocacy. This would weaken current law and allow issue ads to be directly coordinated with candidates.
7/30/98	Delay media consultants amendment is withdrawn	No	Weakens the anti-coordination provisions in the bill by allowing candidates to use the same media consultants, pollsters, etc., as outside groups, without the activity being considered coordination.

7/30/98	Delay legislative matter communication amendment fails, 195–218	No	Weakens the anti-coordination provisions in the bill by exempting any communication with a member or staff on a pending legislative matter, regardless of whether the intent is to influence an election.
7/30/98	Gutknecht amendment is withdrawn	Neutral	Prohibits fund-raising on federal property.
7/30/98	Schaffer amendment is withdrawn	No: poison pill	Adds Paycheck Protection Act to the bill, undermining support for the legislation. The Shays-Meehan substitute already deals with union influence in elections, and applies the rules equally to corporations.
7/30/98	Horn amendment fails, 117–294	Lean no	Adds a cost of $25 million to the bill (thus potentially undermining the coalition of support for Shays-Meehan) by allowing candidates to send two low-cost mailings per household.
7/30/98	Upton amendment is withdrawn	No: poison pill	Opposed by many candidates in minority and low-income districts because of concerns it harms their ability to run an effective campaign (thus breaking apart coalition of support for Shays-Meehan). The amendment prohibits candidates from raising more than 50 percent of their contributions from PACs.

continued

BOX 3-3 Proposed Amendments to the Shays-Meehan Bill *continued*

Date	Action	Shays-Meehan Position	Shays-Meehan Assessment
7/30/98	Nick Smith broadcasters amendment is withdrawn	No	Imposes unnecessary burden on broadcasters by requiring them to report to the FEC information about the cost and sponsor of "political ads." The Shays-Meehan bill already significantly increases disclosure of campaign ads, and brings sham "issue ads" into the campaign system, where disclosure is required. The amendment is vague and overreaching.
7/30/98	Shadegg amendment passes by voice vote	Neutral	Allows candidates to go directly to court to file claims of election law violations close to an election.
7/30/98	Delay voter guide amendment is withdrawn	No: poison pill	Guts bill's provisions that treat sham "issue ads" as campaign ads, for any printed communication that deals with a candidate's voting record.
7/31/98	Shaw in-state amendment fails, 160–253	No: poison pill	Opposed by many candidates in minority and low-income districts because of concerns it harms their ability to run an effective campaign (thus breaking apart coalition of support for Shays-Meehan). The amendment requires all candidates to raise at least 50 percent of their contribution from within their home state.

7/30/98	Kaptur constitutional amendment is withdrawn	No	Establishes procedures for expedited consideration of a constitutional amendment to establish spending limits if any portion of Shays-Meehan is found unconstitutional. The amendment is beyond the scope of the substitute, which does not deal with spending limits.
7/30/98	Kaptur foreign-controlled PACs amendment passes, 341–74	No	Limits the ability of some Americans to participate in the political process, by prohibiting PACs (including those set up by U.S. subsidiaries of foreign companies) sponsored by foreign-controlled corporations. Directly conflicts with the Gillmor amendment to Shays-Meehan, which passed June 19 by a vote of 395–0.
7/30/98	Nick Smith foreign money penalties amendment is withdrawn	Neutral	Increases penalties for violations of foreign money ban.
7/31/98	Stearns modification of the Fossella amendment passes, 385–29	Yes	Modifies the Fosella amendment (which passed July 14) to permit permanent resident aliens serving in the armed forces to make campaign contributions.
7/30/98	Stearns conspiracy penalty amendment passes by voice vote	Neutral	Increases the penalty for conspiracy to violate presidential campaign spending limits.

continued

BOX 3-3 Proposed Amendments to the Shays-Meehan Bill *continued*

Date	Action	Shays-Meehan Position	Shays-Meehan Assessment
7/31/98	Stearns presidential public financing amendment passes, 368–44	Neutral	Bans solicitation of soft money by presidential and vice presidential candidates who receive public financing. Because the bill already bans the solicitation of all soft money, the amendment is redundant (but not harmful).
7/31/98	Whitfield amendment to triple contribution limit fails, 102–315	No: poison pill	Triples the individual contribution limit (from $1,000 to $3,000). Because of the concern that tripling the limit would increase the role of wealthy contributors, the amendment would undermine support for the bill. The amendment is strongly opposed by groups advocating the bill, including Public Citizen, Common Cause, the League of Women Voters, and US PIRG.
7/31/98	Whitfield amendment to revert to "magic words" only fails, 173–238	No: poison pill	Guts bill's provision that treats sham "issue ads" as campaign ads by amending the definition of "express advocacy" to mean magic words only, reverting to our wholly inadequate current law.

7/31/98	English bundling amendment fails, 134–276	No: poison pill	Imposes a partial ban on "bundling" contributions (thus breaking apart the coalition of support for Shays-Meehan). While some Shays-Meehan supporters oppose bundling, the provision was removed from earlier version of the legislation to increase support for the bill.
7/31/98	Gekas amendment passes by voice vote	Yes	Improves FEC enforcement by requiring "tainted money" be deposited in an escrow account rather than immediately returned to the contributor.
7/31/98	Miller amendment is withdrawn	No: poison pill	Requires additional reporting and disclosure of union financial activities.
7/31/98	Doolittle attorney's fees amendment is withdrawn	Neutral	Permits courts to require the FEC to pay attorney's fees in certain cases.

Source: Adapted from "Shays-Meehan Campaign Finance Reform Status of Amendments/Recommended Votes," prepared by the offices of Representatives Shays and Meehan, July 1998.

4

STRATEGIC CONSIDERATIONS
Issue Leaders, Policy Entrepreneurs, and Issue Networks

One of the many strategy sessions for the Shays-Meehan campaign finance reform effort got under way in a meeting room at the Capitol. It was late spring 1998 and the key reform House members and their staffs had gathered to talk about strategy for securing passage of the Shays-Meehan bill. Representative Shays opened by thanking the members for attending. He explained that this was a first step in a long process to bring together reform members from both sides of the aisle (that is, from both parties). The House members discussed strategies and asked for guidance from Representatives Shays and Meehan about what they would accept as amendments to their bill and how the coalition of support would be held together. By the end of the meeting, the participants agreed that a network should be created to share information and to stay ahead of those opposed to passage of the Shays-Meehan bill. Shays and Meehan would emerge from this meeting more than just members of Congress; now they were issue leaders in their own right and becoming policy entrepreneurs in the legislative process.

As leaders of the reform coalition, Shays and Meehan were uniquely placed to carry out the different strategies needed to pass a limited, but meaningful campaign finance reform bill in the House of Representatives. For instance, the Republican Christopher Shays was able to mediate many of the often-heated disputes between the Republican leadership and Republican members of the reform coalition. Not all House members are in an appropriate position to negotiate between feuding camps, especially when one is the party leadership. Likewise, Democrats, including the party leaders, trusted Marty Meehan to represent their interests in the reform coalition.

However, Shays and Meehan were far from the only visible legislators involved in the campaign finance reform process. Other issue leaders on both sides of the debate played important roles in the process. They all provided voting cues for other members, suggesting how the other members should vote. They also crafted and disseminated the most convincing and compelling arguments and sought to use outside interest groups and the media in support of their positions. Additionally, they mobilized their core supporters to reach out to their fellow partisans to persuade them to vote their way on key amendments.

Yet Shays and Meehan stood out among the many issue leaders and eventually emerged as the recognized policy entrepreneurs of campaign finance reform in the House of Representatives. Shays and Meehan worked with the institutional constraints and opportunities that dotted the landscape through which the reformers and their opponents navigated, and the eventual outcome was characterized by these factors. For instance, by defeating the series of poison pill amendments that were part of the Republican leadership's death-by-amendment strategy described in the last chapter, the reformers had many opportunities to show the strength of support for their bill and to increase the size of the reform network they had built. In this chapter we discuss how Representatives Shays and Meehan met the challenge of policy entrepreneurship, organized an issue network, and led it to victory in the House. Theirs is a good case study of the importance of policy entrepreneurs in the contemporary policymaking process.

Issue Leaders and Policy Entrepreneurs

For a bill to succeed after being introduced in Congress, it generally has to be championed by an *issue leader* advocating some policy change—a senator or House member who devotes his or her time and resources to an issue and introduces legislation to address some perceived policy problem.[1] Thousands of bills are introduced every year. Some never make it past this stage and join the many measures that remain in relative obscurity. Indeed, most bills are referred to a committee and die there, never to be seriously considered. An issue leader will attempt to avoid this fate for his or her legislation and work to publicize the need for the policy change and gather support for the bill. Still, most of the measures proposed never see the light of day or may take many years to make it onto the active political agenda of items that receive serious consideration in Congress.

Popular policies with a good chance of legislative success and some clear electoral benefit for their sponsors are the most likely ones to attract issue leaders. For example, as health care and the regulation of health maintenance organizations (HMOs) became issues of top concern to the American public in 1999, lawmakers from both parties rushed to promote legislation calling for a "patients' bill of rights." Other, less popular and less electorally beneficial proposals, although they may be good policy, do not always attract legislators to champion their cause.

Issue leadership quite often is motivated by goals other than reelection, however. Issue leaders sometimes emerge on policy issues that cut across party lines when the majority party leadership and its members are divided. An issue leader can move to fill the resulting vacuum between leaders and members and work to create a coalition of support with members from both parties. Thus, a legislator championing a particular bill or cause may defy his or her own party leaders, as was the case with the GOP campaign finance reformers in the 105th Congress. If successful, an issue leader who opposes the party's position can gain influence, but he or she also will draw the wrath of the party leaders, who might see such a member as a maverick within their ranks. That is why issue leaders often pursue the support of outside groups and organizations that can help provide "cover" from any threats of sanctions from the party leaders. These outside supporters can, for example, obtain favorable stories in the media and, therefore, help sway public opinion in favor of the issue leaders, and party leaders are wary about acting against public opinion.

An issue leader may be a legislator aspiring to higher office and, therefore, may be promoting a cause to gain distinction from congressional colleagues and to attract interest group and media attention. Committee chairpersons and party leaders who want to preserve their reputations for influence will sponsor legislation and seek support from colleagues to ensure that someone else does not beat them to it. Additionally, issue leaders tend to emerge on issues to protect or bolster the institution of Congress. For example, under the heat of scandal, congressional leaders pushed through legislation to ban gifts to House members in 1995. The gift ban was not popular with many legislators, particularly since it implied that members were being influenced by gifts, such as extravagant vacations, from lobbyists. Yet congressional leaders understood the importance of maintaining the reputation of the institution of Congress for the sake of all members. Although such "in-

stitutional maintenance" issues may provide some indirect electoral benefits, they generally have few direct electoral payoffs. Indeed, they require
issue leaders who are electorally secure and are willing and able to pursue institutional power and good public policy goals rather than only reelection
ones.[2] Thus, many issue leaders are at a point in their careers where electoral
imperatives are less pressing, or they are somehow able to turn the issue to
some electoral advantage by demonstrating their new-found clout or their
effectiveness to their constituents back home.

Campaign finance reform can be viewed as one of these institutional
maintenance issues. Its passage would provide little direct electoral benefit to
most members. Indeed, constituents back home are not demanding something be done about the campaign finance system, and voting against reform
has not hurt legislators in recent elections. Moreover, under the current system, incumbent senators and House members enjoy a great financial advantage over their electoral challengers, so there is little if any direct electoral
motivation to change the campaign finance laws. Yet enactment of meaningful campaign finance reform legislation would, in the view of many observers, fix a campaign finance system that is broken if not outright corrupt.
For those members concerned about maintaining the reputation of the institution of Congress (as well as those interested in reaping the indirect electoral benefits, if any, that might come from being seen as trying to correct the
institution's problems), campaign finance reform might be a worthy cause
to consider. Thus, for example, many reformers argued that they were not
part of the status quo (the old guard that resisted reform, such as the GOP
leaders). Instead, they were willing to stand "alone" in pursuit of good government while distancing themselves from what is wrong with government.
They presented themselves as part of the solution, not part of the problem.

Campaign finance reform does not enjoy the support of the majority
party leadership in Congress. Thus, it is not the easiest issue for just any legislator to champion. The Republicans had supported at least some proposed
reforms while in the minority, but they were quick to rebuff efforts to enact
reform upon gaining the majority. The Republican leaders in the House and
the Senate have worked hard to derail efforts to reform the current system,
as we saw in Chapters 2 and 3. Campaign finance is a complex issue that requires a good deal of time to understand, and lawmakers have very little time
to devote to projects beyond their already heavy workloads. Thus, campaign
finance reform attracts an unusual group of issue leaders who generally are
not facing serious electoral threat, are willing to devote their time to the
issue, and are able to grasp the complexities of the laws, regulations, and
court decisions they aim to reform.

Issue leaders are a focus point for the public, the media, and fellow lawmakers. An issue leader is someone to look to for expertise and voting cues. They provide key information, and, if they do not have it, they readily know where to find it. Issue leaders have to be willing to help transform other members through education to believe in the effort and be willing to be lieutenants who will go forth and sell the ideas to others.[3]

Just because a legislator decides to take the lead on a particular issue, however, there is no guarantee that the issue will make it onto the agenda of items considered by the House and the Senate. Indeed, those issues that do not enjoy the support of the majority party leadership, such as campaign finance reform, are especially unlikely to receive serious consideration. Members who do achieve some measure of success and become known to specialized publics within and outside of Congress, although they may remain unknown to the mass public, rise to the position of *policy entrepreneur:* those recognized for "stimulating more than . . . responding" to outside political forces in a given field.[4] The terms *issue leader* and *policy entrepreneur* often have been used interchangeably, but we make the distinction here to highlight the extraordinary effort that is usually necessary to pass major legislation. Lawmakers who rise to the level of policy entrepreneurship help create and take advantage of the "policy window" of opportunity in which the circumstances and attitudes for legislative success are present.[5] An issue leader becomes a policy entrepreneur when, for example, along the way the legislator successfully encourages others to support the cause, builds informational and support networks crucial to steering the bill through the legislature, and undertakes internal and external strategies that result in legislative success.

Policy entrepreneurs are "people who seek to initiate dynamic policy change."[6] They strive for support by "identifying problems, networking in policy circles, shaping the terms of policy debates, and building coalitions."[7] Additionally, policy entrepreneurs seek to make contacts with other legislators as well as potential allies outside the institution of Congress, such as interest groups and the media.[8] They develop "networks" to assist them with crafting arguments that aid in building a coalition of support.[9]

In order to be successful, policy entrepreneurs need to build strong coalitions of support for their ideas. They need not only a majority for passage, and indeed quite often a supermajority in the Senate, but also a group of individuals who are committed to the policy goal and who will assist in fending off complex and perhaps unfair rules or dilatory tactics by the opposition. This requires the policy entrepreneur to go a step further than just internal coalition building; he or she must build an *issue network*. This network usually begins to evolve within the institution of Congress. Key legislators and their staffs are tapped to assist in lobbying other lawmakers and their respective party and allied caucuses (for example, the Congressional Black Caucus) to vote in particular ways on the issue. The most successful issue networks, however, are those that have both an internal and external component, support from both inside and outside the institution of Congress. Such an external network includes outside interest groups, the media, and governmental actors such as the president and others in the executive branch.

An expansive issue network provides an informational advantage to those who participate within the network and a disadvantage to those who are excluded or are in opposition to it. Thus, there is an incentive for legislators to join. This sort of network also is able to move beyond just the pursuit of votes to play an educational role that assists in widening the support network and, therefore, increasing the likelihood of legislative success. Clearly, creating such a network is a tremendous task that only sometimes results in passage of a bill. Those who rise to the challenge of policy entrepreneurship, therefore, must be extraordinarily committed to their cause, as Representatives Shays and Meehan proved to be.

The Issue Leaders, Policy Entrepreneurs, and Issue Networks of the Campaign Finance Reform Debate

Each senator and House member has dealt personally with the complex rules and regulations that govern the financing of their campaigns. As a result, most lawmakers have their own thoughts about what, if anything, is wrong with the system and what, if anything, should be done to reform it. Furthermore, reformers themselves disagree on the needed remedies. As with other policy problems, there is no one clear solution, nor do the various solutions divide along conventional battle lines such as party or region. Moreover, as was the case in the 105th Congress, the different bills introduced often are not amenable to combination and their sponsors are not open to compromise. Therefore, there was a good deal of competition among the campaign finance reform issue leaders to rise to the level of policy entrepreneur—that is, to be the leaders of the coalition that would become the one recognized by those inside and outside of Congress as *the* reform coalition.

Despite the lack of reform proposals from the Senate and House committees investigating the alleged campaign finance violations arising from the 1996 election, more than 134 campaign finance bills were introduced during the 105th Congress. Of those, several received attention along the way. Among the issue leaders in the House were the coauthors of the Bipartisan

Campaign Reform Act, Christopher Shays and Martin Meehan. Moreover, several key members of the Shays-Meehan reform coalition emerged as leaders on specific subissues. For example, Tom Campbell, R-Calif., and Barney Frank, D-Mass., were the Shays-Meehan reform coalition's leaders on constitutional and procedural questions, respectively. Others emerged as leaders of specific subcoalitions. For instance, Minority Whip David Bonior, D-Mich., and Democratic Caucus chair Vic Fazio, D-Calif., did much of the party's work on the issue. Reps. Sander Levin, D-Mich., and Sam Gejdenson, D-Conn., were effective liaisons between the Shays-Meehan coalition and the Democratic Caucus. Reps. Michael Castle, R-Del., Marge Roukema, R-N.J., and other GOP moderates worked to bring fellow moderate Republicans into the reform effort, and Zach Wamp, R-Tenn., encouraged conservative GOP lawmakers to join.

Issue leaders also emerged around other campaign finance reform bills, and others arose in opposition to reform. Tom Allen, D-Me., and Asa Hutchinson, R-Ark., were the primary cosponsors of the Freshman bill in the House and the most active and visible advocates for that proposal.[10] John Dingell, D-Mich., Carolyn Maloney, D-N.Y., and Rick White, R-Wash., championed the Commission bill.

The key players in opposition to campaign finance reform in the House were Majority Whip Tom DeLay, R-Texas, Majority Leader Dick Armey, R-Texas, John Doolittle, R-Calif., and the Conservative Action Team (the CAT is a group of conservative Republican House members who work to move their party to the right on major policy issues). These GOP opponents were powerful players, representing not only the party leadership but also the strong coalition of conservative Republicans that in 1997 almost brought down Speaker Newt Gingrich, R-Ga., in a coup attempt. Additionally, although Bill Thomas, R-Calif., had been a respected leader on reform issues generally, he was seen in the context of campaign finance reform more as a member of the Republican leadership than a reform advocate.

In the Senate, John McCain, R-Ariz., and Russell Feingold, D-Wis., offered the lead reform bill, the companion bill to the Shays-Meehan bill in the House. These senators spent a great deal of time and effort early in the 105th Congress on campaign finance reform and were responsible for generating much of the initial interest, both in Congress and outside, in passing reform legislation. Although McCain's and Feingold's efforts may not have resulted in legislative success in the Senate, they provided the spark that enabled Representatives Shays and Meehan eventually to pass their bill in the House.

Other senators, such as Olympia Snowe, R-Me., and James Jeffords, R-Vt., also emerged as key players in the consideration of the McCain-Feingold bill. As discussed in Chapter 2, they helped secure votes by offering useful amendments and brokering deals that made the bill acceptable to more senators. Each of these Senate reform proponents continued working with House reformers and interest groups to secure passage of reform in the House even after the McCain-Feingold bill went down to defeat in the Senate. Heading up the opposition was Sen. Mitch McConnell, R-Ky., chairman of the National Republican Senatorial Committee, the party committee responsible for electing Republicans to the U.S. Senate. McConnell was a fierce opponent for the reformers, particularly since, as in the House, the GOP leadership supported the effort to kill campaign finance reform legislation. McConnell also served as a key adviser to those House members who opposed reform. In both the House and the Senate, these various issue leaders competed with one another for the votes of their colleagues, the approval of interest groups, and the favorable attention of the media. Indeed, as House Speaker Newt Gingrich learned, negative media attention does not serve one's cause well.

Although each of these lawmakers was seen as a leader on the issue of campaign finance reform, only Representatives Shays and Meehan rose to the level of policy entrepreneur. What set Shays and Meehan apart from other leaders, such as the Freshman bill sponsors Tom Allen and Asa Hutchinson, or even from Senators McCain and Feingold, was the fact that they moved beyond competing with other reform and antireform efforts within Congress to creating an issue network, a network that included key figures from the other reform camps as well as from important groups and issue leaders outside of Congress. The existence of an effective issue network is often a necessary step to legislative success, particularly for issues, such as campaign finance reform, that are not high on the list of those most important to the American public.[11]

The Shays-Meehan bill differed from the eleven other substitute bills that were offered in the House in that the bill had support from across levels of seniority and from both parties (although mostly from the Democratic Party). More senior members, such as Rep. Jim Leach, R-Iowa, and Minority Leader Richard Gephardt, D-Mo., joined newcomers such as Republican Zach Wamp and Democrat Lois Capps to support the Shays-Meehan bill over other bills. On the Democratic side, party leaders and rank-and-file members were behind the bill. Additionally, several conservatives joined moderate Republicans to provide a degree of bipartisan support for the bill and, more important, to provide enough votes to obtain a majority. Just as important was the support of key outside interest groups, such as Common Cause and other good-government groups, that had come to define what constituted real reform and what fell short of it. If the reform interest groups did not approve of some provision or thought that a bill was too weak, the measure had little chance of going anywhere. These public interest groups exercised quite a lot of power in the effort to pass campaign finance reform, sometimes making it difficult for reformers inside of Congress to secure the compromises needed to gather more support for the bill.

The media were also a powerful external asset to the reform effort. In part because the good-government groups had sanctioned the Shays-Meehan bills as the true reform bill, the media did the same. The press demonized the opponents of reform, such as Speaker Newt Gingrich and the House GOP leadership, as corrupt hypocrites bent on preserving a broken system that had become detrimental to our representative democracy. The ability to bring all these disparate internal and external forces together as an effective issue network in support of one bill over other alternatives, and to maintain that network, set Representatives Shays and Meehan apart as true policy entrepreneurs.

Moreover, Shays and Meehan behaved like policy entrepreneurs. They brought energy and vitality to the process, and they were personally invested in it. They staked their personal and professional reputations on their efforts to pass the Shays-Meehan campaign finance reform bill, and they risked their share of institutional power by going up against some formidable opponents, such as the majority party leadership and the American Civil Liberties Union. When they lacked the ability or credentials to influence a certain group of legislators or potential allies outside of Congress, Shays and Meehan sought out others to help counter their weaknesses. Educating others is a necessary ingredient in the process of translating interest into support, and Shays and Meehan worked hard to educate other lawmakers, lobbyists, and members of the media about the details of this complicated policy area.

The Shays-Meehan Issue Network

The issue network that developed around the Shays-Meehan campaign finance reform effort in the House evolved gradually. Initially, this effort involved no more than several cosponsors. A few "issue leaders" began the process, but no one initially emerged as a policy entrepreneur. The process of this transformation was slow and would in the end happen only for Shays and Meehan, not for the other issue leaders such as the sponsors of the Freshman bill or those of other bills. This transformation of Shays and Meehan from issue leaders to policy entrepreneurs helps us to understand why their effort was successful and other campaign finance reform efforts in the House were not.

Becoming Policy Entrepreneurs

Shays and Meehan both were recognized issue leaders on campaign finance issues prior to the 105th Congress. They had in previous Congresses highlighted the issue and worked with Senators McCain and Feingold on their more prominent effort in the Senate. But because most of the initial activity, hope, and promise for reform was in the Senate, much of the early focus was on the efforts and issue leaders there. Although this situation initially relegated the two House members to relative obscurity, as the chances of passage in the House increased, the media began referring to the endeavor as the McCain-Feingold/Shays-Meehan effort. Eventually, the attention shifted to the House, and the media and others started to refer to it as the Shays-Meehan campaign finance reform effort. The change in the media's focus from McCain and Feingold to Shays and Meehan reflected a subtle transition but an important one that contributed to the transformation of Shays and Meehan into policy entrepreneurs. Shays and Meehan were becoming the story to follow.

In the Senate battle, as opposition to reform had mounted, others had joined in to push for reform, such as Democratic minority leader Daschle and GOP senators Snowe and Jeffords. Although each had added his or her own expertise to the process and laid some of the groundwork that allowed Shays and Meehan to succeed in the House, none had been able to rise to the level of policy entrepreneur. Unlike their House counterparts, these issue leaders had not been able to overcome the formidable procedural roadblocks, such as the filibuster, put in their way by the Republican leadership.

Reformers in Congress and allied interest groups outside of Congress initially expected that the Senate would pass the McCain-Feingold bill and then the House would take it up. House and Senate reformers worked to build support for reform in the House in anticipation of passage of the bill in the Senate. Representatives Shays and Meehan participated in the development of the Senate strategy with Senators McCain and Feingold through a bicameral, bipartisan working group. This type of cross-chamber, bipartisan ad hoc organization is a relatively unusual way for legislators to pursue policy success. The two congressmen's participation in this group allowed them to gain exposure to the type of opposition their measure might face in the House and provided an opportunity to learn from all aspects of the failed Senate process. In addition, it demonstrated their commitment to reform, helped them build their reputations for expertise on the issue, and enabled them to develop many important contacts with the relevant interest group and media people. When the focus shifted to the House, Shays and Meehan already were considered by many to be key issue leaders on campaign finance reform.

Shays and Meehan built their reputations internally in the House as well. Not only did they work within their own party caucuses to gain support for their bill, they also developed an extended group of reformers from both parties who helped to craft some of the initial language of the bill and forge compromises with sponsors of the other major pieces of legislation. Even when compromises could not be reached, Shays and Meehan were able to bolster their position in the process. For example, in February 1998 Shays and Meehan tried to strike a compromise with the sponsors of the Freshman bill. Although negotiations broke down, this effort to rectify differences aided both reform camps in clarifying their own positions and strengths. This preliminary negotiation would be an ironic foreshadowing of the House's eventual debate. Because Shays and Meehan were so familiar with the Freshman bill and its sponsors' strategies, when the real debate began they were in a better position to anticipate the freshmen's positions and to use their bill's weaknesses to promote the Shays-Meehan bill.

Representative Meehan in particular made many attempts within his own party's caucus to get his party leaders and key members to endorse the Shays-Meehan bill exclusively and publicly. He also was vital in gaining the support of the White House. Yet Meehan did not receive the level of media attention that Shays did, in part because Shays was defying his own party's leaders by pushing for campaign finance reform. As one might expect, the media found it much more interesting to report on the battle between Shays the maverick, bucking his own party leaders, and Speaker Newt Gingrich, the often harsh GOP party boss, than on an issue leader who had the support of virtually all his Democratic colleagues. However, Meehan's efforts as a policy entrepreneur, particularly within the Democratic caucus, were vital to the eventual passage of the Shays-Meehan bill. For example, he obtained formal resources from the Democratic Party, such as leadership support and whipping, to promote the bill. He also obtained the support of many Democratic freshmen at the expense of their own bill.

Reforming government and making it accountable were issues that Shays had pursued since his days in the Connecticut state legislature, and he continued these reform efforts after being elected to Congress in 1987. During the campaign finance reform debate, Shays worked with a small cadre of Republican reformers to build a larger coalition of GOP legislators in support of reform. He successfully appealed to many moderates in the party by reminding them of the Republicans' own 1994 rhetoric from the Contract with America that cast them as the party of reform. He, therefore, highlighted the differences between what the GOP party leaders said they would do in 1994 and what they actually did in the course of the campaign finance reform debate. As Shays noted at one press conference, "When the Republicans took over, we said things were going to be different, but I have not seen that to be the case."[12]

Publicly, Shays tried to emphasize the reform effort more than himself. In fact, he usually referred to the Shays-Meehan bill as the "Meehan-Shays" bill or the "House version of McCain-Feingold." This attempt to deflect attention no doubt contributed to his diplomatic effectiveness. Still, those outside of Congress identified Shays with the House reform effort. The "David versus Goliath" character of Shays's challenge of his own party's leaders was irresistible fare for the media. For example, the media did not miss the particularly prickly exchange on the House floor in March between Shays and Majority Leader Dick Armey in which Shays openly challenged the party leader's sincerity and motives regarding campaign finance reform. One of Shays's home state newspapers began depicting him as "Super Shays," a crusader on the issue of reform, and even carried a superhero cartoon of him (see illustration). The *New York Times* also noted that "Good-government groups, Democrats and editorial writers are calling him a hero for defying his party leadership."[13]

Despite his increasingly favorable reputation outside of Congress and the fact that he had been seen as a dedicated party member, Shays had to fight his own party leaders and fend off often-hostile attacks from his own party caucus.[14] At the urging of House conservatives, Speaker Gingrich warned Shays that his (and other moderate Republicans') committee assignments were at risk if he worked with the Democrats on campaign finance reform.[15] Majority Whip Tom DeLay criticized Shays for wanting to "use the government to shut down campaigns."[16] DeLay also endorsed an effort by Rep. Robert L. Ehrlich Jr., R-Md., advocating sanctions against Republicans who violated the "continued unity to [the Republican] conference" by signing Democratic discharge petitions.[17] Even Shays's relationship with Gingrich, bolstered by his early support of Gingrich during the coup attempt against the Speaker by conservatives in 1997, became strained, leading Shays to ask his friend in a very public moment "Do you and I have a problem?"[18]

Illustrator: John Coutinho

Super Shays

Building the Issue Network

The process by which the Shays-Meehan reform effort transformed from an internal congressional coalition into a full-fledged issue network was a gradual one. As Shays and Meehan began to exercise more entrepreneurial authority, it became necessary to have a network to sustain and build support. Constructing a network of internal and external supporters of campaign finance reform required a good deal of time and staff resources to educate and recruit potential issue network members. For the Shays and Meehan offices in particular, getting campaign finance reform passed required *all* staff members to work on the issue in addition to their regular duties. Shays, Meehan, and their core support group circulated many Dear Colleague letters seeking members, for example, to "join [them] in supporting a fair and open debate on bipartisan campaign reform that will truly put an end to the soft money system."[19]

The Shays-Meehan reform team also tried other approaches in their outreach efforts. For example, the reform network followed up the leadership's failed attempt to pass "sham" reform legislation in March 1998 with "an informational briefing including important handouts" for congressional staff two weeks later.[20] Aimed at educating and recruiting legislative staff, and thus indirectly their bosses, this meeting brought together key staff from the offices of Shays, Meehan, Scotty Baesler, D-Ky., the Blue Dog Democrat Coalition leader who sponsored the discharge petition, and Jim Leach, R-Iowa. Staff from the Congressional Research Service (the extensive collection of researchers and resources established to serve Congress exclusively) and representatives from leading public interest groups, such as Common Cause, the League of Women Voters, the Public Interest Research Group (PIRG), and Public Citizen, also were present. With this meeting, the reformers sought to provide answers for "all those questions you've been getting about the discharge petition and what is next for campaign finance reform."[21]

The favorable media coverage that the reformers, Shays in particular, received also provided another tool that the Shays-Meehan network could use to educate and attract new members. Members of Congress crave positive attention from the media, especially *local* media. The favorable media attention that flowed to Shays and Meehan showed other members that they too could benefit from joining the reform effort, and that this could be parlayed into an enhanced reputation with their constituents.

As the House moved toward debate on the Shays-Meehan bill, the Freshman bill, and other pieces of reform legislation in late May 1998, the Shays-Meehan network shifted its educational and recruitment operation to other efforts. First, the reformers worked to counter arguments that were expected to be raised by opponents of the Shays-Meehan bill. For example, the Shays-Meehan network circulated numerous Dear Colleague letters countering the opposition's arguments, such as one written by Tom Campbell, R-Calif., and Blue Dog Coalition member Charles Stenholm, D-Texas, stating that the Shays-Meehan bill "does not ban speech." This was an effort to head off charges that the bill violated First Amendment free speech rights.[22] And Shays and Brian Bilbray, R-Calif., sent a detailed letter to members of the GOP conference dealing with a key issue for many Republicans—how labor union money was addressed in the Shays-Meehan bill—in an effort to counter objections to the bill that hinged on this issue.[23]

Second, the Shays-Meehan network informed other legislators how the members of the Shays-Meehan coalition intended to vote on various bills and amendments expected to come up for a vote during debate on campaign finance reform. The Shays-Meehan bill had to survive the GOP leadership's death-by-amendment strategy to ensure that it would be the Queen of the Hill, or the bill that received more votes than the Freshman bill (the base bill) and all the other substitute bills. To that end, Shays and Meehan distributed to any member who wanted it a detailed analysis of each proposed amendment and their recommendation on how to vote. Many amendments were considered poison pills, or provisions that, if added to the Shays-

Figure 4-1 Voting Cue Card

Ensure the Shays-Meehan Substitute is "Queen of the Hill"

Vote "NO" (or "Present") on all substitutes!

Prepared by the Office of Representative Christopher Shays

Source: The Office of Rep. Christopher Shays.

Meehan bill, would destroy the fragile coalition of support for the measure. For instance, an amendment offered by Rep. Bill Paxon, R-N.Y., to impose costly new accounting and reporting procedures on labor unions (but not on corporations and interest groups) would have caused many Democrats to drop their support of the Shays-Meehan bill if the amendment had passed.

Voting cue cards also were provided on the floor of the House during debate to ensure that members who had not received the advance notice of vote recommendations would be able to follow the lead of Shays and Meehan easily when it came time to vote on each item. (See Figure 4-1.) With so many amendments often considered in rapid succession and often quite late at night, it was important to keep it simple so that a member who had already decided to support the Shays-Meehan effort could easily and quickly vote in a way that was consistent with that commitment. If a member had a question about a particular vote, Shays, Meehan, other key reform members, and several staffers were always on the House floor to respond during the debates to questions about the various bills and amendments.

The success of the Shays-Meehan network rested in part on the fact that it included organizations and entities outside of Congress. Shays, Meehan, and other members in the reform coalition encouraged the public interest groups to build networks among each other as well as to reach out to recruit new groups, and by mid-May at least thirty-two public interest groups had endorsed the Shays-Meehan bill.[24] Many of the most prominent proreform public interest groups, such as Common Cause, the League of Women Voters, and Public Citizen, also served as useful resources for reform legislators and staff. These groups assisted in crafting the legislation, provided congressional network members with quick and reliable information, and helped shape the Shays-Meehan response to the many proposed amendments the bill faced on the floor.

The media also were key to the success of the Shays-Meehan issue network. Presidents have long used the media to take their case directly to the public to pressure Congress to act on their policy agendas. By "going public" via the media, presidents have been able to mobilize public opinion in their favor, and Congress often follows by responding to such public pressure.[25] The Shays-Meehan network adapted this technique to Congress and quite effectively used the media to keep the issue of campaign finance reform alive and to pressure the GOP leaders to abandon their attempts to marginalize the reform effort.

Prominent newspapers such as the *New York Times* and the *Washington Post* helped keep the issue on the political agenda by carrying stories, often front page stories, on campaign finance and on reform events in Congress. Perhaps more important were the editorials and editorial cartoons carried in these and other papers that advocated campaign finance reform in general, endorsed the Shays-Meehan bill in particular, and criticized the Republican leadership's efforts to block reform legislation. The media provided details, cover, support, and well-timed pressure urging many House members to join the reform effort by pointing out the potential consequences of not joining. For example, newspaper editorial boards across the country, spurred on by Common Cause on behalf of the Shays-Meehan issue network, urged their local House members to sign the discharge petition that would have forced a vote on campaign finance reform. Of these efforts, the one with the highest profile was an unusually forceful editorial in the *New York Times* on April 18 that listed the names of those House members who had signed the petition and those who had not. The media also helped legitimize the Shays-Meehan reform effort by portraying Shays in particular as the courageous public servant, someone who was willing to go against his own party's leaders in the name of good government. This positive media coverage can be traced back, in large part, to the media strategy used by the Shays-Meehan issue network, including Common Cause and other interest groups, in its efforts to pressure the Republican leadership into allowing campaign finance reform to come to the House floor.

Communication within the network was also vital to its success. To coordinate the extensive effort needed to broaden the issue network, educate

House and other network members, and pass its reform legislation in the House, the Shays-Meehan network held regular meetings on the status of the reform effort. Sometimes these meetings were for House members and their staffs only. Other times, the core public interest groups were included as well. As the debate heated up and the need for quick access to information increased, Shays's and Meehan's offices became the informal headquarters for the issue network. While the House members and key legislative staff of the Shays-Meehan network worked on the floor of the House to build and maintain support for the bill, other staff and representatives from the public interest groups watched the events unfold on C-SPAN in Shays's and Meehan's offices. The staff on the House floor would phone those in the offices with information that would be instantly translated into analyses of vote totals, handouts for distribution on the House floor, action lists for follow-up the next day, or thank-you notes to members for their support on key votes.

This working group allowed the Shays-Meehan team to anticipate moves by the opposition as well as to react instantly. At follow-up meetings the next day, network members and staff would develop strategies on how to handle the results from the night before. For instance, a press release might be issued highlighting how the reformers successfully defeated poison pill amendments offered by the opposition in an effort to kill the Shays-Meehan bill. These informational sessions provided all the issue network members with up-to-date information on the progress of the reform effort and generated instructions for necessary actions to be taken.

Triggering Events

Many times throughout the reform effort in the House, the Shays-Meehan issue network benefited from what some scholars refer to as "triggering events." A triggering event is a "precipitating event such as a disaster or political happening [that] puts a different light on certain issues by making them seem more intense or more pressing than they were before."[26] The occurrence of several such events and the ability of the policy entrepreneurs Shays and Meehan to take advantage of them helped build momentum for the reform effort. The first set of triggering events, and perhaps the most important, was the many promises broken by the House Republican leaders as well as their attempt to claim that campaign finance reform had been considered by bringing up so-called reform bills under suspension of the rules.[27] In Chapter 3 we saw that these events cost the Republican leaders, especially Speaker Newt Gingrich, any credibility they might have had on the issue of campaign finance reform. The public interest groups and the media labeled this GOP attempt to bury the reform effort a "sham," thereby lending legitimacy to

Shays, Meehan, and other reformers and allowing them more forcefully to pressure the leadership to take up "real" campaign finance reform. Even those who were not enthusiastically supportive of the Shays-Meehan effort reacted negatively to the heavy-handed tactics of the Republican leadership.

The actions of the GOP leaders were not a gift that fell into the laps of those seeking to pass significant campaign finance reform legislation. Instead, their actions were responses to the increased pressure that they were feeling from all reformers—not only Shays and Meehan—to have a fair and open vote on campaign finance reform legislation. The prospect of losing control of the floor debate to the Democrats as a result of the discharge petition was not acceptable to the GOP leaders. They decided hastily to give reformers what they wanted—a vote. The scheduling of the leadership bills under suspension of the rules was a way for the leadership to teach rank-and-file GOP moderates a lesson on agenda control. They would allow a vote "as promised," but one for which they could control the outcome. The GOP leaders did not realize that this use of the rules would benefit the reformers by becoming a symbol of oppression, a symbol to fight against, and a message to which the media and the public would pay attention.

The leaders' failed strategy in turn led to a revitalized discharge petition effort. After helping to create this triggering event, Shays, Meehan, and their fellow reformers built on the momentum now in their favor. Conservative Republican Zach Wamp, in explaining why he signed the discharge petition, likened this momentum to a tornado: "When you hear the tornado coming you move."[28] More important, this triggering event took discussion of campaign finance off the insiders' table and placed it onto the kitchen tables of everyday Americans. Heightened media awareness became a vital tool for the reformers to use to get their message across, to call the leadership's actions into question, and to use as cover for others to join in the effort. In the media, words such as *dictatorial, obstructionist, hypocrisy,* and *cheating* were associated with Gingrich and the other GOP leaders.[29] Meanwhile, the reformers were portrayed positively, even glowingly, by those in the press who both supported reform and opposed Gingrich's tactics.

The success of the Shays-Meehan network in keeping the issue alive and gaining support for the bill both within and outside of Congress led to a second key event—the agreement with the GOP leadership to allow debate on campaign finance reform with the Freshman bill as the base bill. This event shared one trait with the leadership's "sham" vote, namely, the leaders' desire to maintain control of the floor during any campaign finance reform debate. Yet the agreement provided the reformers with an opportunity for a

House vote on the Shays-Meehan bill. With that, the Shays-Meehan network could concentrate its efforts on achieving success on the House floor.

Employing Successful Legislative Strategies

The Shays-Meehan reformers also acted strategically in identifying potential competitors, structuring the terms of the debate, and working to develop a winning scenario. For example, Shays-Meehan supporters (most notably, Shays himself) were key in selecting the Freshman bill as the base bill for consideration, and getting other bills, including the Shays-Meehan bill, onto the agenda. Although some Shays-Meehan supporters objected to this agreement, because they feared the Freshman bill might get more votes than the Shays-Meehan bill, the Freshman bill provided a good foil and a known quantity off which the Shays-Meehan network could work. First, because the Freshman bill, like the Shays-Meehan bill, dealt with soft money and issue advocacy, the tone of the debate centered on these reforms, as opposed to others that the Shays-Meehan bill did not address. Further, Shays and Meehan garnered support and momentum for their bill at the Freshman bill's expense. They eventually persuaded Democrat Tom Allen, one of the main cosponsors of the Freshman bill and a sponsor of the Shays-Meehan bill, to join the effort to pass the Shays-Meehan bill. Meehan followed this up by persuading other Democratic freshmen to support the bill. Finally, since Republican Asa Hutchinson, the remaining key sponsor of the Freshman bill, was unwilling to compromise and wished to go it alone, he became marginalized in the process and was seen by some as a supporter of the GOP leadership and therefore associated with "sham" reform.

Another example of successful legislative strategy was the deal that Meehan and Shays brokered with the Commission bill sponsors (Democrats John Dingell and Carolyn Maloney) to vote "present" rather than "aye" on their own bill. In exchange, the Shays-Meehan team agreed to accept the Commission bill as an amendment to their bill. Because the Shays-Meehan bill and the Commission bill approached campaign finance reform differently, the two bills could be merged without either of their sponsors giving up what they believed to be crucial components. As a result, Shays and Meehan eliminated a substitute bill that might have knocked their bill off as Queen of the Hill. More important, they added to their network of supporters more members who would be willing to fight for their bill's passage. The Shays-Meehan effort benefited from the decision of the Rules Committee chairman, Gerald B. H. Solomon, R-N.Y., to allow this last-minute deal to become a reality when he permitted Carolyn Maloney to submit her Commission bill as an amendment to the Shays-Meehan bill after the designated deadline. In return, however, the Shays-Meehan supporters were forced to accept the amendments of other latecomers as well.

Furthermore, Shays-Meehan reformers were able to persuade some amendment sponsors not to offer their amendments to the Shays-Meehan bill or to reach acceptable compromise language. A key effort along these lines was the combination of the six amendments regarding voter guides offered by Rep. Linda Smith, R-Wash., which closed the door to many similar amendments. One of the strongest objections to the Shays-Meehan bill was its perceived effect on voter guides, printed flyers that compare candidates on a series of issues. Critics argued that the Shays-Meehan bill would ban voter guides, and the Smith amendments aimed to ensure that voter guides would not be limited in any way. Many conservative House members were not willing to support the bill if it limited the Christian Coalition's ability to distribute its voter guides. Combining Smith's voter guide amendments and making them acceptable to Shays and Meehan took the wind out of the opposition's arguments that the Shays-Meehan bill would ban voter guides. This deal also further expanded the Shays-Meehan issue network, bringing in as a key supporter Representative Smith, a member who previously had criticized the discharge petition process as a waste of time and a "fruitless effort."[30] Once again, the Shays-Meehan effort turned a potential threat to its success into a source of strength.

Another key component of Shays's and Meehan's success as policy entrepreneurs is that at several steps along the long road of consideration of the Shays-Meehan bill, the two congressmen (as well as their supporters) demonstrated the ability to adapt to changing circumstances. This ability to adapt allowed the reform network to take advantage of political events and potential avenues for success. By doing so, they also built the perception that momentum was on their side. For example, the reform effort appeared to win a key victory when the leadership agreed to a "fair and open process" using the reformers' choice, the Freshman bill, as the base bill for the process. Also when their strategy that there be no amendments to the bill became politically untenable, the Shays-Meehan reformers switched gears and began to work out a way to handle the vast number of potential amendments that would be offered, rejecting only some of them as poison pill amendments.

The reformers further adapted by taking advantage of efforts by Rep. Bill Thomas, chairman of the House Oversight Committee, to negotiate a unanimous consent agreement regarding the universe of amendments that might be offered. The agreement was an attempt to limit the number of amendments offered and, by stipulating them in advance, to make their content known. The flexibility of the issue network, along with its ability to know others' moves quickly because of its preparation before the floor debate and its multiple sources of information, allowed it to react to and, in many instances, to anticipate the need for a change in strategy.

Additionally, the members of the Shays-Meehan issue network were very good at controlling the dialogue of the debate. The supporters of the Shays-Meehan bill had learned from the Senate process, in which reform opponents had established the terms of the debate, and they adapted their strategy accordingly. They began to transform the narrative of reform from one that focused almost exclusively on the role of special interests in federal elections to one about reforming the institution of Congress itself. Their effort became perceived fundamentally as a fight to make Congress more open and accessible. The fight for campaign finance reform was about representation, about making everyone's voice heard. It was about equality and opportunity. It was about leveling the playing field. This transformation of discourse helped the reformers debunk the detractors' argument that the Shays-Meehan bill violated the First Amendment right to free speech, in essence making such an argument appear contrived.

Finally, the Shays-Meehan network was well prepared and well informed. Staffers of the reformers met several dozen times throughout the course of the debate in the House. There were strategy meetings, education meetings, and question and answer sessions. A core group of Republican and Democratic House members was formed and each was provided with briefings, extensive briefing books, and staff support. All Shays-Meehan House members were provided with voting guides for each of the proposed amendments that included justifications for the Shays-Meehan position and recommended voting action (see Box 3-3). The production and dissemination of such materials is fairly common for contested legislative debates, but many House staffers noted at the time that the campaign finance reform debates generated far more material and sustained the effort for a longer period of time than usual. This network of support and information was vital for anticipating and preempting arguments from the opposition. It also enabled the Shays-Meehan team to limit any surprises on the floor during debate.

Other Issue Leaders and Why They Failed

As discussed earlier, many issue leaders in the campaign finance reform debate failed to rise to the level of policy entrepreneur. In contrast to the successful effort of Shays and Meehan to pull together the necessary issue network, to control the dialogue, and to educate and recruit fellow lawmakers, the efforts of the other issue leaders fell short in one or more of these key areas.

McCain and Feingold never fully developed an issue network of support in the Senate or interest group support and media attention outside of Congress. Even though the McCain-Feingold bill brought core House and Senate reformers and public interest groups together, the group remained a loose coalition and was not fully prepared to deal with the First Amendment attack launched by GOP senator Mitch McConnell and others. Furthermore, its attempts at innovative legislative strategy, such as the changes made to the original bill and the addition of the Snowe-Jeffords amendment to appease the First Amendment critics, fell short of their mark for several reasons.

First, the process was mostly internal to the Senate and only really involved the traditional public interest groups rather than an expanded and diversified network of external supporters that the Shays-Meehan bill enjoyed. The counter-interests were able to entrench themselves in an institution where individuals rule. Second, although the campaign finance scandals of the 1996 election were potentially powerful springboards for reform, and in fact were used by Senate reformers to support their claims of the need for reform, the McCain-Feingold reformers were unable to turn the scandals into a source of legislative action. They missed their opportunity to use them effectively as triggering events that might have transformed the issue of campaign finance reform from one with only internal importance to one with external support.

Finally, in reporting on reform efforts in the Senate, the media did so in the middle section of the newspaper as opposed to the front page, quite unlike the ongoing coverage and editorial emphasis that the House process received. Even though McCain and Feingold may have received the lion's share of attention in 1997 and early 1998 for being the prominent leaders on the issue of campaign finance reform, the Senate story ultimately was the humdrum one of failed legislation and stalemate. The House process was a classic "David versus Goliath" scenario, a much more interesting story for the media.

In the House, the reform effort behind the Freshman bill failed to develop an issue network, and its leaders did not transform into policy entrepreneurs for several reasons. First, the effort failed to adopt a successful legislative strategy. The Freshman bill leaders took an all-or-nothing approach. They were unwilling to compromise with the Shays-Meehan team and would not change sections of the bill called into question by reformers both inside and outside of Congress. Furthermore, the freshman reformers failed to recognize that the interest groups and the media that could serve as their issue network had already thrown their support to the Shays-Meehan bill. In essence, the freshmen were courting these important external network players too late in the game. Finally, the freshman reformers suffered from divided loyalty. Many of the Democratic members, including Tom Allen, the lead Democratic cosponsor, also supported the Shays-Meehan bill. This support called into question their loyalty to the Freshman bill, since they had to face consideration of the Shays-Meehan substitute bill first. As might be expected, the freshmen found it difficult to muster support for their bill once the Shays-Meehan substitute bill passed so overwhelmingly and appeared to be the only viable reform package that stood a chance of becoming law, especially given the late timing in the Senate.[31] The other substitute bills offered would suffer the same fate, for momentum was clearly behind the Shays-Meehan effort.

Even though Rep. Bill Thomas may have had a reputation of supporting government reform issues, his efforts on campaign finance reform were seen from the outset as a tool of the GOP leadership. The hearings under his watch in the House Oversight Committee dragged on and led many to believe that they were going nowhere. The brokered deal that Thomas tried to put together between the leadership and the reform groups fell apart under the weight of the leadership imperative that "paycheck protection" be a part of the base bill.[32] Later, when his bill and the three other so-called reform bills were offered under suspension of the rules, they were seen again as tools of the leadership that were designed to derail "real reform." The last-minute brokering on the language of the Thomas bill as well as the fact that the committee members had only an hour to review the bill before markup (when the final language of the bill is crafted) also lent credence to those who were suspicious of the GOP leadership's motives. Thomas would later be instrumental in negotiating the unanimous consent agreement that helped limit the number of amendments offered to the Shays-Meehan substitute bill, but he would be relegated for the most part to the fringes and was seen by many as an enemy of reform.

Conclusion: The Guides through the Labyrinth

Issue leadership, entrepreneurship, and networking were vital factors in the House passage of campaign finance reform in the 105th Congress. As in other ventures, there are many ingredients in legislative success; and in the contemporary era of unorthodox lawmaking, there is not just one recipe for success but many possibilities as well as numerous potential pitfalls. Today's legislative process requires innovative methods and leaders who are savvy about using them, leaders who have what it takes to be policy entrepreneurs. In the case of campaign finance reform in the 105th Congress, many legislators took on the topic as issue leaders. Yet only Representatives Shays and Meehan rose to the level of policy entrepreneur.

The qualities that characterize a policy entrepreneur include: electoral security or a chance of gaining it by establishing oneself as a leading policymaker; the respect of one's colleagues in Congress and of important issue leaders outside of Congress, such as the relevant interest groups; a deep commitment to an issue; a willingness to expend extraordinary amounts of time, energy, and resources on that issue; and a superb sense of timing. Political scientists often speak of a "policy window" of opportunity for an issue whose time has come.[33] Yet such an opportunity may go untapped if astute and capable legislators do not take advantage of it. The ability to recognize when the time is right to move on an issue and how to best go about doing so at various points along the way are also important qualities that a policy entrepreneur must possess.

Representatives Shays and Meehan and their core group of reformers worked to bring together their talents, energy, and connections to potential supporters both inside and outside of Congress to form an effective issue network for steering the Shays-Meehan Bipartisan Campaign Reform Act through the House of Representatives. Of course, they did not control all the events that affected the fate of their reform bill, such as the GOP leadership's many attempts to kill reform in the House. But the Shays-Meehan reformers responded to the various events strategically and turned many into triggering events that helped raise the profile of the reform effort and built support for the Shays-Meehan bill.

The reformers' ability to cultivate a rather wide issue network of support was key to their success. The external components of this issue network were particularly important. Many well-respected public interest groups helped promote the reform effort by lobbying within Congress to recruit more supporters and by advocating outside of Congress to bring the issue home to representatives' districts and keep it alive in the press. The media remained interested in the story, especially as the GOP leaders continued to call attention to their antireform strategy by breaking promises to take up campaign finance reform and attempting to sweep the issue under the rug by presenting what were perceived as one-sided reform bills to the House membership. Yet if the Shays-Meehan team had not effectively taken advantage of such opportunities to advance their cause they probably would not have navigated successfully through the many obstacles to the bill's passage.

No legislative process is exactly like another, yet the story of the Shays-Meehan bill's journey through the House reveals valuable lessons about what it takes to be an effective policy entrepreneur and about the kind of efforts that are necessary for legislative success. These require a good deal of energy and resources, but perhaps more important is the right kind of personality to rise to the challenges of policy entrepreneurship. Congress is a collection of people with many goals and varying abilities, and not all of them will become policy entrepreneurs, which should not be surprising considering the effort required. Another essential ingredient is the right timing. Even if a lawmaker possesses all the qualities necessary for policy entrepreneurship, he or she might not get anywhere with a chosen cause if the time is not ripe for the topic to enjoy serious consideration by Congress. For example, if the issue is not perceived by fellow legislators, the public, relevant interest groups, and the media as a problem that needs a policy solution, it will be extremely difficult to develop an internal and external issue network to push for change. Likewise, if triggering events do not occur to help propel an issue to the active political agenda, the issue is not likely to emerge from the obscurity to which most legislative proposals are doomed. Moreover, given the pronounced partisanship of contemporary Congresses and the often overly cautious approach of many legislators who fear losing their seats, many measures die in a stalemate. Despite the legislative success the reformers achieved in the House, campaign finance reform eventually died in the Senate. One can see why many policy proposals stay on the policy agenda for years before finally becoming law.

5

A HIGH-STAKES PARTISAN BATTLE
The Role of Political Parties
in the Campaign Finance Reform Debate

Minority party members in Congress are sometimes referred to as "bomb throwers," and majority party members are often called the "dictators" of the policy process. The partisan lines are drawn even more vividly when issues of election, incumbency, and control of the Congress lie in the balance. That is why party leaders on both sides of the aisle may profess to want campaign finance reform, but each side requires that it be *their* version of reform. Since the mid-1990s the parties in Congress have become more contentious, making passage of any proposal that splits along party lines much more difficult.[1] Thus, it is clear why the simple handshake deal between Speaker Newt Gingrich and President Bill Clinton to establish a commission to offer a campaign finance reform proposal was a lot more difficult to accomplish than it looked on the surface.[2] Indeed, the stakes were high as both parties saw the other party's version of reform as harmful to their bottom line, that is, to their ability to wage and win campaigns.

Although American voters have gradually moved away from strong identification with a particular political party, parties and partisanship are still the currency of choice on Capitol Hill. In many ways, party is everything. The primary goal of the minority party is to achieve majority status, and the majority party guards its control of the chamber jealously. A lawmaker's partisanship is the best indicator of how he or she will vote on most issues, and party loyalty in Congress has increased in recent years.[3] It should come as no surprise, therefore, that the debate over campaign finance reform was basically a partisan one. Yet it is not that simple, because a healthy number of Republican House members and senators joined virtually every Democratic lawmaker in support of campaign finance reform, enough of them to build a majority in support of reform in both chambers.

In this chapter we discuss questions that help shed some light on the character of parties and partisanship in the contemporary Congress. For example, why did some Republican senators and House members defy their party leaders to support and, in some cases, sponsor campaign finance reform legislation? Why did a small number of House Democrats oppose the leading reform bill when an overwhelming majority of their fellow partisans and their party's leaders supported the measure? Why did the GOP leaders pull out all the stops in their attempts to kill campaign finance reform efforts in Congress, creating a major rift in their party's ranks and drawing heavy criticism from good-government groups and bad press from the media? Why did Democratic leaders wait as long as possible before endorsing one of the many campaign finance reform bills that Democratic lawmakers had introduced? What role did President Bill Clinton play during the campaign finance reform debates? In addressing these and other questions about the activities of the parties and their partisans, we pay particular attention to the crucial support for campaign finance reform provided by a small group of Republican legislators despite opposition from their party leaders in both chambers. This dynamic significantly shaped the course and outcome of the congressional battle over campaign finance reform during the 105th Congress.

Setting the Stage

In 1994 the Republicans won control of the House of Representatives for the first time in four decades. The elections gave them a 230- to 204-seat advantage over the Democrats, an impressive 52-seat gain. With Newt Gingrich leading the way as Speaker of the House, the new GOP majority began the 104th Congress (1995–1997) with an ambitious agenda and a good deal of party unity to accomplish that agenda. Many of the GOP freshman House members believed that they owed their elections in part to Gingrich, who had stepped up the party's efforts to recruit and assist candidates. Gingrich also devised the Contract with America, the party's manifesto that most Republican candidates signed before the 1994 elections, particularly those seeking to unseat Democratic incumbents. Many sophomore legislators also credited Gingrich with helping the party rise to majority status in the House after forty long years in the hinterlands of minority status. After the 1994 elections, freshman and sophomore legislators constituted over 50 percent of the House Republican membership, giving Gingrich a strong base of support to pursue his party's ambitious legislative agenda.

This heightened level of loyalty to the party, as well as to its leader, and the revolutionary tone of the changing of the guard enabled the House GOP to pass all but one of the ten planks of the Contract with America in the first three months of the 104th Congress, an extraordinary pace in the usually lumbering and incremental House.[4] Never mind that most Americans had not even heard of the Contract with America on election day, Gingrich and his new majority party claimed that they had a mandate from the people to consider the Contract in the House within the first 100 days of the 104th Congress, and they had the votes to do it. Republicans also took control of the Senate with the 1994 elections. Not only were Republicans now in charge of both chambers of Congress, but also the Democratic president was substantially weakened. After failing to enact his sweeping health care reform bill during the 103d Congress despite Democratic control of the House and the Senate and barely winning approval of his economic stimulus plan, President Clinton was at a decided disadvantage with the 104th Congress.[5]

A few years later, however, the political landscape changed significantly. The Republicans still held a majority of House seats in the 105th Congress (1997–1999) following the 1996 elections, but their majority had shrunk to a mere twenty-seat advantage, the smallest margin of control since 1952. The Republicans picked up two seats in the Senate, but their margin of control was still small at fifty-five to forty-five seats. The House Republicans were no longer riding high on the revolutionary spirit of the 1994 elections and the Contract with America. In fact, public reaction to the Republicans' rhetoric of revolution had soured.[6] President Clinton had vetoed Republican budget legislation, effectively shutting down the federal government in November and then again over the Christmas and New Year holidays in 1995. The public blamed the Republicans in Congress, not the Democratic president, for the shutdowns. Clinton and the Democrats in Congress had successfully pointed out that the Republicans' proposed $245 billion tax cut was suspiciously close to the $270 billion the Republicans wanted to cut from the popular Medicare program, and support for the GOP tax cut faded.[7]

Gingrich had become an increasingly unpopular and controversial figure. His harsh style did not sit well with voters and his popularity ratings plummeted. Gingrich also spent much of 1996 under a House Ethics Committee investigation of GOPAC, a Gingrich organization to recruit and fund candidates and to promote House Republican priorities. Then in July 1997 about a dozen young conservative legislators led an aborted coup effort to oust Gingrich from the Speakership because they felt he had given in to President Clinton and the Democrats by compromising too much during the budget negotiations earlier that summer.[8] This challenge from within his own ranks was a clear indicator that Gingrich had lost the ability to command party loyalty from the diminished GOP majority in the House. With a smaller margin of control in the House, only a slight advantage in the Senate, and a highly factionalized collection of party members, GOP leaders were unlikely to achieve much legislative success on their own. At the same time, Democratic Party cohesion had grown stronger. After losing control of both chambers to the Republicans and finding themselves rather powerless to stop GOP initiatives, Democratic lawmakers saw the value of unifying against their opponents. This was the climate in which campaign finance reform emerged as a serious issue in Congress in 1997. Both of the political parties significantly affected the long and often contentious debate, and senators and House members from both parties were key players on both sides of the issue.

Although the Republicans controlled both chambers of Congress during the 105th Congress and the party's leaders were strongly opposed to campaign finance reform legislation, it gained the support of a majority of legislators in both the House and the Senate (but not the sixty votes required to overcome a GOP filibuster in the Senate). The alliances of legislators from both parties that developed on this issue and the lack of support from the majority party leadership ensured that the battle for reform would be especially contentious.

Parties and Partisanship in Congress

Congress is a partisan institution. Whichever party holds the majority in the House or the Senate controls the top leadership positions and the agenda of the chamber. The majority party also enjoys majorities on all committees and subcommittees, and majority party members are the chairpersons of all of them. As we saw in Chapter 1, being the majority party is a more powerful distinction in the House than in the Senate, but in both chambers majority status brings with it significantly more power than minority status. Indeed, a party generally cannot enact its policy priorities unless it is the majority party in at least one chamber of Congress.[9]

The degree to which a party achieves legislative success in Congress is most often a function of the degree to which its members vote with the party. As shown in Figure 5-1, party unity has increased in recent years. Party unity is measured here as the degree of cohesion or adherence to the party's

Figure 5-1 Average Party Unity Scores, 1966–1998

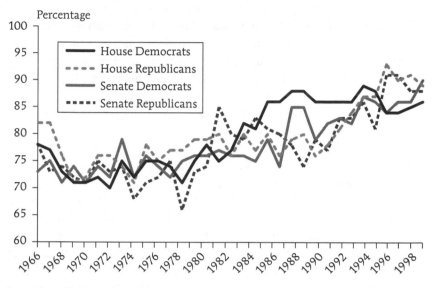

Source: Compiled from data in Norman J. Ornstein, Thomas E. Mann, and Michael J. Malbin, *Vital Statistics on Congress, 1999-2000* (Washington, D.C.: AEI Press, 2000), 202–203.

Note: Data show the percentage of members voting with a majority of their party on party unity votes. Party unity votes are those roll-call votes on which a majority of a party votes on one side of the issue and a majority of the other party votes on the other side.

position on votes that elicit a partisan split, when a majority of one party votes on one side of an issue and the majority of the other party votes on the other side.[10] Party leaders generally have an easier time accomplishing the party's collective legislative goals when party unity is high and a more difficult time when it is low and there is little agreement on what the party's priorities should be. The data in Figure 5-1 suggest that the parties have been more cohesive in recent years and, therefore, able to act in unity more effectively and more often than in past decades.

Yet partisanship and majority power are checked in many ways. Even if a party enjoys a large margin of control and a high level of party unity, it may not always succeed in enacting its legislative priorities. Congress is highly partisan, but at the same time it is an individualistic institution, particularly the Senate. Although the general goals of a party are shared by most if not all of its members in Congress, legislators also have individual goals that may, at times, conflict with the goals of their party. The most obvious of these individual goals is reelection.[11] Most lawmakers do not choose to act with their party if they believe that doing so will jeopardize their reelection. House members and senators generally do not follow their party's position on bills when that position would be detrimental to a large number or a powerful group of their constituents back home. For instance, a House member from Wyoming is not inclined to support an increase in the fees ranchers pay to graze their cattle on federal lands even if the rest of his or her party supports the measure. Meanwhile, a congressperson in the same party from New York City would face little if any objection from the folks back home to increased grazing fees.

Party leaders also recognize the importance of the reelection goal and they often advise legislators whose constituency interests clash with the party's position to "vote your district" rather than to follow the party line. Party leaders realize that the party's primary concern is to retain that legislator's seat, for the party will be less able to affect policy outcomes if it does not first gain or maintain majority status.[12] Campaign finance is an issue especially sensitive to such reelection concerns, for a change in the rules could have a significant effect on the parties' electoral fortunes. The debates over campaign finance reform during the 105th Congress suggest that this reelection concern is the primary motivating factor behind each party's position on the issue.

Party unity also may be weakened because lawmakers pursue goals other than reelection. Reelection is and must be every legislator's proximate goal, that is, it is the "goal that must be achieved over and over if other ends are to be entertained."[13] Yet lawmakers also strive to achieve influence in Congress.[14] Legislators may defy their party's recommended vote in order to gain influence in Congress. For example, if a lawmaker aspires to a party leadership position, he or she might challenge the sitting leaders by opposing their policy priorities. Or a committee chairperson may want to stake out his or her ground on an issue that falls under the committee's jurisdiction. A lawmaker may gain respect from his or her colleagues with this kind of action. Moreover, such independence from one's party leaders may draw media and interest group attention, enhancing a lawmaker's profile on an issue and expanding his or her influence among colleagues and with the public.

Lawmakers are interested in making good policy as well, and the desire to pass good public policies may pit a legislator against party leaders.[15] This final goal helps us understand why some Republican legislators supported comprehensive campaign finance reform despite their party's strong objections that such reforms would hinder the GOP's election prospects and despite some serious threats that they would be punished for their active participation in the reform effort. For example, a group of House GOP loyalists, led by Rep. Robert

Ehrlich, R-Md., asked Speaker Gingrich in May 1998 to punish the twelve Republican members who had signed the discharge petition designed to force a vote on campaign finance reform legislation.[16] At a Republican Conference meeting Gingrich did scold Banking Committee chairman James Leach, R-Iowa, the only full committee chairperson to sign the discharge petition, in front of his GOP colleagues. Gingrich accused Leach of betraying him. The Speaker argued that if the petition succeeded, the Republicans would lose control of the debate to the Democrats.[17] Indeed, defectors had cost the Republicans victories on several key votes during the 105th Congress. One GOP aide remarked, "These guys get plum committee assignments, and then they screw the [Republican Conference] on these key votes."[18]

Gingrich had already shown that he was willing to reward loyalty and punish disloyalty in very tangible ways. When he first took office as Speaker, Gingrich passed over some senior members to appoint loyal freshman and sophomore legislators to high-powered committees and in some instances disregarded the seniority system in appointing committee chairpersons.[19] Thus, it might have been a risky proposition to defy Gingrich on an issue he wanted to bury, such as campaign finance reform. By the time campaign finance reform emerged as a key issue in 1997, however, Gingrich's influence was weaker than in the first "glory days" of the Republican revolution following the 1994 elections. Defying Gingrich on campaign finance reform, therefore, was a less serious risk than it would have been in 1995. There were also growing frictions between Republicans in the House. Conservatives thought Gingrich had betrayed their conservative agenda, and they tried to bring him down. Moderate Republicans thought that Gingrich was too rigid on issues such as campaign finance reform. And Republicans of all stripes had become increasingly concerned about the decreasing popularity of their leader, particularly as they got closer to the 1998 midterm elections.

Voters also registered negative opinions about the campaign finance system, but they were not focused on or demanding campaign finance reform. If voters had expressed a strong desire for campaign finance reform, perhaps the Republican Party leaders would have been more inclined to support reform in order to protect their majority status in Congress. The issue did have some clear partisan electoral implications, however. For example, the Republican leaders argued that the reforms proposed in the McCain-Feingold and Shays-Meehan bills would be detrimental to their party's ability to wage campaigns. Thus they insisted that any reform measure include a provision to restrict the fund-raising capabilities of labor unions, which, they said, would level the playing field between the two parties (that is, the so-called paycheck protection measure).[20] Likewise, many Democrats believed that reform must include both a soft money ban and restrictions on campaign-like issue ads. They argued that if only a soft money ban became law, the Republican advantage in fund-raising would increase because of the GOP's ability to raise far more in hard money. Democrats also were unwilling to accept restrictions on labor unions' political activities, especially if similar restrictions were not placed on corporations and nonprofit groups.

These perspectives guided each party's approach to the issue of campaign finance reform. They cannot explain fully, however, why a small but significant number of GOP members defied their party's leaders to join virtually every congressional Democrat in support of campaign finance reform and, therefore, helped achieve a majority for reform in both chambers. Many of the GOP members who actively supported campaign finance reform were in part pursuing the goal of good public policy. They were driven to improve what they considered a faulty system of regulating campaign finance activities.

Yet their active support for reform also served their reelection goals and their desire to gain influence in Congress. The desire to enact good public policy often motivates lawmakers to become issue leaders and policy entrepreneurs, as we saw in Chapter 4. The rise of policy entrepreneurs Christopher Shays and Martin Meehan was a crucial development that contributed to passage of their campaign finance reform bill in the House. Yet both Shays and Meehan were also electorally secure, and they represented districts that favored reform of the system. In fact, Shays had been an active advocate of such reforms since his days in the Connecticut state legislature, and his districts' voters no doubt expected him to continue to pursue reform issues when they elected him to Congress. Likewise, Meehan, who has long supported campaign finance reform, says he was first drawn to the issue because of the reform efforts of the late Rep. Mike Synar, a populist Democrat from Oklahoma, who fought for campaign finance reform from the mid-1970s until his defeat in the primary election in 1994.[21]

Partisanship, Bipartisanship, and Crosspartisanship

A minority party in Congress is not often able to form a majority with the help of members from the other party. This is particularly true in the House, where the tools at the disposal of majority party leaders are effective means for controlling the agenda. Yet occasionally, majority coalitions that consist of members from both parties do emerge. Sometimes, these coalitions even defy the wishes of the majority party's leaders. One of the best examples of this is the coalition that formed in support of the tax cuts proposed by Republican president Ronald Reagan shortly after he took office in 1981.

Although Reagan's proposal for tax reduction ran counter to the long-standing goal of progressive taxation advocated by the Democratic Party, a large number of Democratic House members voted with the minority party Republicans in support of President Reagan's tax plan.[22] It helped that the issue came before the House early in the congressional session during what has come to be known as a new president's "honeymoon" period—the first few months of a president's administration when even legislators from the opposition party are willing to give the new president some leeway to try to enact his policy agenda. More important, however, was the particular composition of the coalition that supported the tax cuts: conservative Democrats joined House Republicans to form the majority coalition that passed the tax cut legislation.

The 1980 elections featured a powerful group of voters known as Reagan Democrats, who voted for the Republican for president while still voting to reelect their Democratic House members (that is, they split their tickets). The message seemed clear to many House Democrats, especially those from districts where Reagan had won: voters wanted them to move to the right on both social and economic issues. It was no surprise that most of these Democrats were from the South, where the Republican Party had made deep inroads into this formerly Democratic stronghold. Since the civil rights era of the 1960s, southern Democrats had combined with Republicans to form a *conservative coalition* to promote more conservative social and economic policies. The bipartisan group that passed the Reagan tax cuts tapped into this well-established coalition of House Republicans and Democrats.

Other issues, however, do not have such strong and established bipartisan coalitions behind them, generally because powerful differences exist between each party's approach to an issue. If a majority of one party votes on one side of an issue and a majority of the other party votes on the other side of that issue, the parties are said to be acting in a partisan, not a bipartisan manner. Thus, even if some members of one party vote with the other party, it may not reach the level of true bipartisanship. *Bipartisanship* is a term reserved for situations in which a majority of one party votes with a majority of the other party, that is, when majorities of both parties agree with each other. Such bipartisanship is fairly rare in the contemporary Congress, particularly on major legislation.[23] Yet when it occurs, bipartisan policymaking in Congress can be a powerful impetus to significant policy change.

Lawmakers like to claim that the legislation they are advocating has bipartisan support, for this suggests that there is a broadly based consensus for the proposal. Projecting an image of consensus helps build support for a bill, because legislators generally do not want to be on the "wrong side" of an issue if so many people seem to be on the other side. Moreover, bipartisanship reflects a cooperative rather than a combative working relationship between the two parties on Capitol Hill, something that voters say they want. Partisan combat over high-profile issues often leads to deadlock, and voters become frustrated when their elected representatives cannot effectively address pressing policy problems. Legislators are naturally inclined to seek bipartisan support for their legislation, particularly in this era of divided government (that is, when one or both chambers of Congress is controlled by one party and the presidency is controlled by the other party). When government is divided, the party in control of Congress is less likely to have a bill vetoed by the president if some of his own party's legislators also support the measure.

True bipartisanship, however, does not occur often. More common is what the political scientists Joseph Cooper and Garry Young call "crosspartisanship," when a minority of one party votes with the majority of the other party or minorities in each party vote in the same direction.[24] The coalition organized around campaign finance reform during the 105th Congress is more accurately described as crosspartisan, not bipartisan, for only a minority of GOP members joined nearly every Democrat to pass the Shays-Meehan bill in the House and to deliver a majority in support of the McCain-Feingold bill in the Senate. Indeed, campaign finance reform was an issue that split the Democratic and Republican Parties in a very partisan way: the majority of Democrats and the party's leaders supported reform; and the majority of Republicans and the party's leaders strongly opposed reform. Only 61 of the 227 Republicans (27 percent) voted for final passage of the Shays-Meehan bill in the House, and only 7 out of 55 GOP senators (13 percent) joined an overwhelming majority of Democrats in favor of a vote on the McCain-Feingold bill in the Senate—hardly a strong show of bipartisanship, for clear majorities of Republicans voted against the measures.

Despite the numbers, however, reformers characterized their efforts as bipartisan and even used the word *bipartisan* in the titles of their bills: the official title of the McCain-Feingold and Shays-Meehan bills was the "Bipartisan Campaign Reform Act" and the Freshman bill was titled the "Bipartisan Campaign Integrity Act." The reformers hoped to gain the benefits of true bipartisanship, such as increased support for their bills, by suggesting that there was a broadly based, bipartisan consensus for their measures. Campaign finance reform in the 105th Congress did require support from both parties if it was to be successful, because as the minority party the Democrats could not pass a reform bill alone. Yet true bipartisanship was neither necessary nor likely to emerge.

Congressional Democrats had long supported campaign finance reform and had, in fact, passed a comprehensive reform bill in 1992 (when the Democrats still controlled both chambers of Congress), but the bill was vetoed by Republican president George Bush and the Senate failed to override the veto. It generally was understood, however, that the Democrats were able to pass this comprehensive reform bill in 1992 in part *because* everyone knew it would be vetoed, thus allowing the Democrats to use the GOP president's opposition to reform as a campaign issue later that year. Nevertheless, while the Democrats controlled both chambers of Congress from 1987 to 1994 they generally did not have to recruit supporters from the other side of the aisle to pass legislation. But by the 105th Congress the Republicans were the majority party in both the House and the Senate, and Democrats needed Republican votes to pass any legislation, especially if it was not supported by the GOP party leaders. Republican leaders in both chambers strongly opposed campaign finance reform and would never voluntarily bring the issue to a vote. Therefore, out of necessity, the proreform position did not belong to the Democrats exclusively. The leading reform bills were championed by some respected senior GOP senators and House members as well as some of the newest legislators.

The Republicans and Campaign Finance Reform

As we saw in Chapter 2, John McCain was the leading Republican advocate for campaign finance reform in the Senate. His reputation as an independent thinker made him a natural issue leader for an issue that would pit him against his own party leaders and GOP colleagues. In fact, McCain seemed at times to revel in defying his party's leaders, and his maverick tendencies did not seem to affect negatively his reputation with his constituents back home in Arizona. McCain won reelection in 1998 with nearly 69 percent of the vote. When McCain ran for the Republican presidential nomination in 2000, he was equally defiant of the mainstream Republican Party, for he dared to challenge the party's anointed choice, Texas governor George W. Bush. In fact, Bush had already secured the endorsement of many GOP governors and state legislators when McCain officially entered the race. Although McCain did not win the nomination contest, he did make campaign finance reform part of the campaign dialogue, forcing Bush, as well as the Democratic candidates, to discuss an issue they might otherwise not have paid so much attention to. After the nomination season ended, McCain continued to press for campaign finance reform in the Senate, and he enjoyed some measure of success.

As a conservative, McCain may seem like an unlikely supporter of reforms that many of his GOP colleagues say will hurt the Republican Party. Yet McCain sees campaign finance reform as an issue conservatives should advocate. He believes that the current campaign finance system allows the "special interests" to determine policy outcomes, and conservatives, and everyone else for that matter, should not permit wealthy corporations, labor unions, and powerful and wealthy interest groups and individuals to overrun representative democracy. In the spirit of this argument, during his presidential campaign, McCain ran a television advertisement touting his reputation for "taking on the special interests," and he promised, "I'm going to give the government back to you."

Other GOP senators who supported campaign finance reform, such as Olympia Snowe, R-Maine, James Jeffords, R-Vt., John Chafee, R-R.I., and Arlen Specter, R-Pa., came from the moderate wing of the party. As moderates, these senators were less inclined to follow the party's more conservative leaders, such as Senate majority leader Trent Lott, R-Miss., on this and other issues. For instance, Senators Jeffords and Snowe teamed up with Democratic senators Christopher Dodd, D-Conn., Patty Murray, D-Wash., and Barbara Boxer, D-Calif., to offer child-care legislation in the 105th Congress that was a good deal more liberal than the child-care measures supported by the GOP party leaders.[25] Yet opposing their leaders on campaign finance reform may have been a bit more difficult. Campaign finance reform was an issue that Senate GOP leaders did not want to consider *at all.* Joining Democrats to support reform was, therefore, a more serious defiance of their leaders' wishes. Of course, the Senate is the more individualistic chamber, where senators, who must represent the more diverse constituencies of entire states, generally are more independent than House members, who represent smaller, more homogeneous districts within states. Moreover, party leaders in the Senate, even those of the majority party, are less able to induce party loyalty because a minority of senators can block a majority from voting for cloture, which requires an extraordinary majority of sixty votes, to end a filibuster. Therefore, senators have always tended to be more independent than their colleagues in the House. As indicated in Figure 5-1, party unity generally is lower in the Senate than in the House.

In the House, Christopher Shays, the primary Republican cosponsor of the Shays-Meehan bill, led the GOP rebels. Shays was known to be a strong supporter of Speaker Newt Gingrich and the Republican revolution that began in the 104th Congress. In fact, throughout the reform debate Shays was inclined to give Gingrich the benefit of the doubt and urged other reformers to accept the Speaker's promises to bring campaign finance reform to the floor for debate. For example, when Gingrich promised a vote on reform in April 1998, Shays and ten other Republican reformers agreed to take their names off the discharge petition that would have forced consideration of campaign finance reform legislation. Yet Shays's faith in Gingrich eventually faded after the Speaker's repeated broken promises and attempts to kill reform. By June he was less willing to trust that his party's top leader was sincere about allowing a fair vote on meaningful campaign finance reform measures. Gingrich's attempts to control tightly the House debate on campaign finance reform actually energized the reformers and forced the GOP leader to allow a second round of debate on the issue. Shays noted in early June that "campaign finance was dead as a doornail until the leadership resuscitated it through stalling and attempting to manipulate the process."[26]

Like McCain, Shays had strong reform credentials. He was the lead sponsor of the first bill to become law in the new Republican Congress in 1995, the Congressional Accountability Act, one of the Contract with America items. The Accountability Act places Congress under some of the health, labor, and civil rights laws that apply to the private sector. Shays also was instrumental in the House adoption of a ban on virtually all gifts from lobbyists and in enactment of a law to increase significantly the reporting requirements of lobbyists to include such information as what issues they work on and who pays them. Furthermore, Shays had frequently sided with Democrats on some high-profile issues since coming to Congress in 1987. For instance, as a fiscal conservative Shays favored cutting some military and space exploration spending in order to balance the budget and accused some of his fellow Republicans of supporting big increases in military spending without offering ways to pay for them.[27] Shays seems comfortable in many different camps, depending on the issue. On fiscal issues, he is as conservative as they come. On social issues, such as gun control and abortion, he is decidedly more liberal than most of his fellow Republicans, and he often votes with GOP moderates on a variety of issues.

Shays was among a small number of Republicans who supported the reform bill that passed in 1992 but was vetoed by President George Bush. The same core group of about twenty Republican reformers emerged as leaders on the issue once the GOP became the majority party in 1995. As in the Senate, the House Republican coalition of reformers in the 105th Congress came from different factions of the party. It was made up of an unusual mix of moderate and conservative Republicans. Many Republican moderates, most of them from the Northeast, had long supported campaign finance reform, so it was not surprising that they were ready to form a crosspartisan coalition with the Democrats. Their ranks included the leader of the GOP reform coalition, the sometimes-moderate Chris Shays, as well as Marge Roukema, R-N.J., Nancy L. Johnson, R-Conn., Michael N. Castle, R-Del., Constance A. Morella, R-Md., and others. These moderates were joined by some of the most conservative Republican members of the House of Representatives, such as Zach Wamp of Tennessee and Brian Bilbray and Tom Campbell of California. Zach Wamp, for instance, was one of the Republican freshmen elected in 1994 when the Republicans took control of the House for the first time in more than four decades. He appreciated his party's traditional support for reform, such as the efforts championed by President Teddy Roosevelt to clean up government in the early part of the twentieth century, and Wamp took seriously the party's recent promises to change the way politics operate in Washington.

GOP Leaders

Speaker Gingrich and the other GOP leaders, who were so strongly opposed to campaign finance reform, had couched their promotion of the Contract with America in the rhetoric of reform—welfare reform, tax reform, tort reform, and congressional reform. They had pledged to get government off the people's backs and to clean it up. The House Republican leaders were presenting themselves as good-government reformers intent on stamping out corruption while they were refusing to consider serious campaign finance reform legislation. This is especially ironic because of the Republicans' full-scale attack on the Democratic Party's fund-raising practices during the 1996 elections. Congressional Republicans conducted high-profile investigations of the fund-raising scandals in both chambers of Congress, and they never missed an opportunity to call attention to the charges of illegal foreign campaign contributions, influence peddling, and illegal fund-raising in the White House. For example, they introduced resolutions in Congress that chronicled the alleged Democratic violations. Yet the Republicans had some campaign finance problems of their own. The party had been accused of money laundering, accepting foreign contributions, influence peddling, and conspiring with outside groups to evade campaign finance laws, among other things.[28] One would think that, given these issues, the GOP leaders would be at the forefront of the reform effort.

Instead, House and Senate Republican leaders did everything in their power to try to kill campaign finance reform. The GOP antireformers argued that the ban on soft money and restrictions on issue advocacy advertising in the McCain-Feingold and Shays-Meehan bills were unconstitutional, that these provisions violated the First Amendment right to free speech. They even had some, but not all, of the leaders of the traditionally liberal American

Civil Liberties Union (ACLU) behind them on this argument.[29] Yet most of the interest groups that took their side were Republican-leaning groups that ran issue advocacy ads and contributed soft money to the Republican Party. Most observers of the battle over campaign finance reform were under no illusions about the more important reason for the GOP's opposition: that banning soft money contributions to political parties would disproportionately hurt the Republican Party because it collected far more in soft money than the Democratic Party; and that many Republican Party committees on both the national and state levels and many Republican-leaning groups take advantage of the looseness of the law to run issue advocacy ads that are virtually indistinguishable from campaign ads.[30] A front page story in the *New York Times* in June 1998 made no mention of the First Amendment arguments, but instead reported that the "Shays-Meehan measure—and a companion bill in the Senate—have been fiercely opposed by the top Republicans, who see it as an effort to cut into their party's traditional advantage in fundraising."[31] The *Washington Post* put it more bluntly in an editorial: "The Republicans have spent a year and a half denouncing the abuses even as they block the legislation that would end them. The truth is, they like the system; they're the better fund-raisers."[32] As the majority party after many years in the minority, the Republicans were particularly motivated to keep their fundraising advantage in order to retain their majority status. Thus, the status quo served Republican interests quite well, so why tinker with it?

As organizations with one primary goal, to win elections, political parties are pragmatically driven to protect any advantage they have in pursuing that goal. Thus, Republican opposition to the McCain-Feingold and Shays-Meehan bills was a rational stance for a party focused primarily (and out of necessity) on the electoral goal. Likewise, those disadvantaged by some aspect of the electoral system will try to change that aspect. The Democrats were disadvantaged in both soft money fund-raising and issue advocacy advertising, and the party leaders indeed supported legislation that would eliminate those disadvantages. Because this reform effort posed a threat to the Republicans' ability to retain their majority status, elimination of this threat became a primary concern for GOP party leaders.

GOP Strategies

As we saw in Chapters 2 and 3, Republican Party leaders used a variety of strategies to try to defeat campaign finance reform. In the Senate, Majority Leader Trent Lott attempted to keep consideration of campaign finance reform off the Senate's calendar altogether and then filibustered the issue to death when it did arise. In the House, GOP leaders attempted to kill reform by using their considerable control over the chamber's scheduling and rules for debate. For instance, after making repeated promises to bring the issue to the floor for a vote, House Republican leaders stalled for as long as they could. Al Hunt of the *Wall Street Journal* explained it this way:

> The House Republican leaders have broken their word and abused the rules in a desperate effort to fend off any campaign finance reform this year. With legislative duplicity unprecedented in recent times, Speaker Newt Gingrich, Majority Leader Dick Armey and others sanctioned a months-long filibuster to sabotage the measure. . . . The GOP strategy is clear: procrastinate long enough until it's so late in this already abbreviated session that it's impossible to pass a bill that then might bring pressure on the Senate.[33]

This stalling also allowed plenty of time for the GOP leaders to mobilize lobbying efforts against the Shays-Meehan bill. They helped organize more than fifty-three organizations, such as the Christian Coalition, the National Rifle Association, the National Right to Life Committee, and the Southern Baptist Convention, to fight the bill. These groups were motivated to do so in part because the Shays-Meehan bill would restrict their use of radio and television issue ads in the last sixty days before an election.[34]

Once House GOP leaders were forced to schedule campaign finance reform for a vote, they shifted their strategy to the "death-by-amendment" plan discussed in Chapter 3. As Rep. Ray LaHood, R-Ill., noted: "We tried squelching it first. Now we're trying to talk it to death."[35] Originally, Republican leaders were going to allow a minimum of 258 amendments, many of them poison pill amendments designed to split the coalition behind the Shays-Meehan bill. Then those were whittled down to 55 amendments, but many of them were still killer amendments. GOP leaders also allowed eleven other bills to compete with the Shays-Meehan bill and imposed a "Queen-of-the-Hill" rule on the process so that even if the Shays-Meehan bill passed it could be trumped, and therefore killed, if one of the other bills received more votes. The House leaders hoped to fractionalize the reformers into several camps, by, for example, forcing GOP reformers to choose between the Freshman bill and the Shays-Meehan bill. The Queen-of-the-Hill rule also made some of the other substitute bills a very real threat to the Shays-Meehan bill. For example, the Commission bill was a politically appealing if less sweeping reform proposal that worried the reformers considerably. When the deal was struck to attach the Commission bill to the Shays-Meehan bill, the reformers avoided one of the biggest land mines placed in their path. All the GOP leaders' strategies were designed to kill the type of reform proposed in the Shays-Meehan bill. In the end, however, the reformers were able to get around the many obstacles placed in their way.

The Democrats and Campaign Finance Reform

Like the Republicans, the Democrats acted in their party's best interest with their support of reforms that were likely to help level the campaign finance playing field between the two parties. The reforms proposed in the Shays-Meehan bill would curb the advantages enjoyed by the Republican Party under the current system. Therefore, the overwhelming majority of Democratic legislators supported the McCain-Feingold and Shays-Meehan bills (and other reform bills, such as the Freshman bill, that addressed both the soft money and issue advocacy problems). Yet Democratic support for campaign finance reform was not absolute.

Opposition from Within

One very telling objection to the Shays-Meehan bill came from a key House Democrat. Rep. Martin Frost, D-Texas, opposed the bill because, he said, as written, the Shays-Meehan bill did not serve the best interest of the party in that it possibly would not, in fact, level the playing field between Democrats and Republicans. Frost was chairman of the Democratic Congressional Campaign Committee during the 105th Congress. As head of the organization that raises and spends money for the sole purpose of electing Democrats to the House of Representatives, he was perhaps the one person who was most concerned with the impact of reform on the party's ability to assist congressional candidates. Frost expressed concern about the Shays-Meehan bill because it contained a *severability* clause. Since sections of the bill were severable, if any part of the bill were declared unconstitutional by the courts, all other parts of the bill would remain in effect. Whereas, with a non-severability clause, if one part of the bill were struck down, then the rest of the bill would also be voided; one part, in effect, could not be severed from the others.

Frost argued that if the issue advocacy provision of the bill were, in fact, found to violate First Amendment free speech rights and declared unconstitutional, then the ban on soft money that would still remain law (since there was no non-severability clause) would disproportionately benefit the Republicans and hurt the Democrats. Interest groups and political parties would be able to run issue advocacy ads, but not to give or spend soft money. With its greater level of hard money resources and wealthier allied interest groups, the Republican Party and its allies would be able to far outspend the Democratic Party and its allies, and the Democrats would not be able to make up the difference by raising more soft money or by relying on the help of labor unions.

Frost understood that both major planks of the Shays-Meehan bill, both the soft money and issue advocacy planks, must be in effect in order for the bill to improve the campaign finance situation of the Democratic Party. Of course, most other Democrats understood this as well, but some of them were confident that the courts would not strike down the issue advocacy restrictions contained in the bill and therefore would leave both the soft money ban and the issue advocacy limits intact. Others argued that some reform is better than no reform at all, and even if only the soft money ban survived it was at least a first step toward meaningful campaign finance reform. Many Democrats also quietly acknowledged that the bill had little chance of passing in the Senate, especially since it had gone down to defeat earlier in the year. Thus, they reasoned, why not support the Shays-Meehan bill, even without a non-severability clause, and be able to claim that they worked for campaign finance reform? In the end, after trying but failing to attach a non-severability clause to the bill, Frost himself voted for final passage of the Shays-Meehan bill.

Another major Democratic objection to the Shays-Meehan bill and some of the other campaign finance reform measures came from the Congressional Black Caucus (CBC). Some black lawmakers argued that a ban on soft money would disproportionately hurt candidates in minority and low-income areas, where citizens are less inclined to vote. Soft money has been used quite effectively for voter registration and get-out-the-vote drives in these areas, and the loss of soft money would mean that the party would have fewer resources with which to conduct these activities. As CBC member Rep. Albert R. Wynn, D-Md., who represents a majority black district in the Washington, D.C., suburbs, said: "I think [soft money is] a legitimate source of money for party-building activities such as voter registration, which are particularly important in minority communities."[36] Marty Meehan and Democratic Party leaders put forth much effort to bring this important group of lawmakers on board. In the end, Wynn and most of the other members of the Congressional Black Caucus did vote for the Shays-Meehan bill.

A final core of opposition came from a small group of Democrats who oppose abortion. These legislators had been swayed by the arguments made in a hard-hitting campaign waged by the National Right to Life Committee (NRLC) and other nonprofit, issue-oriented groups such as the Christian

Coalition, the American Conservative Union, the Eagle Forum, the Family Research Council, the National Rifle Association, and the U.S. Business and Industry Council. These groups worked with the House Republican leaders to try to weaken the issue advocacy provisions in the Shays-Meehan bill. They claimed that the Shays-Meehan bill violated their First Amendment right to free speech by restricting their ability to comment on the policy positions of federal officeholders and office seekers. They favored an amendment offered by Rep. John Doolittle, R-Calif., that would "fix" the issue advocacy provisions of the Shays-Meehan bill. The Shays-Meehan reformers pointed out that their bill already contained a provision that allowed such groups to distribute printed voter guides as long as the guides did not expressly advocate the election or defeat of any federal candidates. Nevertheless, these groups, almost all of them allies of the Republican Party, felt that the bill was too restrictive of their activities, and they lobbied heavily for the Doolittle amendment.

Republican leaders attempted to gain Democratic support for the Doolittle amendment by asserting that traditionally Democratic-leaning groups such as the NAACP would be gagged. For instance, House majority whip Tom DeLay distributed a Dear Colleague letter entitled, "Protect the NAACP's Scorecards: Vote for the Doolittle Amendment."[37] In the letter, DeLay asserted that "if the NAACP voter guide were published on one member of Congress, it would be banned [and the] Shays-Meehan bill would impose a chilling effect on the distribution of material that reports our votes and where we stand on issues."[38]

The not-so-veiled threats from the interest groups and Representative DeLay that they would bring down legislators who did not support the Doolittle amendment did have some effect. The Doolittle amendment was considered on July 14, and the slim margin of defeat (201 for and 219 against) indicates that the campaign to amend the Shays-Meehan bill in a way that would substantially weaken the issue advocacy provisions worked to some extent. Since Shays and Meehan considered the Doolittle amendment a poison pill, this close call was an important victory for the reformers. Indeed, some antiabortion Democrats did vote for the Doolittle amendment and against the Shays-Meehan bill despite the efforts of Democratic Party leaders and key House reformers to persuade them otherwise.[39] Yet the number of Democrats who voted against final passage of the bill was so small, only 15 of the 205 Democrats who voted, and the effort required to get those last few votes was so great, that in the final days before the vote on the Shays-Meehan bill very little energy was spent on trying to win them over.

Democratic Party Strategies

An interesting aspect of the Democrats' strategy was the party leaders' handling of the many Democratic House members who had introduced their own campaign finance reform legislation. All these members wanted the party leadership to support their bills. They especially wanted the benefits of the party's resources, such as the whip operation and the enhanced media attention afforded the party leaders. This presented somewhat of a problem for Minority Leader Dick Gephardt and the other Democratic Party leaders. For example, they did not want to minimize the efforts of the freshman legislators who had worked with some of the GOP freshmen to craft a comprehensive campaign finance reform measure. First-term lawmakers generally do not and are not expected to jump right into sponsoring major legislation, and Gephardt did not want to take the wind out of their sails. Democratic leaders also probably wanted the freshmen's seal of approval on whichever bill they did endorse, because the freshmen were seen as sincere and not yet tainted by the ways of Washington. In addition, one of the main bills contending with the Shays-Meehan bill was the Commission bill, sponsored by John Dingell, a very senior and visible Democratic legislator, and Carolyn Maloney, and their bipartisan efforts deserved acknowledgment. Another bill, sponsored by Scotty Baesler, a leader of the Blue Dog Coalition of conservative Democrats, would have been considered as the base bill if the discharge petition forcing a vote on campaign finance reform had succeeded.[40] Yet the Shays-Meehan bill was fast becoming the leading reform measure as it gained support from outside interest groups and the attention of the media. When the Shays-Meehan bill was reintroduced in amended form in early 1998 to mirror the McCain-Feingold bill in the Senate, the bill was strategically positioned as the measure with the best chance of clearing both chambers.

Democratic Party leaders avoided endorsing one bill over the others until somewhat late in the process. At Democratic Campaign Finance Reform Task Force meetings and Democratic Caucus meetings, the party leaders encouraged open discussion of all campaign finance reform bills sponsored by Democrats. Sponsors of the various bills pitched their proposals and tried to persuade their colleagues to support them. At one meeting of the full Democratic Caucus, Shays-Meehan supporters thought that the party leaders finally were going to announce their endorsement of the Shays-Meehan bill. Instead, Gephardt announced support for both the Shays-Meehan *and* the Freshman bills. He encouraged both groups of reformers to keep pushing hard for reform. This angered many Shays-Meehan supporters, who thought that the Democratic leaders already had pledged their support, but after tempers simmered down it became clear that it was just too early to commit to one measure over all others. Until momentum gathered behind one option, the leaders were going to advocate campaign finance reform as a general goal without specifically endorsing a particular version of reform.

Throwing their support behind one bill might have made sponsors of some of the other bills feel that their measures were not considered fairly by their party's leaders, and this might have led them to refuse to support the party-endorsed bill. Another possible explanation for a delayed endorsement of a bill is that party leaders sometimes want a particular piece of legislation to fail so that it can be used as a campaign issue in the next election. In this case, the Democrats could have, for example, blamed the Republicans for blocking reform legislation that would have cleaned up campaigns for federal office, accusing them of promoting the corrupting effect of millions of dollars of soft money in America's campaigns. Sometimes it is better to make the other party look bad and pick up more seats on election day than to pass a bill, even if it is an important policy goal for the party.

Of course, House Democratic Party leaders never expected to lead the way on campaign finance reform. Most observers had thought that the Senate would pass a campaign finance reform bill first, and the House would consider whatever the Senate passed. Instead, the McCain-Feingold bill died in the Senate in October 1997 and then again in February 1998, even though it had gained the support of a majority of senators. The House then took up the issue despite its failure in the other chamber. Eventually, House Democratic leaders came out in favor of the Shays-Meehan bill and it emerged as the leading reform bill in the House, in part because it mirrored the McCain-Feingold bill. Significant resources of the party were dedicated to its passage, and the leaders hoped that if the House passed the bill, it would garner enough votes to pass when it was sent back to the Senate.

The party's resources were considerable indeed. For example, Dick Gephardt devoted a staff person to the issue who became, along with the campaign finance staffers from Shays's and Meehan's offices, one of the point people on campaign finance reform. She dealt with interest groups and the media as well as the internal coalition of House members who supported the Shays-Meehan bill. Minority Whip David Bonior conducted numerous whip counts to help defeat the many poison pill amendments and substitutes such as the so-called paycheck protection measure. Democratic Caucus chairman Vic Fazio held regular Democratic Caucus Campaign Finance Reform Task Force meetings. These meetings kept the issue at the forefront of the party's activities and allowed for frank discussion of the issue among partisan colleagues before and after the party leaders endorsed the Shays-

Meehan bill. These efforts helped build and sustain momentum among Democrats for reform in the House.

The President's Role

Another partisan player in the battle to pass campaign finance reform legislation was President Bill Clinton. The president favored campaign finance reform and eventually endorsed the McCain-Feingold and Shays-Meehan bills. Yet many legislators and proreform interest group leaders complained that, as president, Clinton could have done more to advance the cause of reform. A proreform lobbyist for one of the good-government groups commented that Clinton "really spent the minimum level of political capital on this issue."[41]

Scholars of the presidency tell us that presidents actually have very little influence over what Congress does, yet many presidents have enjoyed a good deal of success in getting Congress to enact their policy priorities. Many factors affect how successful a president will be in dealing with Congress. For example, the particular circumstances at the time, such as the state of the economy or whether Congress is controlled by the president's party or the opposition party, can significantly affect a president's level of influence with Congress. The stage in a president's term also matters, because most newly elected presidents enjoy a honeymoon period, when Congress, the press, and the public are willing to give the new president a chance to enact his policies.

Bill Clinton's influence was diminished during the 105th Congress because of the highly partisan GOP investigations of the 1996 fund-raising scandals, and because of the emerging scandal surrounding his affair with White House intern Monica Lewinsky that hit the newspapers in January 1998. Clinton also faced a Congress controlled by the other party and was at a stage in his presidency way beyond the honeymoon period. These factors certainly decreased Clinton's sway over Congress. Yet given what a president can do to influence Congress, and what Clinton had done for other issues, many were disappointed with his efforts on campaign finance reform.

One of the most effective tools presidents use to influence the actions of Congress is called "going public," when, instead of bargaining with Congress, a president appeals directly to the American public for support and asks citizens to urge their senators and House members to support the president as well.[42] Ronald Reagan was a master of this technique, and Bill Clinton has used it effectively at times as well. Shays, Meehan, and the external issue network pushing for reform adapted the technique to Congress to mobilize public support for their bill. Proreformers in and outside of Congress had hoped that Clinton might make such a public appeal on campaign finance reform. Yet, as one might guess, a president cannot "go public" for every issue. He must reserve such appeals for his top priorities, for he cannot expect the American people to help him persuade Congress to act very often.

Despite his restricted capacity for influence, the president did provide some assistance to help keep the issue on the front pages of leading newspapers and on the legislative agenda of Congress. Yet his efforts were limited to a few, highly visible events. President Clinton's campaign finance reform activities began with the well-publicized handshake between Clinton and House Speaker Newt Gingrich on June 11, 1995, in Claremont, New Hampshire. The two leaders agreed to work together to establish a bipartisan commission to propose a reform measure to Congress for an up or down vote, but the commission was never created. Later, the president appointed former vice president and senator Walter Mondale and former senator Nancy Kassenbaum Baker to lead an effort to promote campaign finance reform. He never funded their effort, however, and the Aspen Institute and the Pew Charitable Trusts stepped in to provide funding for the project.

In September 1997 Clinton again helped promote reform when it began to look like GOP leaders were going to let the Senate adjourn for the year before considering the McCain-Feingold bill. He sent a letter threatening to take the historic step of reconvening Congress if senators left town before voting on campaign finance reform. Minority Leader Tom Daschle used this letter to push Majority Leader Trent Lott to put reform on the Senate's calendar. Two days later, Lott announced that the debate on campaign finance reform would begin.[43]

Clinton publicly endorsed the McCain-Feingold bill and called on Congress to pass it in his State of the Union address in January 1998, a few weeks before the Senate debated the bill for a second time. He said, "Everyone knows elections have become too expensive, fueling a fund-raising arms race. . . . A vote against McCain-Feingold is a vote for soft money and the status quo. I ask you to strengthen our democracy and pass campaign finance reform this year." Yet, like the House Democratic leaders, President Clinton waited quite some time before endorsing the leading campaign finance reform bills. The Senate had already debated the McCain-Feingold bill once before Clinton endorsed it, and he did not endorse the Shays-Meehan bill in the House until April 22, 1998.

President Clinton also made some special appeals to encourage legislators to support campaign finance reform and later to thank them for their votes in favor of reform. For example, on May 20, 1998, in a letter personally addressed to individual House Democrats, President Clinton urged his partisan colleagues to support the Shays-Meehan bill: "[O]nly Shays-Meehan represents real, comprehensive, bipartisan reform. . . . Talking about reform is easy; this week, the House of Representatives has a rare and fleeting opportunity to act. . . . I urge you to make this the year that Congress confounds public cynicism and passes bipartisan, comprehensive campaign finance reform." Note the repeated references to bipartisanship when in fact the measure had a relatively small number of GOP House members behind it. The president too scored points with the public for cooperating with the other party, so portraying his favored legislation as bipartisan may have helped boost his approval rating.

Advocating campaign finance reform was also a useful political strategy for the president because he was under the glare of congressional investigations of his and his party's fund-raising practices. Some saw his support for reform as less than genuine. Others, however, viewed the GOP-led investigations as partisan witch-hunts and praised the president for supporting solutions to a campaign finance system out of control while the Republicans merely pointed fingers. Much as John McCain was said to be promoting reform in part to overcome his own past entanglement with a campaign finance scandal, Bill Clinton also needed to improve his image on the issue. All in all, however, President Clinton's efforts were helpful but limited, and some reformers are convinced that more pressure from the president may have helped McCain and Feingold secure the few additional votes they needed to defeat the GOP filibuster against their bill.

Conclusion: The Place of Parties in the Labyrinth

The particular nature of the partisan climate at any given time can have a significant effect on the outcome of a policy proposal. Timing is an important factor that influences all stages of a debate on a policy issue. The circumstances of parties and their members change, and such things as the strength of party leaders, the size of the majority's margin of control, and the partisan balance between the legislative and executive branches provide opportunities or barriers, an atmosphere ripe for policymaking or one hostile to a particular issue. Of course, legislators cannot control all these factors. In fact, they can control few, if any, of them. Yet recognizing whether the partisan climate is favorable or unfavorable will often determine whether lawmakers can successfully navigate a measure through Congress.

With campaign finance reform, the partisan climate appeared hostile on the surface. The public was not loudly demanding a change in the campaign finance laws, so neither party was particularly inclined to take up the cause. The majority party leaders in both chambers strongly opposed the leading campaign finance reform bills, so the chances of getting a vote on the issue were automatically diminished. Even if the reformers did get a vote on the issue, Republican leaders were ready to throw numerous procedural and legislative grenades at the first sign of any progress by the reformers. In the Senate, this was a particularly difficult obstacle to overcome, for a supermajority of sixty votes was needed to shut down the GOP filibuster that eventually killed the McCain-Feingold bill. With such a high threshold to achieve, it is difficult to pass any major legislation through the Senate unless it has strong support from a majority of senators and no strong objection from the majority party leadership. The McCain-Feingold bill met the first requirement, but not the second. Finally, the issue had little support from Republicans, so the reformers needed to get almost all the Democrats on their side. Securing the support of virtually every member in one of the parties is a difficult task for any contested policy debate. President Clinton helped with this task, but some say not enough. Moreover, his efforts were tainted by his own campaign finance and other troubles, thus his influence was limited.

In the House, circumstances were more favorable than in the Senate. It is much more difficult for a minority to stop a majority in the House than in the Senate. Yet House GOP leaders had raised the bar by imposing a Queen-of-the-Hill rule, whereby of the twelve bills to be considered, the one that received the most votes would pass and the others would not, even if they received a majority of votes. Nevertheless, this obstacle proved easier to overcome than the Senate filibuster against reform. Some observers were surprised that the House GOP leaders did not impose the more restrictive King-of-the-Hill rule, which specifies that the last substitute bill to be voted on that passes, wins, even if another bill had received more votes. We believe that the GOP leaders did not use this more restrictive rule because they had already been harshly criticized from virtually all corners, even by some in their own camp, for their earlier efforts to bring "sham" reform bills up under suspension of the rules. Perhaps more important, Rules Committee chairman Gerald Solomon of New York had made clear that now that the Republicans controlled the Rules Committee, they would not use the King-of-the-Hill rule, which was a favored tactic of the Democrats when they were the majority party and was often used by them to the Republican minority's detriment.

Although the GOP leaders in the House were just as opposed to campaign finance reform as their counterparts in the Senate, the diminished influence of Speaker Newt Gingrich and the clumsy way that he and the other GOP leaders handled the issue helped the reformers gain the necessary momentum to pass the Shays-Meehan bill. The many broken promises regarding campaign finance reform and the rather devious attempts to kill the issue with parliamentary procedures and complex rule structures actually energized House reformers, mobilized more support from the reform interest groups, and helped keep the media's attention on the issue.

Probably the most important factor for legislative success is to know when to take advantage of opportunities in the partisan environment and when to save one's energy. If the partisan climate is right, an effective policy entrepreneur needs to be poised to ride the wave of opportunity and make as much headway as possible on the issue. If the partisan environment is inhospitable, it may be best to wait until circumstances improve. If reformers had attempted to push for campaign finance reform in 1995, when the Republicans had just taken control of both chambers of Congress and Newt Gingrich in particular was enjoying a high level of influence among his fellow partisans, the issue would have gone nowhere. In fact, Linda Smith, a first-term Republican House member, tried to persuade Gingrich and her party's other leaders to bring campaign finance reform legislation to a vote during the 104th Congress when the partisan climate for the issue was quite hostile. She even spearheaded a discharge petition drive to force the issue to a vote, but she failed miserably. Smith appears to have suffered for her independence on this and other issues, for she lost her position as the first Republican women ever to chair a subcommittee in her first term (the Subcommittee on Small Business).[44] By 1997, however, the partisan climate had shifted dramatically, and the issue saw much greater success.

Yet, in the end, campaign finance reform did not succeed in the 105th Congress. Despite the improved partisan climate, it was killed three times in the Senate, where, even with the support of a majority of senators, a measure may go down because of the procedural tools that allow a minority of senators to prevail. When that minority has the majority party leadership on its side, as was the case with campaign finance reform, the majority supporting a bill may find it incredibly difficult to impose its will. Thus, both the rules of the chamber, which were designed by senators to protect the rights of minorities and guard against the tyranny of the majority, and the partisan circumstances revolving around an issue can have a tremendous impact on its chances for legislative success.

6

THE EXTERNAL ISSUE NETWORK
Interest Groups and the Media

Congressperson A: Can I count on you to support my bill?
Congressperson B: I like the idea, but do the important interest groups support it?

Congressperson A: I'm not sure.
Congressperson B: Such a change is definitely needed, but do the poll numbers show the public wants it?

Congressperson A: I don't think so.
Congressperson B: It is an important policy problem, but has the issue received a lot of media attention?

Congressperson A: Not really.
Congressperson B: Then why should I support your bill?

This exchange could happen in regard to any one of the thousands of bills that never really make it onto the policy agenda in Congress. Unless there is an external network of support for some policy change—support from relevant interest groups, favorable public opinion, and attention from the media—lawmakers usually generally have little motivation to disrupt the status quo. As we saw in Chapters 3 and 4, a well-developed external issue network that includes the relevant interest groups and the national media can greatly enhance the likelihood of legislative success. Interest group advocacy for a policy change and positive media attention can go a long way to mobilize favorable public opinion. If the drive for some legislative action exists only inside the halls of Congress, its advocates might have difficulty persuading enough of their colleagues to vote for the measure to pass it. Support and attention from interest groups and the media can help legislators gain the votes they need from their colleagues by building the momentum necessary to overcome the many obstacles that dot the legislative labyrinth.

The external issue networks that developed around both sides of the campaign finance reform debate had a discernible impact on the course of reform legislation during the 105th Congress. The proreform interest groups were helpful in the early stages of crafting the McCain-Feingold bill in the Senate. Later, during the final days before the vote on the Shays-Meehan bill in the House, they actively lobbied lawmakers. The interest groups opposed to reform assisted GOP leaders in their effort to defeat proposed reforms once it became clear that a bill actually might pass in the House. The attention given to the issue by the media and the generally positive proreform editorial commentary from leading newspapers helped keep the issue alive even as Republican congressional leaders tried to kill it. As effective policy entrepreneurs, Representatives Shays and Meehan were able to expand the proreform external issue network and use it to their benefit. This ability to nurture and manage a powerful external issue network is what set them apart from other campaign finance reform issue leaders.

Although most textbooks on Congress devote some attention to the role of interest groups in policymaking and a little to the potential effect of the media on the policy process, we argue that these external players can and often do have tremendous influence.[1] In the case of campaign finance reform, a collection of "good-government" public interest groups and many in the national and local media constituted an effective external issue network that helped raise the profile of the issue, assisted in keeping campaign finance reform on the policy agenda in Congress, and contributed to the success of the Shays-Meehan bill in the House.

Interest Groups and Congress

Interest groups can play a vital role in the policymaking process. They often provide information, resources, a conduit to the media, and of course targeted pressure on undecided or wavering lawmakers. When they work closely with legislators inside Congress, the coordinated effort can be quite effective. Most of these organizations engage in direct, or "inside," lobbying, where they develop and maintain close contacts with government officials to influence their decisions. Lobbyists provide useful information, testify at hearings, and help legislators shore up support from other lawmakers for their legislation. Traditionally, inside lobbying has been considered the most effective means of pressing for a group's concerns, for it puts lobbyists directly in touch with lawmakers. It is also a very expensive method of lobbying, and only those groups with sufficient resources are able to engage in extensive inside lobbying activities. The contemporary interest group system is dominated by economic interests, particularly business interests, that have the resources to win out over less wealthy interests.[2] Many of the public interest groups that work for campaign finance reform argue that the proposed changes would help "level the playing field" by diminishing some of the advantages enjoyed by groups with lots of money. They appeal to the general belief that moneyed special interests should be held in check, much as John McCain argued during his presidential campaign.

Yet other means of lobbying also can be quite potent. Interest groups also engage in "outside" lobbying, whereby an interest group puts public pressure on policymakers. With outside lobbying, interest groups often tap into the power of numbers. The idea is to convince lawmakers that the group's policy position has broad public support, and that opposing the group's position may harm a legislator's chance for reelection.[3] Outside lobbying involves grassroots activities such as encouraging the group's members and the public in general to write, call, fax, e-mail, or, better yet, visit their representatives in Congress; suggesting that the group's members and other voters support particular candidates in elections; and pursuing favorable coverage from the news media for the group's position and the government officials who support it.

Interest groups also use issue advocacy advertising as a means of outside lobbying. These ads are controversial when aired close to an election, and the leading campaign finance reform bills sought to curb them if they mention a candidate for federal office. Yet issue ads were originally allowed more legal leeway than conventional campaign ads because issue ads are supposed to be used to state a person's or a group's position on some issue and sometimes to encourage citizens to contact their lawmakers about the issue. The intent is to motivate citizens to lobby their elected representatives, much like presidents will "go public" by taking their case for some policy change directly to the public and asking citizens to pressure Congress to support the president's proposal.

Many interest groups also provide information regarding the voting records of members of Congress on the groups' key issues. Some interest groups offer "scorecards" to their members and the public, which are powerful tools that groups use to influence policy and the outcome of elections. Interest groups often warn legislators that their vote on some particular bill will be "scored"; that is, it will be included on the groups scorecard of key votes and tabulated with other votes to give each legislator a score from 0 to 100 percent. This score indicates how much the legislator conforms to the groups policy positions. Such a warning is a not-so-subtle suggestion that the legislator better vote the "right" way on that bill or suffer the potential consequences at the next election. Some interest groups distribute "voter guides" that list how one or more candidates stand on issues important to the groups. A candidate's positions on the group's issues are taken either from the candidate's voting records or from the candidate's responses to the group's questionnaire. Voter guides became one of the most contentious issues of the campaign finance reform debate, because the GOP leaders and others opposed to reform—namely, the nonprofit groups that use voter guides—charged that the Shays-Meehan bill would ban voter guides.

Interest groups on both sides of the campaign finance reform debate used all these inside and outside lobbying techniques to get their messages across and to influence the outcome of the legislative process. Of course, interest groups also are quite active in campaigns.[4] They give campaign contributions from their political action committees, provide workers to help candidates win their elections, mobilize voters to vote a particular way, and attempt to influence voters' opinions of candidates and parties through personal contacts, mailings, telephone calls, voter guides, and radio and television ads. Some of these activities are the focus of the efforts to reform the campaign finance system.

Taking Sides on Campaign Finance Reform

Just as each party's view of reform was based on the potential effect various reforms might have on the party's ability to win elections, many interest groups too came down on one side of the issue or the other based on the impact they thought reforms would have on their activities during elections. For instance, numerous nonprofit groups thought the issue advocacy restrictions in the McCain-Feingold and Shays-Meehan bills would hinder their ability to communicate with voters using materials such as voter guides. They joined the Republican leaders in opposition to reform. On the other side, a group of thirty-five business executives who formed the Business Advisory Council of the Campaign Reform Project supported the Shays-Meehan bill, because they believed that modern campaigns were too costly and that the soft money system encouraged party leaders to "shake down" corporations for large, unregulated contributions.

The so-called good-government public interest groups that advocate campaign finance reform, such as Common Cause and the League of Women Voters, would neither benefit nor suffer materially if campaign finance reform were to be enacted. A public interest or citizen group is a special type of interest group whose members are not motivated by some material benefit to participate in politics. Public interest groups press for policies that they believe will benefit the public at large. In this case, the public interest groups viewed their participation as an effort to improve the political process and to enhance the chances for good government. People join public interest groups for the "purposive" benefits that membership in such groups provide, not because their membership will give them some material benefit: "Thousands of organizations across the country offer members only one thing: satisfaction that they have done their part to make the world a better place."[5]

Some citizen groups were on the other side of the reform debate. For example, the Christian Coalition is not an economic interest group that people join for personal material benefits. Rather, it is a nonprofit organization that attracts members primarily because of the purposive benefits that it offers. For instance, the Christian Coalition presses for policy change on abortion, a goal that the group asserts would benefit unborn children and the public at large, not necessarily the members of the Christian Coalition. The Christian Coalition and other nonprofit groups opposed the leading campaign finance reform bills because they believed the proposals would limit their issue advocacy and voter guide activities. Many nonprofit groups that conduct the same activities, however, supported reform.

The Proreform Public Interest Groups

The public interest groups that advocate campaign finance reform are a well-established coalition of groups that have worked for reform for years. Many of the lobbyists of today's good-government groups are veterans of the reform movement of the 1970s that led to enactment of the Federal Election Campaign Act. These people were around for every previous attempt at reform throughout the 1980s and 1990s, only to be disappointed when reform measures never made it out of Congress, or, if one did, when it was vetoed by the president. As is true of many issues before Congress, some of these lobbyists have a better understanding of the issue, and more experience dealing with it, than many of the legislators who now advocate reform in Congress. Needless to say, their knowledge and experience were valuable resources in the battle to pass campaign finance reform during the 105th Congress.

The Shays-Meehan campaign finance reform effort involved several public interest groups that were core members of the reformers' issue network. These

groups were there from the beginning of the effort, helping to draft the legislation and providing the initial lobbying that helped place campaign finance
reform on the congressional policy agenda. The clear leader among these
groups was Common Cause, and its lobbyists were intensely involved in the
reform effort. Other core interest groups included Public Citizen, the League
of Women Voters, and the U.S. Public Interest Research Group (US PIRG).

The leaders of these reform public interest groups had extraordinary access to House reformers and their staffs. These groups were part of the essential external issue network, the counterpart to the internal network, of
support for the Shays-Meehan bill. Without a strong external issue network,
the Shays-Meehan reform coalition within Congress may not have succeeded in passing the bill. These groups were represented at key briefing
meetings that took place on Capitol Hill, and they (particularly Common
Cause) were sometimes invited to smaller, more private meetings with key
members of Congress.

The reform groups provided needed information and expertise to lawmakers and their staffs. A few of the proreform lobbyists had valuable institutional memory of past attempts to enact reform and brought to the table
known pitfalls and snags to avoid. The close working relationship the House
reformers had with these lobbyists helped prepare them for the many angles
of attack from the antireformers. Such experience and insight were especially helpful because many of the key reform legislators had not been in
Congress or even working on the issue during the 1970s, 1980s, or 1990s. In
the Senate, however, the reformers did not build as strong a link to lobbyists
in an external issue network. These public interest groups were also well-
established Washington players, and their lobbyists had developed working
relationships with many legislators. Thus, these lobbyists often had access to
legislators who were reluctant to meet with their colleagues sponsoring reform measures. The groups were very good at identifying potential supporters in Congress and lobbying them for assistance on key votes. This was of
great help during the amendment process, when Shays-Meehan supporters
had to fight off a number of poison pill amendments. Additionally, Common Cause and other organizations offered the legal expertise of some of the
nation's leading campaign finance attorneys.

The public interest groups also provided key grassroots efforts by mobilizing their many volunteers throughout the country to pressure lawmakers to
support campaign finance reform. These volunteers were key to reaching
people outside Washington, D.C., and, therefore, to reaching members of
Congress in their home districts. For example, the reform interest groups or-

ganized mass postcard mailings and e-mail alerts in key states. Volunteers also staffed phone banks to call other group members to action on the issue.[6] When legislators hear something from the folks back home, they are more inclined to listen than if they hear it only from lobbyists in Washington. One Republican House member, Thomas M. Davis III of Virginia, said that even though his party's leaders clearly disapproved, he decided to sign onto the Blue Dog Democrat discharge petition to force a vote on campaign finance reform because a Common Cause volunteer urged him to do so at a meeting back home in his district.[7] Another Republican member of Congress, Brian Bilbray of California, caught the wrath of Speaker Newt Gingrich for signing the discharge petition. In clear view of his colleagues on the floor of the House, Bilbray and Gingrich had it out. Making a gun-to-the-head motion, Bilbray told Gingrich he had "pledged to his constituents to take a stand on campaign finance reform, and the only thing worse than reneging 'would be putting a gun to my head and blowing my brains out.' "[8] The groups' grassroots efforts also helped translate the issue into one that people could understand. Reform group volunteers around the country helped educate the public about why such reforms were important to them and to preserving their voice in the political process, a message that would not have been easily conveyed by debates and speeches on the floor of the House of Representatives.

The public interest groups worked both alone and together as a coalition in support of reform. For example, on May 5, 1998, five proreform groups led by Common Cause sent a letter, titled "Pass Shays-Meehan—The Test of Real Campaign Reform," to all House members urging them to vote for the Shays-Meehan bill. The other groups were the League of Women Voters, US-PIRG, Public Campaign, and Public Citizen. The next day, the groups held a press conference with Shays, Meehan, and other House members to endorse the bill. The letter and press conference were intended to persuade House members to support the Shays-Meehan bill *instead of* the Freshman bill. The letter noted that in the groups' opinion, the Freshman bill and others did not sufficiently address soft money and sham issue ads. For this reason, the groups chose not to endorse any reform bills except the Shays-Meehan bill.

The reform interest groups knew that if the proreform vote were split in Congress, then no reform bill would pass. Thus they decided to throw all their support behind one bill, often a risky strategy because endorsing one bill naturally alienates the sponsors of other competing bills. Supporters of the Freshman bill were, as expected, not pleased about the interest groups' endorsement of the Shays-Meehan bill. One of the primary sponsors of the

Freshman bill, Asa Hutchinson, R-Ark., issued a press release in response that accused Common Cause of

> trying to stifle debate on reform. . . . Common Cause has called other bills "phony reform" and has cynically described them as efforts "to kill reform." . . . Common Cause's Shermanesque strategy of burning everything in their path leaves no room for debate, consensus, good will, compromise, or success if their ideal bill does not receive a majority. It is counter productive to everything we have worked so hard to achieve. . . . We need to work together, not against each other, to pass reform this year.[9]

This rift in the reform coalition brought reformers dangerously close to breaking up. In the end, however, with concessions made to the freshmen the Shays-Meehan bill did pass. The primary Democratic sponsor of the Freshman bill, Tom Allen of Maine, voted for the Shays-Meehan bill, but Hutchinson did not. This incident illustrates how tricky it is for outside interest groups to know, when it comes down to the line, which lawmakers to work with and also how important it is for issue leaders in Congress to cultivate strong ties with outside interest groups in order to build an effective external issue network.

This story also illustrates the power that established and influential interest groups can have in the policymaking process. Regarding campaign finance reform, Common Cause, which was effectively the leader among the public interest groups, had quite a lot of power. Its authority was based in part on its ability to mobilize citizens around the country, its long-term relationships with many lawmakers, and its expertise on the issue. More important, Common Cause, with the support of the other public interest groups, all but defined what qualified as legitimate campaign finance reform. In fact, congressional reformers sometimes complained that every provision of a reform bill had to pass the Common Cause "smell test" or be doomed. The sponsors of the Freshman bill were all too aware of this. Even some on the Shays-Meehan reform team expressed frustration when any changes under consideration had to pass the "smell test" or suffer the same fate as the Freshman bill. This potentially limited lawmakers' ability to alter their own legislation, even if they were trying to compromise in order to broaden support for their measures.

The power of Common Cause and the other groups was further enhanced because virtually all the media turned to them to gauge the merits of the various reform bills. Throughout the campaign finance reform debate, the press followed the groups' lead. If the groups labeled a bill "sham reform," so did the media. When the groups endorsed the Shays-Meehan bill, so did editorial boards all over the country. In congressional politics, this is power.

It was also a useful strategy for the Shays-Meehan reformers in Congress, because the media generally are not inclined in their reporting (as opposed to their editorial commentary) to follow the policy recommendations of some legislators over others or one party over the other. The good-government groups, particularly Common Cause, acted as outside validators for the press in a way that promoted the Shays-Meehan bill. This is quite possibly the groups' most important contribution to the reform effort, and its effectiveness enhanced the potential for success in the House. For example, news stories on the campaign finance system or on the reform effort frequently featured quotes from a Common Cause lobbyist. Behind the scenes, Common Cause worked hard to get editorial boards not only to write about campaign finance reform but also to endorse the Shays-Meehan and McCain-Feingold bills. This is the kind of press that most legislators can only dream of and a clear illustration of the necessity for a strong external issue network.

To keep the media's attention focused on the reform debate that dragged on for so long in Congress the reform groups provided background material, updates, and access to key lawmakers. They made it easy for reporters, with whom they had established working relationships, to follow the story without doing much legwork. The groups also sent numerous "blast faxes" to targeted radio stations in the districts of key legislators they hoped to persuade. Moreover, Washington staff members of the interest groups would travel to meet with the editorial boards of newspapers in key states and provide op-ed pieces to papers in other states. In House members' districts, local chapter members of Common Cause wrote letters to the editors of local papers and met with their editorial boards to keep the issue in the local news as well as to put public pressure on their members of Congress to support reform. Common Cause's extensive network of volunteers throughout the country aided in the effort to pass campaign finance reform legislation in Washington, D.C.

The core public interest groups were also quite helpful in reaching out to other groups and expanding the campaign finance reform external issue network. The groups held organizational and recruitment meetings with other potentially affected and interested groups. By actively reaching out to other organizations for support, the good-government groups provided the organizers of the effort within Congress a way of reaching those that might have remained inaccessible. One major effort was the organization of numerous church groups and one of the nation's largest and most influential interest groups, the American Association of Retired Persons (AARP), to back the Shays-Meehan bill. To demonstrate this wide-ranging support for their bill, Representatives Shays and Meehan issued a Dear Colleague letter on May 13, 1998, listing thirty-two interest groups that had endorsed their bill (see Figure 6-1). The list included the public interest groups discussed above as well as such diverse groups as the Children's Defense Fund, the Environmental Defense Fund, and the American Heart Association. Support from these and other organizations signaled to many in Congress that momentum was building for campaign finance reform. This momentum contributed to a bandwagon effect and encouraged some wavering lawmakers to join the reform effort.

The Core Reform Interest Groups

Before moving on to discussion of other groups involved in the campaign finance reform debate, we provide brief descriptions of each of the core pro-reform groups and examine some of their specific contributions to the reform effort.

Common Cause

John Gardner, former Secretary of Health, Education and Welfare, founded Common Cause in 1970 as a multi-issue, public interest group. The organization was premised on the idea that grassroots volunteers, buttressed by professional lobbyists in Washington, D.C., would provide a nonpartisan initiative for reform. Today, Common Cause has more than 200,000 members nationwide and is financed by dues and contributions from its members.

Common Cause has made campaign finance reform one of its priority issues. Its lobbyists in the Washington, D.C., office are among the most knowledgeable regarding campaign finance issues. They played a key role in drafting much of the language that was included in the McCain-Feingold and Shays-Meehan bills. Common Cause's president during the campaign finance reform debate in the 105th Congress, Ann McBride, was very vocal at press conferences and issued numerous releases in favor of the Shays-Meehan bill.

Although Common Cause's effort was essential to the issue network that developed around the Shays-Meehan bill, the group's involvement caused some difficulties at times. Many Republicans who applauded their leaders' efforts to end the reform debate used Common Cause's involvement to portray the effort as a purely Democratic one, for Common Cause generally is identified with liberal causes. Furthermore, some legislators and staffers resented

Figure 6-1   A "Dear Colleague" letter from Representatives Shays and
Meehan

Congress of the United States
Washington, DC 20515

Broad Support for H.R. 3526
The (Shays/Meehan) Bipartisan Campaign Reform Act of 1998

May 13, 1998

Dear Colleague:

We would like to take this opportunity to share with you the long list of public interest
groups that have endorsed H.R. 3526, the Bipartisan Campaign Reform Act of 1998.

AARP
The American Heart Association
American Public Power Association
American Society of Public Administration
Campaign for America
Center for Science in the Public Interest
Children's Defense Fund
Church of the Brethren, Washington Office
Church Women United
Common Cause
Consumer Federation of America
Democracy 21
Environmental Defense Fund
The Episcopal Church
Friends of the Earth
Gray Panthers
The League of Women Voters, U.S.A.
Lutheran Office for Governmental Affairs
Evangelical Lutheran Church in America
Mennonite Central Committee, Washington Office
The National Association of Community Action Agencies
The National Community Action Foundation
National Council of Churches of Christ in the USA
The National Farmers' Union
NETWORK: A National Catholic Social Justice Lobby
Presbyterian Church (USA)
Public Citizen
The Union of American Hebrew Congregations
Unitarian Universalist Association of Congregations
United Church of Christ; Office for Church in Society
United Methodist Church, General Board of Church and Society
US PIRG

We hope that you will join us in voting for H.R. 3526 when the House considers
campaign reform in May and June. If you have any questions, or would like to cosponsor
this legislation, please contact us directly or have your staff contact Allison Rak (Shays)
at 5-5541 or Amy Rosenbaum (Meehan) at 5-3411.

Sincerely

Christopher Shays
Member of Congress

Marty Meehan
Member of Congress

the Common Cause "smell test," arguing that this was giving too much power, real or perceived, to an outside interest. Overall, however, Common Cause was a powerful and extremely valuable ally for the congressional reformers. As the leader of the external issue network, Common Cause contributed mightily to the success of the Shays-Meehan bill in the House.

The League of Women Voters of the United States

The mission of the League of Women Voters, which describes itself as a nonpartisan, multi-issue, public political organization, is "to encourage the informed and active participation of citizens in government and influence public policy through education and advocacy."[10] The League was also an important part of the organized effort for campaign finance reform in the 105th Congress. It too provided key lobbying, media attention, and assistance with issue development. The League was especially helpful in the effort to stop the attack on the 1993 National Voter Registration Act (the "motor-voter" law). The motor-voter law required states to make it possible for citizens to register to vote when getting or renewing a driver's license. GOP leaders crafted legislation and several proposed amendments to the Shays-Meehan bill to try to weaken the motor-voter law and therefore make it more difficult to register to vote.

If such poison pill amendments had been added to the Shays-Meehan bill, the bill would have lost crucial support from Democrats and would have failed to pass. The GOP leaders argued that scores of noncitizens had registered and voted in recent elections and that the law was too permissive, making it impossible to defend against such voter fraud. Democrats countered that there was no massive voter fraud problem and suggested that the Republicans were driven by racism and the potential electoral payoff from "wedge" issue politics. The League uncovered a February 5, 1990, Dear Colleague letter from Newt Gingrich, the Republican whip at the time, in support of the original motor-voter bill. The letter was cosigned by Bill Thomas, R-Calif., the vice chairman of the committee on House Administration, and John Hiler, R-Ind., from the Subcommittee on Elections. The letter showed that the GOP leaders' switch of position on the motor-voter law was politically motivated. This helped the reformers defeat the GOP attacks on the law.

Public Citizen

Ralph Nader founded this multi-issue public interest group in 1971. Part of its mission is to ensure a "more open and democratic government."[11] Like the other groups, Public Citizen is funded by members' dues and accepts no government or corporate support. Public Citizen has been involved in the Congress Watch project, a lobbying program that, among other things, is seeking "to ensure a strong democracy by exposing the harmful impact of money in politics and advocating for comprehensive campaign finance reform."[12] Specifically, Public Citizen worked extensively through its Congress Watch program to highlight the problem of phony issue ads (that is, ads that purport to be purely informational or educational but have all the markings of campaign ads). Public Citizen was quite helpful in explaining this confusing aspect of the reform debate to legislators, their staffs, the media, and the public at large. With so much misunderstanding about the various types of campaign finance tactics and the details of the complex campaign finance laws, this clarification and other efforts by Public Citizen were quite useful for the congressional reformers.

The United States Public Interest Research Group (US PIRG)

This is the national office of the state PIRGs. Another Ralph Nader organization, PIRG employs approximately 400 staff nationwide and has 300,000 members and 70 chapters based on college campuses across the country. State PIRGs "have been advocating for and organizing on public interest issues for over 25 years."[13] Among their priorities is the "Democracy Program," which places campaign finance reform as a key agenda item. PIRG supports campaign finance reform at all levels of government and looks to limit contributions and funding from outside of a candidate's district. PIRG provided volunteers for the reform effort, assistance in lobbying efforts, and media support. Moreover, PIRG's state-level successes enacting campaign finance reform helped PIRG lobbyists provide vital information and key insights into what types of reforms work and what types do not.

Other Proreform Groups and Organizations

Other groups and organizations supported the campaign finance reform effort in one way or another, groups such as the Project on Government Oversight (POGO), the National Legal and Policy Center, the National Right to Work Legal Defense Fund, OMB Watch, the Arab American Institute, the National Council of La Raza, the AFL-CIO, Campaign for America, Public Campaign, and the Episcopal Church Office of Government Relations. Many of these groups were willing to proclaim their support publicly in their own news releases and to sign on to Dear Colleague letters like the one shown in Figure 6-1.

Other organizations, such as the Brennan Center for Justice and the Center for Responsive Politics (CRP), provided legal and other expert information and advice regarding the current campaign finance picture. The legal experts at the Brennan Center offered invaluable insight into the constitutional issues involved. The CRP issued a key study in November 1997 that highlighted the money and power shift on Capitol Hill, whereby campaign money followed the Republicans into power once they took control of Congress in 1995.[14] Additionally, foundations such as the Pew Charitable Trusts, the CATO Institute, and the Brookings Institution sponsored grant projects to study campaign finance activities and possible reforms and hosted events for Hill staffers to learn about the research firsthand.

One such effort was the Aspen Institute's Campaign Finance Reform Project. The Aspen Institute is a think tank that provides a forum for local, national, and international leaders to discuss policy problems. It "seeks to improve the conditions for human well being by fostering enlightened, responsible leadership."[15] During the 105th Congress, the Aspen Institute sponsored the Campaign Finance Reform Project. President Clinton originally had appointed former vice president and senator Walter Mondale, a Democrat, and former senator Nancy Kassenbaum Baker, a Republican, to lead an effort to promote campaign finance reform. When the White House failed to come up with the resources to sponsor the Mondale-Kassenbaum Baker Commission, the Aspen Institute, in connection with the Pew Charitable Trusts, stepped in to back their efforts. Mondale and Kassenbaum Baker were particularly active during the Senate deliberations. They testified before the Senate Committee on Governmental Affairs (called the Thompson Committee for its chairman Fred Thompson, R-Tenn.), met with members on Capitol Hill, engaged in numerous Hill briefings and press briefings, published a couple of op-ed pieces timed to influence the legislative debate, and built a coalition of former members of the Senate and the House in favor of reform. The Aspen Institute also sponsored a retreat for House staff members in January 1998 to discuss reform proposals away from the pressures and media scrutiny of Capitol Hill.

In another effort, thirty-five business executives, including Warren Buffett, chairman of Berkshire Hathaway, and Jerome Kohlberg, of Kohlberg and Company, formed the Business Advisory Council of the Campaign Reform Project, creating a particularly high-profile group in support of campaign finance reform. Backing from the business community was especially important because most business interests sided with the Republican leadership on this and other issues. For example, the Chamber of Commerce opposed and worked against the Shays-Meehan bill. These proreform business executives, however, sent an important message to congressional Republicans that some of their most powerful constituents favored reform. As Kohlberg said, business leaders are "working to shatter the myth that business is interested only in perpetuating the system. We are involving other business leaders by explaining that the rapidly rising cost of access [to elected officials] may soon price them out of the political marketplace."[16] Some of these corporate leaders sent personally addressed letters to House members advocating reform. Buffett sent one to House members who had voted to defeat the first poison pill amendment proposed to the Shays-Meehan bill. In the letter, Buffett commended the lawmakers for voting to keep campaign finance reform alive. He called them courageous and principled and urged them to vote for the Shays-Meehan bill.[17] The business leaders also placed a paid advertisement in major newspapers in support of campaign finance reform, thus very publicly proclaiming not just their support for reform, but in effect their challenge to the GOP leaders.

All these groups filled the political marketplace with increasing support for reform, lending credence to many reformers' claims that there was a problem here worth addressing and that the public was concerned about it. As the collection of interest groups and organizations that supported the Shays-Meehan bill expanded, the Republican leaders felt more pressure to do something about the issue. One of the things they did was marshal their own groups and organizations to work against campaign finance reform.

Groups That Opposed Campaign Finance Reform

The campaign finance reform effort had its detractors. Once it became clear that support for reform was growing, those against reform inside the House of Representatives looked for outside group support to counter the Shays-Meehan and Freshman bills—sometimes provision by provision. In effect, these groups and their antireform partners in Congress wanted to maintain the status quo, an easier thing to do than to change existing policies. All proposals to enact new policies or alter existing ones must combat this "defensive advantage."[18] As the political scientist John Wright notes, the "numerous procedural steps required to move a bill through Congress . . . provide multiple opportunities for groups to forestall or block legislation antithetical to their interests. . . . Change-oriented groups must win repeatedly, at each step of the process, while status quo interests have to win just once."[19] Shays himself stated, "There are a 100 ways to kill our bill and very few ways to pass it."[20] Moreover, campaign finance reform actually faced an even stiffer challenge than many proposals, because the majority party leadership was united in opposition to it in both the Senate and the House. With all this working against campaign finance reform, it was quite an accomplishment that the measure actually passed the House and won the support of a majority of senators.

Several key groups emerged in response to the effort to reform the campaign finance system. The first was the National Right to Life Committee (NRLC), which attempted to persuade pro-life and other senators and House members to vote against the McCain-Feingold bill, the Snowe-Jeffords Amendment, and the Shays-Meehan and Freshman bills. The NRLC calls itself the "nation's largest pro-life group with affiliates in all fifty states and over 3,000 chapters nationwide."[21] With such a large membership spread throughout the country, the NRLC has a presence in every senator's and House member's district. Although it is not a particularly wealthy interest group and does not offer its members economic or other obvious material benefits, the NRLC (and other groups such as the good-government groups and the Christian Coalition) makes up for this lack of financial resources and incentives with its large membership.

The NRLC made campaign finance reform a right-to-life litmus test by warning lawmakers that a vote for reform would damage their pro-life record, a serious threat for many GOP lawmakers and pro-life Democrats.[22] In fact, the NRLC even ran harsh radio ads against Arkansas representative Asa Hutchinson, the GOP co-sponsor of the Freshman bill, who otherwise had impeccable pro-life credentials.[23] The NRLC was working against the McCain-Feingold and Shays-Meehan bills in 1997, but this nonprofit antiabortion organization stepped up its efforts in the spring of 1998 when it began to seem possible that the Shays-Meehan bill just might pass. The NRLC expressed its opposition to the Shays-Meehan bill in a letter to House members on May 12, 1998, stating that the bill violated the First Amendment right to free speech and would penalize the exercise of this protected right. Reformers had heard these First Amendment arguments before when GOP senator Mitch McConnell used the First Amendment to fight reform in the Senate earlier in the year.

The NRLC was part of a coalition of interest groups that included organizations such as the Christian Coalition, the National Rifle Association, the Center for Military Readiness, and the U.S. Business and Industry Council. As we saw in Chapter 3, this coalition worked closely with House GOP leaders to try to amend the Shays-Meehan bill with the Doolittle amendment because, they argued, the Shays-Meehan bill would violate their First Amendment right to free speech. This coalition of fifty-three groups combined their efforts to form a powerful external issue network for the GOP leaders inside of Congress. The groups mounted a hard-hitting campaign of media events, legislative alerts, faxes, and letters to urge legislators to support the Doolittle amendment and to vote no on the Shays-Meehan bill. Of course, the coalition members knew quite well that if the Doolittle amendment was attached to the Shays-Meehan bill many Democrats would drop their support of the bill and it would fail. In Box 6-1 are listed the fifty-three groups that signed a joint letter to members of Congress on July 13, 1998, urging them to vote no on the Shays-Meehan bill. In the letter, the groups argued that the Shays-Meehan bill would stifle their right to communicate on the actions of candidates and elected officials and to conduct grassroots lobbying. The letter contained a clear statement that anyone who voted for the bill would have to answer to their constituents for trying to dictate how and when interest groups may comment on their voting records. In a separate communication to House members, the Christian Coalition asserted that the Shays-Meehan bill "places in legal jeopardy any organization that communicates where they stand on the issues."[24] The NRLC, the Christian Coalition, and some of the other coalition groups also threatened to "score" legislators' votes on the Doolittle amendment and the Shays-Meehan bill.[25]

The Christian Coalition was another effective opponent of campaign finance reform. The Christian Coalition presents itself as the "largest and most effective grassroots political movement of Christian activists in the history of our nation." The organization encourages "conservative people of faith to participate in the democratic process ," and one of its priority efforts is opposing campaign finance reform.[26] Like the NRLC, the Christian Coalition argued that if the McCain-Feingold and Shays-Meehan bills became law, "organizations that utilize voter guides [such as the ones distributed by the Christian Coalition in thousands of churches across the country on the Sunday before election day] and score cards would not be able to inform their members and supporters where they stand on the issues."[27] Although the reformers argued that this was not true, the Christian Coalition quite effectively persuaded many legislators, especially pro-life Republicans, to oppose campaign finance reform.

In response to the efforts of these groups, one proreform interest group suggested that the close affiliation between the GOP and the National Right to Life Committee was more than ideological. In a letter to House members on July 13, Common Cause revealed that since 1994, the Republican National Committee (RNC) had given nearly $1 million to the NRLC. This included a $650,000 transfer from the RNC to the NRLC in October 1996. Common Cause suggested that the NRLC's opposition to the Shays-Meehan

BOX 6-1 Interest Groups That Opposed the Shays-Meehan Campaign Finance Reform Bill

The following fifty-three groups signed a July 13, 1998, letter to members of Congress asking them to vote "no" on the Shays-Meehan bill:

Abraham Lincoln Foundation

American Association of Christian Schools

American Conservative Union

American Council for Immigration Reform

American Family Association

Americans for Hope, Growth and Opportunity

Americans for Tax Reform

Association of Concerned Taxpayers

California Pro-Life Council

Catholic Alliance

Center for Military Readiness

Center for Security Policy

Christian Action Network

Christian Coalition

Christian Voice

Citizens for a Sound Economy

Citizens for Reform

Coalition for Constitutional Liberties

Coalition for Cultural Reform

Coalitions for America

Competitive Enterprise Institute

Concerned Women of America

Conservative Victory Fund

Coral Ridge Ministries

Council of National Policy

Eagle Forum

Empower America

Ethics and Religious Liberty Commission of the Southern Baptist Convention

Family Policy Network

Family Research Council

Free Market Committee

Gun Owners of America

Gun Owners of California

High Frontier

Home School Legal Defense Assoc.

International Ministries Fellowship

Life Advocacy Alliance

Life Issues Institute

Madison Project

Media Research Center

National Center for Home Education

National Defense Council Foundation

National Family Legal Foundation

National Legal and Policy Center

National Rifle Association

National Right to Life Committee

Of the People

Project Reality

Traditional Values Coalition

U.S. Border Control

U.S. Business and Industry Council

U.S. Family Network

bill therefore might be based more on its political and financial self-interest than on its view of the First Amendment.[28] The proreform and antireform groups, along with their party counterparts in Congress, were fighting head-to-head over the Doolittle amendment and the Shays-Meehan bill. Both sides were playing political hardball.

One traditionally liberal interest group joined the antireformers in their effort to defeat campaign finance reform. The leaders of the ACLU (American Civil Liberties Union), the authoritative civil rights organization, made the argument that any restriction on communications that did not expressly say such things as "vote for" or "vote against" violated the First Amendment right to free speech. The ACLU, founded in 1920, describes itself as a "non-profit, nonpartisan, 275,000-member public interest organization devoted exclusively to protecting the basic civil liberties of all Americans."[29] The ACLU argued that the Shays-Meehan bill:

. . . was patently unconstitutional;
. . . would have a chilling effect on issue advocacy speech that is essential in a democracy;
. . . would impermissibly limit soft money;
. . . would be a deterrent to small contributors and a gross invasion of political privacy;
. . . [would] make it harder for ethnic and racial minority, women and non-mainstream voices to be heard prior to an election; [and]
. . . [would create] a "Big Brother" governmental regime for political speech.[30]

Upon seeing the title of a Dear Colleague letter from House majority whip Tom DeLay, "Christian Coalition Joins ACLU to Prevent Reform," one proreform House member commented at a Shays-Meehan briefing meeting that these were "strange bedfellows." Another noted that "you get hit on this issue from both the right and the left. What's the winning position?" A discussion ensued in which House members considered the potential costs they would incur from openly supporting campaign finance reform. Although many acknowledged the threat of these two powerful groups joining hands, most were willing to take the "hit" on the groups' scorecards. Some, however, were shaken by the power of such an unlikely alliance, and the reform team and the proreform public interest groups promised to provide cover for their stand by pursuing favorable press for the reform effort.

The ACLU supplied valuable legitimacy to reform opponents both in and outside of Congress. Many critics believed that the Republican leaders opposed reform not because they were concerned about its potential effect on the First Amendment, but because the party stood to lose its financial advantage over the Democrats if the Shays-Meehan and McCain-Feingold bills became law. Many of the nonprofit and ideological groups that used the First Amendment argument also saw the reform bills as a threat to their activities. If the bills had become law some of these groups would have lost their valued nonprofit tax status because their activities would have been considered campaign activities. They also would have been required to disclose the names of their contributors, something many of the religious groups in particular strongly opposed. Given the political benefits that reform opponents were in line to lose if campaign finance reform had been enacted, the First Amendment argument was not the primary concern of all of them. Thus, the ACLU's blessing was valuable indeed.

Yet the ACLU's position on campaign finance reform was controversial as well, tainting the opposition coalition's efforts somewhat. These ACLU leaders viewed the reform effort as an attack on free speech. Virtually every previous leader and many current members, however, held a different view of the constitutionality of the campaign finance reform proposals before Congress. The former ACLU leaders agreed with the proreform advocates in Congress that legislation such as the Shays-Meehan bill did *not* violate free speech rights. They publicly expressed their disagreement with the current ACLU elite in an editorial piece in the *New York Times*.[31] Despite this disagreement within the ACLU, the GOP leadership used the ACLU leaders' opposition to reform whenever they could. For example, Majority Whip DeLay distributed many Dear Colleague letters to his fellow House members highlighting the ACLU's position. One, for example, was titled, "ACLU on Shays-Meehan: It's Patently Unconstitutional." Another Dear Colleague letter from DeLay asked, "What's Wrong with Shays/Meehan? Ask the ACLU." This letter was sent with the ACLU's "Campaign Finance Reform Fact Sheet #4," which detailed the ACLU's opposition to the bill.[32]

House GOP leaders helped organize a large and formidable collection of groups opposed to reform in a relatively short period of time. Pressure from these outside groups clearly affected the debate over campaign finance reform. For example, many pro-life Republicans and some pro-life Democrats opposed the Shays-Meehan bill in part because of the arguments made by the National Right to Life Committee and its coalition partners. The coalition of fifty-three groups that pushed for passage of the Doolittle amendment succeeded in gaining many votes for that measure, yet not enough to pass it. These groups' efforts against reform in general and the Shays-Meehan bill in particular gave proreformers a run for their money by making them work especially hard to secure victories such as barely defeating the Doolittle amendment.

The Role of the Media

Many congressional policy debates are characterized by a substantial amount of interest group activity, but, for the most part, regular citizens hear little about these policy debates because generally they are confined to the halls of Congress. In the case of campaign finance reform, both sides had developed strong external issue networks, which prompted lively interest group activity. Yet the issue also attracted a good deal of media attention, more than for other issues that, like campaign finance reform, were not leading the polls as one of the most important public policy issues. This media attention, strongly encouraged by the interest groups pushing for reform, helped keep the issue alive in Congress.

The Media and Congressional Politics

The press is an interesting player in congressional politics. Members of Congress certainly pursue positive media attention for their constituency-focused activities in Washington, D.C., and at home. Sometimes, however, lawmakers try to stay out of the limelight when working behind the scenes to enact or block some legislative measure, especially if that measure is controversial. Lawmakers often prefer the coverage they get from local news outlets to the attention they receive from the national press. Legislators' constituents back home are more likely to read their local papers than the national papers. Local reporters are not specialists in particular issues before Congress or in the workings of Congress. Thus, local reporters generally are not as well prepared to pose tough policy questions to legislators. They usually treat national officials with respect and deference and portray them in a favorable light.[33] National news reporters, in contrast, are often specialists in some policy area and follow the norms of investigative journalism. Always watchful for corruption or scandal, they are "on the lookout for stories with good guys and bad guys, winners and losers."[34] It should not be surprising, then, that when asked in a survey whether they would rather get their boss in the hometown newspaper or on the front page of the *New York Times,* press secretaries for members of the House of Representatives almost unanimously chose the hometown newspaper.[35]

Contemporary congressional policymaking is not confined to the back rooms away from the scrutiny of the national media. Party and issue leaders in Congress often work hard to get the attention of the media to help them win public and congressional support for their policy proposals. Roger Davidson and Walter Oleszek, two veteran scholars of Congress, note that "[n]o longer is the 'inside' game—working behind the scenes to line up votes—sufficient to pass major, controversial measures. Also necessary is the 'outside' game—influencing public opinion and creating grassroots support for policy initiatives."[36] These goals are accomplished in part by gaining positive media attention for one's policy initiatives. The media has become an important ingredient for building an effective external issue network.

The media can be a very powerful political tool. The press has long been recognized for its role in educating the public about the workings of politics.[37] News reports about political happenings in Washington, D.C., serve as a vital link between politicians inside the Beltway and citizens outside of it by providing the American public with relatively objective information about politics. We say "relatively objective" because the information is not filtered by the politicians themselves, as was the case in the nineteenth century, during the era of the partisan press, when American newspapers were virtually controlled by the major political parties. Although much has been made of the apparent rise in media bias, the media now present a more objective version of the news than during the 1800s, and most journalists aim to provide facts rather than opinions. Citizens rely on the press to provide impartial information for evaluating politics and politicians. Thus, the media can influence the political process immensely.

What appears in the nation's leading newspapers, such as the *New York Times,* the *Los Angeles Times,* the *Wall Street Journal,* and the *Washington Post,* often has a significant effect on policymaking in Washington. When these news organizations call attention to some issue, that issue is more likely to make it onto the policy agenda in Congress, in part because these elite newspapers set the national agenda for news coverage. In fact, the *New York Times* has been called "the bulletin board" because of the leading role it plays in setting news trends across the country.[38] When one of these major newspapers highlights an issue as important, other papers and electronic news outlets often jump on the bandwagon and also devote coverage to the issue. Thus lawmakers' hometown newspapers all over the country are watching the elite national press for stories about what's going on in Washington. The local papers may put their local spin on the story by, for example, highlighting their House member's position on the issue, but the important thing to note is that the issues selected by these leading papers get coverage at the local level, where lawmakers are most concerned about the reaction to their policy stands.

The media help set the political agenda by choosing what issues to cover and how much and how long to cover them. Those involved in the political process intuitively seem to understand the importance of the media. Office-holders, party leaders, government officials, and interest group leaders devote great energy and resources attempting to get the media to report *their* story. For example, every senator and House member has at least one staff person responsible for press affairs. Yet many observers outside of the political process underplay the influence the media actually exert on Capitol Hill. Some political scientists have suggested, for example, that the media really only clue people into what is going on, and that their influence is only a perception, not a reality.[39] For those active in the political process, however, news coverage is a currency that can be used to purchase support, squelch opposition, or provide cover when it is needed. The press can provide cover by, for example, praising the vote of some group of legislators who may have voted against their party leaders (as they did for some GOP lawmakers on campaign finance reform), a powerful interest group, or even the wishes of their constituents. It is a commodity to use as leverage. Those who get positive press attention can gain the support of the public and, therefore, of fellow lawmakers. Those who cannot or who attract only negative press attention, in contrast, are likely to lose public support and their colleagues' votes.

Both sides of the campaign finance reform debate wanted to convince their fellow lawmakers that the public was on their side. As we saw in Chapter 5, legislators go out of their way to show that there is great support for their proposed legislation. When they claim, for example, that they have bipartisan support for their measure, they make the case that there is a consensus in favor of their position. This, in turn, motivates other legislators to join in that support so as not to be on the wrong side of an issue with strong public support. Both sides presented polling data that supported their views on campaign finance reform. For instance, Roger Wicker, R-Miss., issued a Dear Colleague letter titled, "Forget the Hype!!! Don't Believe Everything You Hear: Campaign Finance Is Not a Critical Issue." The letter featured a huge bar graph that ranked issues in order of their importance to voters beginning with Social Security and Medicare at 16 percent and campaign finance reform at 2 percent. Another Dear Colleague letter, "Ten Big Lies about Campaign Finance Reform," was from Majority Whip Tom DeLay; the first "lie" was "The American people are clamoring for campaign finance reform."

In similar fashion, Shays, Meehan, and seven other reformers (five Democrats and two Republicans) sent a Dear Colleague letter dated May 20, 1998, that announced in bold letters at the top: "Myth: The Public Doesn't Care about Campaign Reform. Reality: Public Opinion Polls Show Overwhelming Public Support for Major Campaign Reform."[40] And Democratic pollster Celinda Lake wrote a piece for *Roll Call* that made the case that "[v]oters may not be clamoring loudly for change now, but let us not be deceived. To the American people, the system is sick and they want it cured."[41] Winning the battle of public opinion is an important element of the successful external issue network. The media attention afforded campaign finance reform in the spring and summer of 1998 raised the profile of the issue and convinced many lawmakers that the public was indeed on the reformers' side.

The media played a critical role in transforming the campaign finance reform debate during the 105th Congress. At certain points along the way, the media provided momentum and gave a needed boost to the efforts of the reformers inside of Congress. Quite often, the interest groups successfully used the media to help advocate changes to legislation under consideration, promote key events such as important votes on the issue, or expose what they viewed as the GOP leaders' less-than-sincere approach to the issue. Thus, the media supplied additional pressure to the debate, and that pressure almost always benefited the reformers. The press has long had a tendency to promote campaign reform, probably in part because stories about political scandal sell papers. A notable exception in the mainstream press to the proreform approach was the *Wall Street Journal*, which often highlighted the arguments of the reform opponents in its news stories and issued some strong editorials against reform proposals under consideration in Congress. The probusiness character of the *Wall Street Journal* usually puts it in the same camp as the Republicans on most issues. Generally, however, the media delineated the two sides debating the issue as a battle between the GOP leaders and the reformers engaged in a classic standoff in which the media kept a close watch to see who would "blink" first.

David and Goliath: The Media's Portrayal of Campaign Finance Reform

On March 27, 1998, the *New York Times* ran an editorial calling the Republican leaders obstructionists to campaign finance reform and Rep. Christopher Shays a "hero" for standing up to his party's leaders.[42] Less than twenty-four hours later, the House GOP leaders announced that campaign finance reform would finally come up for a vote but that the bills to be voted on would be of their choosing and be considered under the suspension-of-the-rules process that requires a two-thirds majority vote for passage. This move by the Republican leaders became fodder for many news stories that featured the maverick, Chris Shays, against his strong-arming party bosses led by Speaker Newt Gingrich. The media turned it into a David and Goliath story that lent much fuel to the campaign finance reform effort in the House of Representatives. These dramatic tones greatly contributed to the media's willingness to cover the story.

The media coverage of the campaign finance reform debate in the 105th Congress began in 1997 with stories about how the issue was likely, once again, to meet defeat in the Senate. These stories generally played up the roles of the Republican John McCain and the Democrat Russell Feingold and their futile attempt to pass campaign finance reform in the Senate, particularly in the face of strong opposition from the Republican leadership, led in battle by Mitch McConnell. McConnell wrapped his arguments in the notion that the reforms proposed in the McCain-Feingold bill would violate the First Amendment of the Constitution. This reference to the Constitution struck a chord with some in the media, for journalists are more inclined to be drawn to stories about big, important issues (such as ones that present some challenge to the Constitution) than to minor, uninteresting issues (such as the intricacies of an already complicated set of laws and regulations for financing federal elections).

On October 9, 1997, when McCain-Feingold supporters had failed three times to get the sixty votes needed for cloture, the bill was pulled from the Senate floor. The issue seemed all but dead, and when the Blue Dog Coalition of conservative House Democrats filed the discharge petition on October 24 to force consideration of campaign finance reform in the House, it received little mainstream media coverage. This important step toward reform initially was covered only by insider publications such as *Roll Call, The Hill,* and *National Journal's Congress Daily.* All are publications directed to the audience inside the Beltway and get little attention from the public at large. Coverage of campaign finance issues continued to focus on the fate of the McCain-Feingold bill when it was taken up again but defeated in the Senate on February 26, 1998.

The other big campaign finance story was the Republican-led investigations of alleged Democratic campaign finance abuses during the 1996 election.[43] This story allowed journalists to perform their "watchdog" role, whereby the media exercise what they see as their responsibility to protect the public from corrupt, incompetent, and deceitful public officials, and therefore "expose any official who violates accepted legal, ethical, and performance standards."[44] Because the investigative hearings focused almost exclusively on the Democrats' activities, however, the media covered few of the campaign violation allegations against the Republicans.

Very little media attention was focused on the House until GOP leaders announced that their hand-picked campaign finance bills would be considered under suspension-of-the-rules in March 1998. This announcement received quite a lot of press coverage as members of the media framed the story as Speaker Gingrich's failure to live up to his promise to have a fair vote on campaign finance reform and his Contract with America promise to reform Congress. Editorials in leading papers scolded the GOP leaders for their cynical strategy. One *New York Times* editorial accused the Republicans of "plotting against reform" and charged that "Mr. Gingrich is working hard to make sure the vote is rigged to come out the way he wants."[45] In other editorials, the GOP's reform legislation and procedural tactics were called "mock reform" (the *Washington Post*), "pseudo reform" (the *New York Times*), and an "embarrassment" (*Roll Call*).[46]

Another *New York Times* editorial included the comment that "Gingrich does not care if his own fraudulent legislation wins or loses. All he seeks is the chance to say the House considered campaign finance reform and was unable to pass a bill. It is a cynical maneuver that will come back to haunt Gingrich and any House member who supports it."[47] This last statement would prove prophetic as the debate over reform dragged on well into the summer. As the *Washington Post* noted in an editorial, the "effort to manipulate the outcome produced a revolt, including among some Republicans who are not necessarily fans of particular reform proposals but think the party should not be in the position of shoving the subject aside."[48] Likewise, the *Los Angeles Times* reported that "[t]he good news is that suppressive efforts by House and Senate leaders seem only to have re-ignited bipartisan enthusiasm for reform below the leadership level."[49]

The exchange between Majority Leader Dick Armey and Representative Shays on the floor of the House in late March (see Chapter 3) also highlighted for the press the unfolding drama of a maverick lawmaker trying to hold his party's feet to the fire. Shays was winning accolades from the press. Although Representative Meehan played just as vital a role as Shays, the media focused most of their attention on Shays. The story the press viewed as worth telling was that of a lone member against his party, not that of both lawmakers leading a large coalition of their colleagues in an effort to pass campaign finance reform, and not a story about a Democrat who had virtually all his Democratic colleagues behind him. For example, in a *Washington Post* op-ed piece, syndicated columnist Mark Shields said of Shays: "It takes some nerve for a House Republican to take on the House leadership, which has openly threatened that the penalty for such a breach of party loyalty could be the member's losing his committee assignment or subcommittee chairmanship."[50] The *New York Times* reported that "[g]ood government groups, Democrats and editorial writers are calling [Shays] a hero for defying his party leadership, which wants to kill his legislation."[51] And many news outlets dubbed the battle for reform "Shays's Rebellion," in reference to the violent revolt in 1786 led by the Revolutionary War veteran and farmer Daniel Shays to prevent foreclosures on farms in Massachusetts.[52]

Once the Republican leaders' much-maligned effort failed to produce a comprehensive reform measure in late March, the reformers in Congress and the proreform interest groups called attention to the GOP's trickery in an effort to gain media attention for the discharge petition process. The discharge petition had been out there since it was filed in October, but it had received little media attention until this time. During the April recess, the interest groups were instrumental in persuading papers across the country to cover the campaign finance reform story and the discharge petition effort. The elite newspapers focused on the discharge petition. For instance, the *New York Times* ran an editorial titled, "A Sign-Up List for Reform," and the *Washington Post* featured one that highlighted the ongoing countdown to get the necessary 218 signatures on the petition to force a vote on reform.[53] Other papers followed suit, running feature stories or editorials on the issue during the April recess. They included the *Boston Globe*, the *Louisville (Ky.) Courier-Journal*, the *Raleigh (N.C.) News and Observer*, the *Fort Worth Star-Telegram*, the *Allentown (Pa.) Morning Call*, the *Portland (Maine) Press Herald*, the *San Francisco Chronicle*, the *Norfolk Virginia-Pilot*, the *Los Angeles Times*, the *Palm Beach Post*, the *Lakeland (Fla.) Ledger*, the *New York Daily News*, the *Baltimore Sun*, the *Atlanta Journal*, and *Copley News Service*. One paper noted that the "chief hope of Shays and his backers is that so much public outrage will surface in April, when Congress takes a two week recess, that House leaders will be forced to allow a vote on their bill later this year."[54] This increased media attention certainly improved the chances that such outrage would materialize.

Of course, news reporters did not dig up these stories all by themselves. They were constantly encouraged by proreform lawmakers, their staff people, and Common Cause and the other proreform groups to cover the campaign finance reform debate. During this period, at the end of March and into April, House members and the groups held press conferences regularly, often more than twice a week. The interest group leaders and staff of key reform legislators were constantly in touch with reporters interested in the issue to ensure that they had the most up-to-date and correct information. One should not underestimate the impact of the interest groups' media strategy. As we saw above, their ability to influence newspapers all over the country was greatly enhanced by the existence of thousands of interest group members in various locations. Many of the state and local leaders of Common Cause, the League of Women Voters, and other groups had well-established working relationships with local reporters. These groups also had thousands of active members to put pressure on their local members of Congress during their visits home in April, to write letters to the editor about campaign finance reform, and generally to help produce public outrage over the need for reform and the GOP's cynical tactics to stop it.

Furthermore, the reform interest groups virtually defined legitimate reform for the press, much as they had during negotiations inside of Congress. One paper even reported that it had been "scolded by Common Cause, the League of Women Voters, PIRG, and Public Citizen for praising [GOP Rep. Bill] Thomas [who had introduced the Republican bill] instead of leaping to support Shays-Meehan."[55] This paper (*Roll Call*) may not have appreciated the groups' reprimand, but it was clear from news reports of the ongoing debate on reform and the steady stream of editorials from various papers around the country that the groups' view of real reform (a measure that would ban soft money and regulate phony issue ads) became the media's standard by which to gauge all reform proposals. The media almost uniformly took the side of the proreformers in their editorials, and the proreform interest groups, especially Common Cause, should get a good deal of the credit for this.

The increased media attention on campaign finance reform also brought more offers for Shays and Meehan to appear on the Sunday morning political talk television programs as well as on CNN's *Crossfire*. These shows gave the reformers a national audience, something most House members never experience. Additionally, the media attention kept the White House interested in the issue and motivated the president to continue promoting reform. Eventually, however, news coverage of the campaign finance reform debate died down as both proreformers and antireformers regrouped in late April. It picked up again in May after the GOP leaders announced that the Shays-Meehan bill, as well as eleven other bills, would get a vote. Efforts to get more signatures on the discharge petition were then dropped, as Shays and most of the other Republicans who had signed took their names off it at the request of Speaker Gingrich who had promised a vote on the Shays-Meehan bill.

Eventually it became clear that the process by which the bills would be considered was a parliamentary nightmare designed to weigh down the Shays-Meehan bill with so many unattractive amendments that it would fail. The press became interested in campaign finance reform once again and reported on the issue as an uphill battle and one that pitted reformers against the GOP leaders in a game of beat-the-clock as the second session of the 105th Congress was coming to an end. One news report described it this way: "Even for Congress, the House's Bipartisan Campaign Integrity Act of 1997 stands as a tour de force of parliamentary esoterica. It has a basic campaign finance reform bill, 11 alternatives, a proposed constitutional amendment, 258 ordinary amendments and a legislative beauty contest known intriguingly as 'Queen of the Hill.'"[56] Again, the media used the good-guy-versus-bad-guy theme to describe the GOP's attempt to defeat reform. The headline on one *New York Times* story about the GOP plan was "House G.O.P. Opens Floodgates on Campaign Finance"; another was titled "When $10 Million Is in Trough, Few Want to Overturn It."[57] The Democrats and the reform coalition did what they could to encourage this type of reporting in the hope that it would provide the added pressure needed to clear the way for passage of the Shays-Meehan bill. Republican leaders tried to make the case that the process they had designed for consideration of that bill and the eleven other bills was "fair and open," but the reformers had more success framing the GOP's process as "death by amendment." Editorials were particularly critical of the Republicans' tactics. Here are the titles of some of the editorials that ran during this last round of fighting over campaign finance reform in the House:

"Campaign Finance Mousetrap," *Washington Post,* June 7, 1998 (p. C6)
"G.O.P. Trickery in the House," *New York Times,* June 8, 1998 (p. A26)
"Dirty Ploy on Campaign Reform," *Los Angeles Times,* June 9, 1998 (p. A10)
"The House Plotters against Reform," *Boston Globe,* June 10, 1998 (p. A22)
"Micro-Muzzling," *Roll Call,* June 11, 1998 (p. 4)
"Talked to Death," *New Republic,* June 15, 1998 (p. 12)
"Mines on the Road to Reform," *New York Times,* June 17, 1998 (p. A30)
"Mr. Gingrich's Killer Amendments," *New York Times,* July 22, 1998 (p. A18).

Some editorial cartoons were even more harsh than the editorials themselves. The following Herblock cartoon ran after GOP leaders announced the "death by amendment" plan. The next one ran in July as the reformers were defeating one poison pill amendment after the other to the Shays-Meehan bill.

"WE'VE GOT TO PRESS ON —
HE'S STILL BREATHING

Source: Herblock: A Cartoonist's Life, Times Books, 1998.

The Republican leaders were beaten up badly by the press, but some might say that they brought it upon themselves. The drama that was playing out in the House, where the GOP leaders were trying to strong-arm their way through the debate and the reformers survived the many battles with renewed strength, was another opportunity for the press to play its watchdog role. The media portrayed the House leaders as hypocritical and the reformers as those who were just trying to save our representative democracy from special interests and big-money fat cats. After a while, it would seem unlikely that the GOP leaders would persist in trying to kill reform, knowing that they would continue to be portrayed badly in the press. Yet they fought hard to bring down the Shays-Meehan bill with unpalatable amendments and to persuade Republican legislators to stay with their party on this issue. The

"I HATE THE WAY YOU KEEP COMING BACK"

press had done a lot to ensure that enough Republicans would vote for the Shays-Meehan bill by keeping the issue in the public eye, presenting the Shays-Meehan bill as the only true reform bill and making it clear how legislators should vote. In turn, this media attention, along with the interest groups' activities, helped generate pressure from members' constituents to pass the Shays-Meehan bill.

With momentum going the reformers' way, the GOP leaders eventually pulled back somewhat. Only DeLay remained in the fray with one last attempt to defeat the Shays-Meehan bill by calling for support of the Freshman bill. But with the final gavel on the amendment process, cheers rang out in the House chamber, and news reports called passage of the Shays-Meehan bill "all but certain."[58] When the Shays-Meehan bill passed in early August other members with reform bills withdrew their measures, leaving the path clear for final passage of the Shays-Meehan bill. The television program *Nightline* highlighted this accomplishment, but the victory was quickly put in its place as news reports noted that the measure was, once again, likely to fail in the Senate, stymied by eight senators who were not willing to vote for cloture.

Conclusion: Help from Outside the Labyrinth

Any legislator who aims to make changes or add to existing law knows that the path will be smoother if there is pressure from outside of Congress to accomplish that policy goal. Successful policy entrepreneurs will make sure that this outside pressure is there by nurturing and managing an effective external issue network of interest group support and positive media attention. With these outside elements engaged in the policymaking process, the issue also may become more salient to the public. If voters can be mobilized by interest group activity and press coverage to demand a policy change, then the chances for legislative success are greatly enhanced. Thus, in many cases, and in the case of the Shays-Meehan bill, these outside players have a significant impact on the fate of legislation inside of Congress.

Extensive interest group involvement in the struggle for campaign finance reform is not surprising. The issue itself affects who has power and who controls government, in part because the rules that govern the financing of campaigns generally tend to give the advantage to incumbents over challengers and often the majority party over the minority party. The specific reforms proposed in the McCain-Feingold and Shays-Meehan bills caused a clear split between the two parties. The Democrats viewed the changes as beneficial to their candidates and supported reform, and the Republicans saw the proposal as detrimental to their interests and generally opposed reform. Many interest groups too have a great stake in who has power and who controls the government in Washington, D.C., and like the parties, the groups that saw the proposed reforms as detrimental to their own activities opposed the McCain-Feingold and Shays-Meehan bills, and those that viewed the suggested changes as helpful supported reform.

Yet another collection of interest groups made the debate over campaign finance reform unique. The public interest groups that supported reform (and some that opposed reform) had no real material stake in the outcome of the battle for reform, yet they were perhaps the most important external force in the process. Some issues, such as campaign finance reform, attract groups that are motivated by purposive rather than material incentives. Although such groups often have a difficult time organizing for or against some issue because they lack the material resources of other groups, they are just as passionate and often just as effective as groups that have something tangible to gain or lose. The coalition of public interest groups that pushed for campaign finance reform during the 105th Congress was highly effective in part because its members worked so closely and so well with proreform lawmakers and their staffs inside of Congress, and because the groups helped draw positive media attention to the issue and its progress on Capitol Hill.

That media attention was vital to the success of the Shays-Meehan bill in the House of Representatives. The proreform interest groups were helpful in attracting press coverage and supportive editorials, but the Republican leaders themselves employed such cynical and strong-arm tactics that the press had little trouble telling the story of the good guys and the bad guys. Moreover, and perhaps more important, was the David and Goliath story of Rep. Christopher Shays's defiance of his own party leaders. Quiet and calm, Shays made a good David in combat with the harsh and bullying Goliath, Speaker Newt Gingrich. The determination of one lone House member against the awesome power of the majority party leadership apparatus made for dramatic news and colorful editorials. Few stories about policymaking on Capitol Hill come so ready-made for the press.

The regular media attention to the progress of campaign finance reform presented within the David and Goliath framework had a discernible effect on the activities of legislators in Congress. For example, after many newspapers issued scathing editorials critical of the GOP leaders' attempt to brush campaign finance reform under the rug by considering "pseudo reform" in late March, and after the press covered the renewed effort to secure enough signatures on the discharge petition to force a vote on "real" reform, Gingrich announced that the issue would be taken up again.[59] Of course, without the real threat posed by the discharge petition that would have, in effect, given control of the floor over to the Democrats, Gingrich may not have relented. Yet the media coverage of these events gave the reformers the needed momentum and helped them successfully push the GOP leaders to agree to a vote on the Shays-Meehan bill.

The ability of Shays and Meehan to nurture and maintain such an effective external issue network was key to the success of their legislation. Their efforts help explain why campaign finance reform succeeded in the House but not in the Senate. Yet reformers in the Senate have more obstacles to overcome than do their colleagues in the House, for a minority of senators may defeat a measure there, whereas in the House a majority generally does rule. To be sure, there are limits to what an external issue network can do, but without strong interest group support and positive media attention, a bill's journey through Congress is an uphill battle indeed.

7

THE 106TH CONGRESS
History Repeating Itself

On September 15, 1999, the reformers cheered as once again the Shays-Meehan campaign finance reform bill passed the House of Representatives, just over a year after their first victory. The celebration would last long into the night, for most knew that, once they stopped, the struggle would begin again in the Senate. The House Republican leaders looked calm, considering they had just been defeated. They knew, however, that they had lost only a "free vote," where the outcome really did not matter, because the measure was sure to be defeated in the Senate. GOP leaders and their antireform allies (and even some quietly among the majority who voted for the bill) waited with anticipation to see campaign finance reform's demise once again. It was history repeating itself.

The campaign finance reform legislative process in the 106th Congress (1999–2001) was well informed by the debate the year before. Echoes of the process from the 105th Congress loomed large, and many actors played the roles preset by their previous interactions on the issue. Here, too, there were procedural wranglings, arguments among coalitions and the House leadership, interest group mobilization, party politics, and the media spotlight. Additionally, the president once again offered some assistance in the attempt to pass a reform bill. But, as in the 105th Congress, the effort to pass comprehensive campaign finance reform legislation in the 106th Congress came to an end in the Senate, defeated once again by a vocal and powerful minority. Yet, while comprehensive campaign finance reform lay dead on the Sen-

201

ate floor, the 106th Congress did pass the first important (albeit incremental) amendment to the nation's campaign finance laws in more than twenty years, giving reformers a glimmer of hope that their issue remained alive.

This Time the House Goes First

The House reformers started early in the 106th Congress when Representatives Shays and Meehan introduced a version of their bill similar to the one that had passed late in the second session of the 105th Congress. The bill, H.R. 417, the Bipartisan Campaign Finance Reform Act of 1999, was introduced on January 19, 1999. The offices of Shays and Meehan prepared a summary of the bill, which we have reproduced as Box 7-1.

The Republican leaders were ready for the fight. They seemed to have learned from their mistakes during the 105th Congress. Unlike the former leaders, Speaker Newt Gingrich in particular, the GOP leaders this time did not allow themselves to be forced to schedule a vote on the bill under threat of a discharge petition. Instead, the new House Speaker, Dennis Hastert, R-Ill., announced that campaign finance reform would be brought up in September. Of course, reformers wanted Congress to address the issue earlier in the session to allow the Senate plenty of time to take it up. Such late consideration by the Senate, so close to the session's end and to the start of the 1999–2000 election cycle, would virtually guarantee that comprehensive campaign finance reform would be filibustered to death again in the Senate.[1]

In late February, Chris Shays urged his party's leaders to bring up the Shays-Meehan bill in between the House's passage of the Budget Resolution in May and its consideration of appropriations in June. For Shays, this represented a "logical opportunity" that provided a "real window of opportunity to get this passed."[2] Marty Meehan added, "This year there is a chance that this legislation might become law, thanks to the support and initiative of people across the country who have voiced concerns to their Representatives."[3] These calls for earlier consideration, however, went unanswered by the House Republican leaders. Therefore, on April 14, 1999, the Blue Dog Democrats announced another discharge petition effort that would, "allow for the House consideration of the 'Meehan-Shays' legislation, as well as other proposals to reform current campaign finance laws."[4] But none of the thirty Republican cosponsors of the Shays-Meehan bill, including Shays himself, signed onto the petition at this time.

Speaker Hastert and the other Republican leaders requested that their party members not sign the petition and defer to their plan to bring the bill

BOX 7-1 A Short Summary of the Shays-Meehan Bipartisan Campaign Finance Reform Act of 1999

The legislation (H.R. 417) makes four major changes to our campaign financing system:

1. *Soft Money Ban.* Completely eliminates federal soft money, as well as state soft money that influences a federal election. Increases the aggregate hard dollar contribution limit from $25,000 to $30,000.

2. *Recognition of Sham Issue Ads for What They Truly Are: Campaign Ads.*
   - radio and TV ads that refer to a clearly identified federal candidate, run within 60 days of an election, or
   - any communication that contains unambiguous and unmistakable support for or opposition to a clearly identified federal candidate, run at any time.

   Ads falling under this definition could only be run using legal, "hard" dollars.

3. *Improved FEC Disclosure and Enforcement.* Requires FEC reports to be filed electronically, and provides for Internet posting of this and other disclosure data. Also provides for expedited and more effective FEC procedures.

4. *Establishment of a Commission* to study further reforms to our campaign finance system (White/Dingell/Franks/Maloney/Horn bill).

Additional reforms included in the legislation:

1. *Foreign Money and Fund-raising on Government Property.* Clarifies that it is illegal to raise not only hard money—but soft money as well—from foreigners or on government property.

2. *Franking.* Expands ban on unsolicited franked mass mailings from the current three months before a general election to six months.

3. *Wealthy Candidates.* Bans coordinated party contributions to candidates who spend more than $50,000 in personal funds on their own campaigns.

continued

Box continued

4. *Voter Guides.* Clearly exempts educational voter guides.

5. *Clearinghouse.* Establishes a clearinghouse of information within the FEC, which includes lobby reports, reports filed under the Foreign Agents Registration Act, congressional witness lists, and gift disclosures. Further strengthens FEC enforcement by requiring suspected foreign donations to be deposited in an escrow account rather than immediately returned to the contributor.

6. *Penalties for Violation.* Further strengthens the foreign money ban by increasing the penalties for violation.

Source: The Offices of Christopher Shays and Marty Meehan, January 1999; online at http://www.house.gov/Shays.

---

up in September.[5] Many Republicans were reluctant to defy their leaders regarding the discharge petition, even those who supported the Shays-Meehan bill. They were hesitant to challenge their new party leader so openly. Indeed, GOP leaders had made it clear that signing the Democratic discharge petition would be "a vote of no confidence in the new speaker."[6] The powerful majority whip Tom DeLay said that Hastert had "been working with [the reformers]. He's been very helpful to them, and, frankly, I think they ought to show him the respect to work through the regular order."[7]

Moreover, the partisan landscape had changed. The Republicans had lost seats in the 1998 midterm elections, making their control of the chamber less secure. Keeping the party's members unified, therefore, became more important. And the fact that, unlike former Speaker Gingrich, Hastert had agreed right away to allow the Shays-Meehan bill to be brought up for a vote deterred Republicans from siding with the Democrats on the discharge petition. As one reporter put it, "Given the newness of Mr. Hastert's leadership and his nonconfrontational style, Mr. Shays and his Republican allies are loath to buck him without good cause."[8] The new Speaker could feel comfortable about allowing the House eventually to consider campaign finance reform legislation, because most observers agreed that, regardless of what the House did, comprehensive reform legislation was sure to fail again in the Senate.[9] Therefore, GOP leaders did not place as many procedural roadblocks in the way of the Shays-Meehan bill as they had in the previous year.

They could leave it to their colleagues in the Senate to kill the measure. Yet House leaders certainly did not give the Shays-Meehan bill a free ride either.

Shays's decision not to sign the discharge petition at first put him between two competing sides. "I feel like it's a tightrope. . . . I just have to be very careful," he noted.[10] On the one hand, interest groups and even editorial writers put considerable pressure on Shays to sign the petition once again. Fred Wertheimer, president of Democracy 21 (a proreform group he established after leaving the post of president of Common Cause), indicated the dissatisfaction that interest groups felt at what they perceived as delaying tactics by the House Republican leadership: "This is the precise same manipulative game plan they used in the last Congress to try to maintain the corrupt status quo."[11] Similarly, the Democrats questioned whether the Republican leaders were not planning procedural roadblocks for the Shays-Meehan bill. A Democratic leadership report released the week of May 7, 1999, stated, "At a May 5 meeting Speaker Hastert made it clear that he had no intention of changing Mr. DeLay's 'death by delay' strategy for campaign finance reform."[12] On the other hand, reform opponents continued to pressure their fellow House Republicans to adhere to the leadership's position. Rep. John Doolittle, R-Calif., responded to the Democrats' report with this statement: "People who sign the discharge petition . . . are really committing treason against the party. That is how strong I feel about that. That's a dangerous position to take and we need to end that talk."[13]

On May 22, 1999, Speaker Hastert confronted House Republican moderates and made it clear that his decision to schedule debate on campaign finance reform in mid-September and no sooner would stand.[14] Many Republican moderates felt that the leadership was forcing their hands regarding the discharge petition. As Shays said, "For me I just think it's absolutely imperative that the legislation come before the August break."[15] To pressure the GOP moderates further, Doolittle organized 100 Republicans to send a letter to the Speaker encouraging him to stand firm on his decision to bring up the reform legislation in September. They wrote, "[W]e urge you to disregard the threat of discharge petitions and other tactics designed to distract Republicans—and you in particular—from accomplishing our shared goals."[16]

Nevertheless, Shays announced on May 26, 1999, that he would sign onto the Blue Dog Democrat discharge petition, and five other Republican members joined him in signing it.[17] The number of signers, however, still fell well short of the twelve Republicans who had signed a similar petition in the 105th Congress. Shays stated in a press release later that day:

> The difficult task for my leadership is that a majority of members in the House support the Bipartisan Campaign Finance Reform Act, but a major-

ity of Republicans oppose it. It appears to some of us the path my leadership has chosen is to delay its consideration and run out the clock on reform. We need to take action now, not later and get the bill to Senators McCain and Feingold. Our campaign finance system is in meltdown. Unlimited, unregulated donations are corrupting the political process. For the sake of our precious democracy, we cannot wait a day longer to act.[18]

Shays also charged that Majority Whip DeLay had offered to contribute money to a primary challenger against him. He cast the issue as a struggle with the powerful DeLay over the soul of the party.[19] DeLay was backing a separate bill to eliminate public financing of presidential campaigns and to eliminate all contribution limits.

Throughout the summer, House members on both sides continued to promote their positions. For instance, at a hearing on campaign finance reform before the House Administration Committee on June 29, 1999, Shays and Meehan testified in support of their bill. Their written testimony pointed to one of the more recent uses of soft money—the raising and spending of soft money by leadership political action committees (PACs). Federal leadership PACs are a new way for congressional leaders and prominent House members and senators to amass influence by raising soft money and spending it on other candidates.[20] Other key actors in the debate over reform participated in these hearings as well, including those who advocated alternative bills, such as Asa Hutchinson, the GOP leader of the Freshman bill effort during the 105th Congress.

House Republican leaders used the summer to try to keep party members in the fold by attempting to convince them that the Shays-Meehan bill would be worse for the Republicans than for the Democrats. For example, the GOP leaders told members during a closed-door meeting that the Shays-Meehan bill "would end their party's traditional fund-raising advantage, which gave Republicans a $39.9 million lead in soft money in the 1997–98 election cycle."[21] In this round of debate over reform, GOP leaders articulated more publicly this partisan argument rather than just the more neutral argument regarding the First Amendment they had used the year before.

This activity on campaign finance reform was not limited to those inside of Congress. External organizations and interest groups continued to play a vital role in the campaign finance reform process. For instance, the American University School of Communications and the Brookings Institution tracked campaign finance data.[22] The core proreformers, the public interest groups, led by Common Cause and including such organizations as Public

Citizen, the League of Women Voters, and the U.S. Public Interest Research Group, once again advocated for campaign finance reform. The proreform groups again sent blast faxes, lobbied members of Congress, and provided statements and editorials as well as grassroots support for the Shays-Meehan and McCain-Feingold bills. The American Association of Retired Persons (AARP) once more came out in support of campaign finance reform. In its July–August 1999 member newsletter the group expressed support for the Shays-Meehan bill, and the AARP legislative director, John Rother, called Shays a "spark plug on campaign finance reform."[23]

Some new supporters also joined the effort to pass a reform measure. For example, the reformers picked up a new spokeswoman who attracted a great deal of media attention. "Granny D," an eighty-nine-year-old great-grandmother, started walking from California to Washington, D.C., on January 1, 1999, to show her support for campaign finance reform. Periodically, news stories would appear about her progress, and when she made it to Washington on February 3, 2000, the national press was there to greet her.

One of the more effective new advocates for reform was the Committee for Economic Development (CED). The fifty-eight-year-old CED is a nonpartisan, business-led public policy and research organization that makes economic and social policy recommendations. Its members include current and retired executives of some of America's leading corporations, such as General Motors, Xerox, Merck, Sara Lee, Goldman Sachs, Solomon Smith Barney, Prudential, State Farm, H & R Block, and Hasbro.[24] The CED released a report in March 1999 that advocated a ban on soft money.[25]

This endorsement of a soft money ban from the business community was an important boost for reformers on Capitol Hill, because on most matters corporate interests side with the Republicans. On the issue of campaign finance reform, however, these corporate leaders defied their traditional allies in Congress. One of the CED's most vocal members, Edward Kangas, chairman of the global board of directors of Deloitte Touche Tohmatsu, expressed the group's views in a *New York Times* op-ed piece:

> [F]or those of us on the receiving end of the soft-money shakedown . . . [f]or a growing number of executives, there's no question that the unrelenting pressure for five- and six-figure political contributions amounts to influence peddling and a corrupting influence. What has been called legalized bribery looks like extortion to us. . . . [I]t's not easy saying no to appeals for cash from powerful members of Congress. . . . The threat may be veiled, but the message is clear: failing to donate could hurt your company. You must

Doris "Granny D" Haddock at the Capitol in Washington, D.C., on February 3, 2000, after walking across the country to promote campaign finance reform.

weigh whether you meet your responsibility to your shareholders better by investing the money in the company or by sending it to Washington.[26]

On July 14, 1999, CED members sent a letter to House Speaker Dennis Hastert urging the House of Representatives to act "as soon as possible" to pass campaign finance reform.[27] Yet the CED became most helpful to the reform movement when, in late July, Sen. Mitch McConnell, the preeminent opponent of reform, sent a letter to many of the CED members accusing the group of trying to "eviscerate private sector participation in politics" by imposing "anti-business speech controls."[28] At the bottom of some of the letters, Senator McConnell hand wrote, "I hope you will resign from the CED."[29] McConnell's letter attracted quite a lot of publicity and actually helped the CED recruit more executives, doubling its membership to 212 by mid-October 1999. Moreover, none of the executives resigned from the

CED.[30] The growing consensus for reform now included many important Republican constituencies.

Interest group activity, however, was not limited solely to those favoring reform. The National Right to Life Committee (NRLC) in particular was out in force fighting against campaign finance reform once again. The NRLC announced that it would "include Shays-Meehan on its pro-life voter scorecard."[31] In response, fifteen House members, led by Rep. Ronnie Shows, D-Miss., wrote to the NRLC urging it to reconsider its position:

> In deciding to score roll calls on such debatable issues as the Shays-Meehan bill, the NRLC is saying, in effect, that the only way one can be truly pro-life is to have a certain opinion about campaign finance. . . . [T]his puts many pro-life members in an untenable position and threatens to destroy a pro-life coalition of Republicans and Democrats that has worked successfully to protect millions of unborn Americans.[32]

A meeting with the NRLC left some pro-life Democrats particularly upset. Rep. Marion Berry, D-Ark., said, "I don't care if you blackmail me; I'm never talking to the National Right to Life again."[33] Proreform representative Zach Wamp, R-Tenn., and thirteen other antiabortion House members sent a Dear Colleague letter that argued that the NRLC was "confusing a commitment to protecting the unborn with extraneous issues that do not involve the sanctity of life."[34] Shays estimated that the NRLC's campaign against his bill would cost him at least ten votes. Indeed, Rep. James Barcia, D-Mich., admitted that he did not sign the discharge petition to force a vote on the Shays-Meehan bill in part to maintain his 100 percent NRLC antiabortion rating.[35]

The media also continued to pay attention to the campaign finance reform debate. National newspapers such as the *New York Times* and the *Washington Post* covered the issue on their front pages and carried on the debate on their editorial pages. Once again, the editorial boards overwhelmingly favored the reformers and demonized the GOP leaders for their attempts to kill reform. News outlets also began including the issue of campaign finance reform in their regular opinion polls. Of particular note was a *Washington Post*/ABC News poll based on a random telephone interview with 1,526 adults between August 30 and September 2, 1999, just before the House was to consider the issue. The poll asked the following questions regarding campaign finance reform, which generated the results reported in Box 7-2. Although the results show that the American public

BOX 7-2 Results of Poll on Campaign Finance Reform

1. And which political party, the Democrats or the Republicans, do you trust to do a better job on each issue? Reforming election campaign finance laws:

Democrats	38%
Republicans	40%
Both equally	4%
Neither	13%
Don't know	6%

2. How important will . . . [r]eforming election campaign finance laws be to you in deciding how to vote in the next presidential election in the year 2000?:

Very important	30%
Somewhat important	40%
Not too important	17%
Not important at all	11%
Don't know	1%

3. I'd like to ask you what kind of attention some issues should get in Congress. . . . For each one, please tell me how important it is for Congress to address [r]eforming election campaign finance laws:

Single most important issue	6%
Very important	35%
Somewhat important	42%
Not important at all	15%
Don't address it	0%
Don't know	2%

Source: Reported in the *Washington Post,* September 9, 1999, and online at http://www.washingtonpost.com/.
Note: Poll results have a margin of error of ± 3 percent.

thinks that campaign finance reform is at least "somewhat important," there is no clear public consensus about which party will do a better job reforming the system. Indeed, both sides of the campaign finance reform debate tried to use the results to bolster their positions.

By the end of the summer, the House was geared up to consider the Shays-Meehan bill once again. The House Rules Committee held a hearing regarding the bill on August 5. Following that, the committee reported a resolution providing for consideration of H.R. 417, the Shays-Meehan Bipartisan Campaign Finance Reform Act of 1999. The bill was to be considered under a structured rule. With a structured rule, restrictions are placed on the debate by the Rules Committee regarding such items as what, if any, amendments will be considered, how much time will be allotted for debate, and who will manage the debate for each side.

The rule provided for one hour of general debate, which was to be equally divided between the chairman and the ranking minority member of the Committee on House Administration. Ten amendments were made in order, and, as before, some of them were poison pill amendments engineered by the Republican leaders to split the delicate coalition that supported the Shays-Meehan bill. For example, one required candidates to raise at least 50 percent of their campaign contributions in their own states. Many representatives from poor urban areas rely heavily on contributions from other states, since their own constituents often do not have the disposable income to make campaign contributions. Thus, if such an amendment were added to the Shays-Meehan bill, representatives from these areas might drop their support for the bill. More dangerous, however, were the three substitute bills allowed by the rule. If any one of these substitute bills passed, the Shays-Meehan bill would be supplanted by that substitute and therefore defeated. One substitute in particular was especially worrisome for the reformers, because it included some attractive reforms. Rep. Bill Thomas, R-Calif., offered a measure that would strengthen disclosure requirements. Yet since it was a substitute bill, reformers had to work to defeat it so that its passage would not trump the Shays-Meehan bill.

On the eve of scheduled debate on campaign finance reform, September 13, 1999, Shays released a statement regarding the pending debate on his bill. He called this debate:

> the moment of truth for all who support reform to our corrupt campaign finance system. It is a debate that is long overdue. . . . [W]e cannot let ourselves be distracted by the seemingly attractive—but ultimately dishonest—poison pill amendments and substitutes that will be offered. It is our fervent hope that tomorrow the House of Representatives will do the right thing, pass the Bipartisan Campaign Finance Reform Act and send it to the Senate.[36]

Right before the House's consideration of the Shays-Meehan bill, President Clinton sent a letter to all House members urging them to support the bill. He said passage of the Shays-Meehan bill would "revitalize the political process by curbing the role of special interests, giving voters a louder voice and treating incumbents and challengers of both parties fairly."[37]

The debate over the series of amendments and the three substitute amendments began on September 14, 1999. One particularly engaging interaction occurred between Rep. Todd Tiahrt, R-Kan., and Representative Shays. Tiahrt, a reform opponent, learned that day that labor unions had bought television time in his district to run advertisements against him. The *New York Times* characterized the exchange as follows:

> Seizing the floor, Shays observed that unions have been prohibited from donating money directly to candidates since 1947. So the commercials planned against Tiahrt must be unregulated issue advertisements, Shays said, the very kind of advertisements that his legislation would restrict.
>
> "Sir," Shays said, "it would be impossible for those ads to run against you if our legislation passed, and that's why I'm dumbfounded you do not support us."
>
> Tiahrt seemed flustered. "I don't expect even if your law passed, there would be any enforcement," he said, as his allotted time expired.[38]

The case against reform was becoming strained indeed.

The voting process, much like that in the 105th Congress, was a complicated endeavor. Proponents of the Shays-Meehan bill had to defeat amendments that would increase individual contribution limits from $1,000 to $3,000, weaken the bill's proposed restrictions on printed issued ads, require candidates to raise at least half of their contributions from their home states, exempt advertisements on the Internet from regulation, and invalidate the entire bill if any part of it were struck down by the courts (the severability issue—see Chapter 5).[39] Of the eight amendments on which the House voted, reform supporters classified six as poison pill amendments that would have broken apart their coalition. All were defeated, showing once again that there was great momentum for reform and that the extraordinary efforts made to keep the coalition together had paid off. Additionally, the reform supporters defeated the three substitute bills that would have replaced the Shays-Meehan bill altogether.

The House did approve two amendments, one it had passed in the 105th Congress prohibiting foreign-born legal permanent residents from contributing to federal campaigns, and an amendment to "require non-officeholders—such as prospective New York Senate hopeful Hillary Rodham Clinton—to pay the full cost of travel when they fly on government planes to campaign."[40] This second amendment was a clear slap at the first lady's campaign activities.[41] Box 7-3 summarizes the disposition of each amendment and the reformers' position on it.

On September 15, 1999, the House passed the Shays-Meehan bill for the second straight year by a margin of 252 to 177. Fifty-four Republicans voted to support the measure despite the opposition of their party leadership. But thirteen Democrats broke with their party, some of them because of the hard-hitting campaign against reform once again waged by the National Right to Life Committee. In a press release Shays announced:

> A bipartisan coalition in the House came together today to pass the most significant campaign reforms in a generation. A majority of the House focused on the task and refused to be distracted by seemingly attractive poison pill amendments and substitutes. Our victory is the result of months of preparation and hard work by all the members of our coalition on both sides of the aisle. These members of Congress joined our cause because they have been through the system, and they have seen its problems close up.[42]

The House reformers no doubt felt somewhat bittersweet about their victory, for they knew that campaign finance reform faced an uphill battle at best in the Senate.

On to the Senate

The 1998 midterm Senate elections did not have any significant impact on the prospects for campaign finance reform in the Senate. The aggregate partisan numbers stayed the same (fifty-five Republicans to forty-five Democrats), and the incumbent senators who were defeated had not been significant players in the reform process. Perhaps the most interesting race in regard to campaign finance reform was the defeat of the Democrat Scotty Baesler by the Republican Jim Bunning for one of the Kentucky Senate seats. Scotty Baesler would have brought strong reform credentials to the Senate. Bunning, in contrast, solidly allied himself with the Republican leaders on the issue.

Reform efforts in the Senate tracked, but lagged behind, the Shays-Meehan efforts in the House. Sens. John McCain and Russell Feingold reintroduced their bill, as it was modified by the Snowe-Jeffords amendment in the 105th Congress. McCain also tried to characterize campaign finance re-

BOX 7-3 Proposed Amendments to the Shays-Meehan Bill, September 14, 1999

Date	Action	Shays-Meehan Position	Shays-Meehan Assessment
9/14/99	Whitfield amendment fails, 127–300	No: Poison pill	Breaks apart the coalition of support for Shays-Meehan by tripling the individual contribution limit (from $1,000 to $3,000). Reform supporters are concerned that tripling the limit would increase the influence of wealthy contributors. 1998 vote: 102–315.
9/14/99	Whitfield amendment fails, 123–302	No: Poison pill	Breaks apart the coalition of support for Shays-Meehan by tripling the aggregate contribution limit (from the current $25,000 to $75,000). Reform supporters are concerned that tripling the limit would increase the influence of wealthy contributors. (Note that the Shays-Meehan bill increases the aggregate limit from $25,000 to $30,000).
9/14/99	Doolittle amendment fails, 189–238	No: Poison pill	Guts the bill's provision that treats sham "issue ads" as campaign ads in the name of protecting voter guides. Voter guides are already protected by the Shays-Meehan bill. This amendment would vastly increase the number of undisclosed, third party campaign ads in elections. Under the Doolittle amendment, any print or Internet ad that mentions a candidate's vote would not be considered a campaign ad—even if the ad contains a clear electioneering message. 1998 vote: 201–219.

Date	Action	Position	Description
9/14/99	Bereuter/Wicker amendment passes, 242–181	No	Undermines the ability of Legal Permanent Residents to participate in the political system. Unlike foreign nationals, Legal Permanent Residents—or "citizens in training"—pay taxes and have military obligations. This amendment would prohibit anyone who is not a U.S. citizen or national from making campaign contributions. 1998 vote: 282–126.
9/14/99	Faleomavaega amendment passes by voice vote	Yes	Clarifies the right of U.S. nationals to make campaign contributions.
9/14/99	Goodling amendment is withdrawn	No: Poison pill	Breaks apart the coalition of support for Shays-Meehan by requiring labor unions to obtain written authorization from all union members before using any portion of union dues for political activity, but does not require corporations to obtain the same written authorization from shareholders before using corporate treasury funds used for political activity. The Shays-Meehan bill codifies the *Beck* Supreme Court decision, which ensures that nonunion workers who pay agency fees to a union have the right to deduct the portions of their dues that are used by the union for political purposes.

continued

BOX 7-3 Proposed Amendments to the Shays-Meehan Bill, September 14, 1999 continued

Date	Action	Shays-Meehan Position	Shays-Meehan Assessment
9/14/99	Shaw amendment fails, 179–248	No: Poison pill	Breaks apart the coalition of support for Shays-Meehan by requiring all candidates to raise at least 50 percent of their contributions from within their home states. Opposed by many candidates in minority and low-income districts because of concerns it harms their ability to run an effective campaign. 1998 vote: 160–253.
9/14/99	Sweeney amendment passes, 261–167	Neutral	Requires nonfederal officeholders who use federal government transportation for campaign activities to reimburse the government at full cost.
9/14/99	DeLay amendment fails, 160–268	No: Poison pill	Creates gaping loopholes in campaign finance laws by allowing unlimited, unregulated, and undisclosed funds from labor unions, corporate treasuries, and other organizations to be used for activities, such as ads, on the Internet. Exempts the Internet from all election guidelines, except for the solicitation or receipt of contributions, thereby allowing unlimited funds to be funneled into undisclosed Internet ads. The Shays-Meehan bill does not regulate the Internet and specifically authorizes the electronic distribution of voter guides.

9/14/99	Ewing amendment fails, 167–259	No: Poison pill	Provides that if any portion of the bill—including any amendment added to Shays-Meehan—were to be struck down, then the entire bill would be invalid. A nonseverability approach is highly unusual, and was found in only three of the thousands of bills passed in the last ten years. 1998 vote: 155–254.
9/14/99	Doolittle substitute amendment fails, 117–306	No: Poison pill	Because it is a substitute, a vote for the Doolittle amendment is a vote to defeat the Shays-Meehan bill. Repeals all limits on contributions, ends the presidential public financing system and requires disclosure of funds transferred to a state or local political party. Requires state and local disclosure documents be filed with the FEC, and electronic filing 90 days before an election. Does not require disclosure of union dues, corporate funds or other money used in sham issue ads. 1998 vote: 131–299.
9/14/99	Hutchinson substitute amendment fails, 99–327	No: Poison pill	Because it is a substitute, a vote for the Hutchinson amendment is a vote to defeat the Shays-Meehan bill. Bans only federal soft money, while allowing state soft money to continue; indexes individual contribution limits; and leaves in place the current loophole through which unlimited corporate and union treasury funds are funneled into federal elections through sham issue ads. 1998 vote: 147–222, with 61 present.

continued

BOX 7-3 Proposed Amendments to the Shays-Meehan Bill, September 14, 1999 *continued*

Date	Action	Shays-Meehan Position	Shays-Meehan Assessment
9/14/99	Thomas substitute amendment fails, 173–256	No: Poison pill	Because it is a substitute, a vote for the Thomas amendment is a vote to defeat the Shays-Meehan bill. Makes FEC reforms, including requiring election year, rather than calendar year, filing cycles; prohibiting foreign nationals from contributing soft money (the same as Shays-Meehan); requiring the transfer of suspect contributions to an FEC account (the same as Shays-Meehan); and requiring the FEC to provide written responses to campaign-related questions. While these reforms are positive, they should not be used as a replacement for comprehensive reforms—banning all soft money and reining in sham issue ads—found in the Shays-Meehan bill.

Source: Adapted from "Recommended Votes on Amendments to H.R. 417, The Bipartisan Campaign Finance Reform Act," prepared by the offices of Representatives Shays and Meehan, 106th Congress, 1st session.

form in terms that would appeal to Republican ideals. He contended that achieving conservative political reforms necessitated reforming the campaign finance system first.[43] McCain also noted that the Republican Party at the grassroots level supported reform: "Republicans all across this country are responding encouragingly to my call for reform."[44] But on the other side of the issue, Senate reform opponents continued to show their disdain for the McCain-Feingold bill. For example, Senate majority leader Trent Lott argued that campaign finance reform constituted "unilateral disarmament" for Republicans and would strip them of their traditional advantage in fundraising.[45] Again, GOP leaders were less reluctant to make such an overtly political argument than they had been during the 105th Congress.

Despite this early posturing, the Senate did not take up campaign finance reform until after the House passed the Shays-Meehan bill on September 15. The agreement between the Senate reformers and Majority Leader Lott provided for an open amendment process that would allow other senators to amend the bill. Once again, Senate reform opponents were ready to filibuster and thus defeat the bill. As a result, McCain and Feingold scaled back their bill in the hope of gaining additional Republican support for a cloture vote to end the inevitable filibuster. They introduced a revised reform bill on September 16, 1999, with the understanding from Lott that the bill would be considered in October. The new McCain-Feingold bill (S. 1593) required a complete ban on soft money as well as a provision regarding using union dues for political purposes. The revised bill discarded the new regulations on campaign-like issue advocacy advertisements. If this revised McCain-Feingold bill passed, it would have to go to the House for approval, for all bills must pass in identical form in both chambers before going on to the president for his signature.

It was the issue ad provision that had inspired the hard-hitting First Amendment criticisms during the last Congress. Yet Sen. Mitch McConnell, who began calling himself the "designated spear catcher on this issue," showed no sign that he would drop his opposition even to the scaled-back bill.[46] McConnell, who headed the GOP's Senate reelection committee, the National Republican Senatorial Committee, argued that his party needed large amounts of soft money to counter the issue ads run by labor unions that overwhelmingly favored Democrats. Even McConnell, the champion of the First Amendment argument, was appealing to his fellow Republicans with this more pragmatic partisan argument. Indeed, without the issue ad restrictions in the bill, the First Amendment argument was no longer relevant. Thus, when foes of reform faced only the soft money provision they were forced to reveal their more strategic and partisan arguments against campaign finance reform.

McCain saw the revised bill as a compromise that provided a ban on soft money, "the bare minimum of reform," that might bring "additional Senators on board prior to coming to the floor in October."[47] Indeed, McCain said that he was a "realist" and acknowledged that a comprehensive reform bill was not likely to pass in the Senate.[48] As it turned out, the scaled-down bill drew new support from only one additional Senate Republican, Sam Brownback of Kansas, and many Democrats were leery of breaking apart the reform proposal to deal only with soft money. The Democrats made the same argument that McConnell did: they are often the target of issue advocacy ads run by GOP allies such as Americans for Tax Reform, Citizens for Reform, and the National Rifle Association, and without the soft money to fight back such attacks, the Democratic Party would be rendered helpless to do anything.[49]

Most observers agreed that it would be the Democrats, not the Republicans, who would suffer most if soft money were banned without new restrictions on campaign-like issue ads. The GOP has long enjoyed a tremendous edge over the Democrats in raising hard money, and that financial advantage would allow the Republicans to spend more on issue ads, independent expenditures, and contributions to its candidates to counter Democratic and labor union attack ads. Nevertheless, the pared-down bill was a gamble that the reformers were willing to take and that the interest groups reluctantly supported.

On the first day the Senate considered the revised McCain-Feingold bill in October, the usually collegial Senate debate turned personal—specifically toward Senator McCain. As before, Senator McConnell led the antireform efforts. McConnell responded to McCain's argument that soft money corrupted Congress by stating: "Someone must be corrupt for there to be corruption. How can there be corruption if no one is corrupt? That's like saying the gang is corrupt but none of the gangsters are."[50] McCain retorted, "Who is corrupted by this system? All of us are corrupted by it because money buys access and access is influence."[51]

McConnell did not stop there. He challenged McCain to come forth with charges of corruption against specific senators. Sen. Robert Bennett, R-Utah, took the confrontation further. He was personally offended by an item on McCain's presidential campaign Internet site that claimed that a $2.2 million sewer project in Utah was "directly related" to soft money. Although Bennett admitted securing the pork barrel project for his home state, he challenged McCain to prove that soft money contributions influenced the

Utah Republican. To this, McCain responded that on the Internet site he did not accuse Senator Bennett of being corrupt, "so no apology or withdrawal is warranted."[52]

Despite the drama of these confrontations on the floor of the Senate, they were not the guiding force that drove the eventual outcome there. Neither were the First Amendment arguments that reform opponents used to help defeat the McCain-Feingold bill in 1997 and 1998. Instead, the Senate's consideration was driven by the use of parliamentary maneuvers. As issues gave way to process, "the campaign finance debate . . . simply degenerated into a procedural battle."[53]

For example, McConnell won approval with a voice vote for a "seemingly innocuous amendment" that modified the Senate rules so that senators had to provide "credible information" regarding corruption.[54] McConnell, in effect, wanted to make the reformers name names and to force them to turn their crusade for reform into a witch hunt. Reform supporters worried that this would hamper their effort to seek reform, because they could not make the generic claim that money in politics is a corrupting force.[55] Another example of the unusual parliamentary tactics employed is an amendment offered by McCain that would have killed his own proposal. His reason for putting forth such an amendment was to demonstrate the support a soft money ban would have and to isolate the senators trying to kill the effort. This tactic failed, however, when opponents of this reform bill joined with the proponents to vote against McCain's amendment, thus keeping the McCain-Feingold bill alive. The opponents could afford to "throw the vote," as Senator Feingold noted, because they knew they would have other chances to defeat the legislation.[56]

In the end, campaign finance reform in the 106th Congress once again fell victim to a Senate parliamentary procedure—the filibuster. Not even a late effort by President Clinton, who sent a letter to Senate Democrats supporting the revised McCain-Feingold bill, could provide enough votes to shut down the opponents' filibuster. On a vote that would have allowed the Senate to consider the House (Shays-Meehan) version of the bill, the reform supporters garnered only fifty-two of the sixty votes needed (again, a supermajority, rather than a simple majority, was needed to proceed). On a second vote that would have allowed the revised McCain-Feingold version to move forward, reform supporters added three new Republican senators to their ranks. But two regular reform proponents voted no, giving the reform supporters a net increase of only one vote.[57] After these votes, Majority Leader Trent Lott proclaimed campaign finance reform "dead for the year."[58]

Incremental Reform: A Small Hope for Comprehensive Reform or an Election Year Strategy?

The political context surrounding the 2000 presidential nomination process called attention to campaign finance reform. McCain sought the Republican nomination and campaign finance reform was his marquee issue. While campaigning around the country on board his "Straight Talk Express" campaign bus, McCain highlighted the need for reform to control the power of special interests and to give the government back to the people. McCain sought to demonstrate bipartisanship on the issue with a handshake promise between him and Democratic candidate Bill Bradley to seek reform. Although neither McCain nor Bradley won their parties' nominations, they did raise the issue of reform high on campaign 2000's agenda. Because of their focus on the issue, both Al Gore and George W. Bush would need to address this issue, and we will see later how each tried to rise to this challenge.

Although McCain did not win the GOP nomination contest, he did gain much attention within the Senate for the surprising level of support he received in the nomination process. McCain hoped to parlay some of this new-found support into passage of campaign finance reform legislation on the Hill. Upon his return to the Senate, McCain began negotiations with the Senate leadership to seek reform once again in the 106th Congress. Having learned from his past tangles with the Republican leadership, McCain decided to take a page out of their playbook: he would seek to change the terms of the debate rapidly and propose a smaller, more incremental campaign finance change.

McCain and Feingold introduced on June 7, 2000, an incremental reform proposal that addressed the so-called 527 groups—tax-exempt, nonprofit groups formed under Section 527 of the Internal Revenue Code. These secret political groups were permitted to raise and spend unlimited amounts of money without disclosure of contributors or spending as long as their communications did not expressly advocate the election or defeat of candidates. McCain was targeted by a 527 group just before the March 7 primaries. A mysterious group called Republicans for Clean Air ran television ads that attacked McCain's environmental record and praised Bush's. Liberal groups use the 527 loophole as well. For example, the Sierra Club operates a 527 organization.

Although 527 groups had not been a primary topic of discussion, the issue did receive some notoriety prior to its introduction into the legislative arena. On May 3, 2000, congressional Democrats filed a federal lawsuit accusing Tom DeLay, the House majority whip, of "engaging in extortion, racketeering and money laundering in his aggressive fund-raising for Republican candidates and causes."[59] The chairman of the Democratic Congressional Campaign Committee, Rep. Patrick J. Kennedy, D-R.I., pointed out that this was the third time that Democrats had sought to curb "massive illegal conduct" by Representative DeLay.[60] The lawsuit was an attempt to apply parts of the Federal Racketeer Influenced and Corrupt Organizations Act, known by the acronym RICO, to DeLay's fund-raising practices through many related nonprofit and other committees.[61] Democrats charged that DeLay's use of these committees was equivalent to "money laundering." Republicans and DeLay argued that the lawsuit was an election year political tactic, but "several legal experts, including Houston law Professor Sandra Guerra, noted that a Supreme Court decision in 1994 indicates that the case could have merit."[62]

McCain reported that the idea for the 527 legislation came to him in the middle of the night, when on the evening of June 5 he decided to try to change the "nature of the campaign finance battle by seizing on one, easily definable area to fix."[63] McCain and Feingold hoped that several senators in tough reelection bids might feel compelled to vote with them on this reform issue. They also hoped that the narrow refinement of a single area of the law would give them the momentum to pass more comprehensive reform, which would include a ban on soft money. McCain and Feingold offered a proposal originally introduced by Sen. Joseph Lieberman, D-Conn., S. 2583, to tighten controls on 527 groups as an amendment to the Defense Department authorization bill, S. 2549, which was open for amendments under a concession that Majority Leader Lott previously made to the Democrats. The Republican leaders tried a procedural motion (a point of order) to block the amendment on the evening of June 7 when it was debated, but they were defeated by a vote of 42–57. McCain's amendment passed later, on June 8, on a voice vote.

Upon passage, Senator Lott and Senator McConnell "attacked McCain's proposal as unfairly narrow, arguing that it would not curb the power of labor unions and other Democratic-leaning political groups."[64] Of the thirteen Republicans who voted with McCain, eight were up for reelection in November.[65] Later, McCain agreed to negotiate with Lott to seek a compromise to broaden the provision. However, McCain was quick to herald the victory for reform with over 200,000 e-mails to his supporters. Days later, McConnell, the leading Senate campaign finance opponent, decided to support this type of reform provided that it be expanded to cover labor unions and business groups. McConnell also took the initiative to cancel a June 14 Rules and Administration Committee markup of a bill (S. 1816) by Sen.

Chuck Hagel, R-Neb., that would increase the limits on hard money contributions to candidates from $1,000 to $3,000 per election and limit soft money donations to national party committees.[66] McConnell did so not because McCain opposed the Hagel bill, but rather because the bill had little chance of passing.

Meanwhile, in the House of Representatives, Reps. Dennis Moore, D-Kan., and Lloyd Doggett, D-Texas, both introduced legislation to require greater disclosure by the stealth 527 groups (H.R. 3688 and H.R. 4168, respectively). Under pressure, the House Republican leaders announced that a vote would take place in the House before the July 4 recess. Chris Shays and others sent a Dear Colleague letter on June 15 stating, "We believe the public—at a bare minimum—has the right to know who is spending money on advertising that seeks to influence elections, be it corporations, labor unions, wealthy individuals or foreign nationals."[67] On June 27, 2000, a leadership compromise bill, H.R. 4762, "To amend the Internal Revenue Code of 1986 to require 527 organizations to disclose their political activities," was introduced by Rep. Amo Houghton, R-N.Y. The bill was moved for consideration under suspension of the rules (requiring a two-thirds majority vote for passage), and just after midnight on June 28, 2000, it overwhelmingly passed the House by a 385–39 vote. The measure was laid before the Senate by a unanimous consent agreement for consideration on June 28 and passed on June 29 without amendment by a 92–6 vote. According to one news report, "Today's vote represented a stern rebuke to House and Senate Republican leaders who tried to kill the measure by offering a much broader bill only to see that plan backfire. By clamping down only on the tax-exempt groups, the leaders hope to dilute support for more extensive reform." Representatives Shays and Meehan agreed that they would continue to fight for broader reforms. "We're not going to let this go," said Meehan.[68] On July 1, 2000, President Clinton signed the law, proclaiming, "this is a good day and this is a good law," however, this is "a step but not a substitute for comprehensive campaign reform."[69]

The new law compels 527 groups to inform the Internal Revenue Service (IRS) of their existence within twenty-four hours after forming. If a group raises at least $25,000 per year, it must report contributors who gave more than $200 or expenditures of $500 or more. Violations of any of the above provisions will be subject to a 35 percent tax on all contributions. The law goes into effect in time to force 527s to submit their first reports by the November 2000 election. Following that, they must file reports four times a year plus one immediately before a federal election.[70] Of course, this law does not cover donations and expenditures that were made prior to its passage; therefore, millions might have already been collected and spent. Additionally, once the president signed the law, many of the 527 organizations indicated that all they would have to do to continue their current practices was to change their tax designation to a different type of nonprofit organization or reorganize as a for-profit entity. A new loophole has started to spring forth already, leading many reformers such as McCain, Feingold, Shays, and Meehan to continue calling for comprehensive campaign finance reform.

Conclusion: The Never-ending Labyrinth?

In reflecting on the battle of parliamentary maneuvers in the 106th Congress, McCain admitted that the reformers' initial gamble of offering a scaled-down reform bill that included only a soft money ban may have been "mistaken." But he placed the blame on opponents who "oppose[d] even the most elemental reform." In October 1999, McCain promised not to give up the fight in the Senate to pass more comprehensive campaign finance reform legislation. He vowed to "take our case to the people, and eventually, eventually, we will prevail."[71] Indeed, Senator McCain did take the issue to the people by making it a top priority in his bid for the Republican nomination for president in 2000. McCain brought the message loud and clear back to the Senate that the American people were interested in this issue. And his efforts helped score a small victory with passage of the incremental 527 reform.

Yet, in the end, this minor change may make very little difference. Congressional reformers and their allied interest groups agree that comprehensive reforms are still needed. Indeed, the law regarding 527 groups may not have any effect if these secret groups find other ways to raise and spend money without disclosing it. Thus, although it appears that campaign finance reform as an issue may now enjoy a higher status and more public support, the 106th Congress ultimately was more of the same. History repeated itself as comprehensive campaign finance reform was defeated by a minority of lawmakers in the Senate.

8

LESSONS FROM THE LABYRINTH

The debates over campaign finance reform in the 105th and 106th Congresses provide insights into many aspects of the legislative process. These journeys through the legislative labyrinth allow us to make some general observations about Congress, politics, and policymaking and about the roles played by interest groups, parties, and the media. What becomes distinctly clear from these efforts to enact campaign finance reform is that there is no clean flow-chart that explains how legislation is considered in Congress. Although such charts are used to illustrate how a bill typically becomes a law, this case study shows us how legislation often follows a less conventional route and may languish over a period of years. We see that the "usual" legislative process is one that often takes time, continued energy, and many attempts at passage. The unorthodox has become the usual, whereby no participant in the policymaking process can map out the likely course a bill will take. Thus, legislators, lobbyists, journalists, and citizens are best prepared to participate in and understand modern congressional lawmaking if they expect the unexpected.

Policy development models, such as those offered by John Kingdon and Barbara Sinclair, and this story of efforts to pass comprehensive campaign finance reform suggest that the methods of congressional policymaking are becoming more diverse.[1] Moreover, Congress has become more decentralized. As a result, individual legislators who ordinarily might be kept in check by their party leaders, particularly in the House, are now freer to pursue their own policy and institutional goals. Interest groups are no longer just seeking access to lawmakers. They are an integral part of issue networks that transcend the boundary between Congress and the world outside. The media often have been relegated by scholars to a secondary role in the legislative process, but we argue that the media have become increasingly important, especially as various political actors use the press as a tool to gain political leverage. With all these factors in mind, we now turn to the many lessons that the campaign finance reform efforts in the 105th and 106th Congresses have taught us.

Institutional Forces

This policymaking story highlights some fundamental institutional dynamics of contemporary public policy development. The debate over campaign finance reform involved not only Congress but also the judicial branch and the president, and their roles in this particular policy battle help us understand more about how they operate in the legislative process. For instance, the bicameral nature of Congress and the differences between the two chambers can have a profound impact on the outcome of legislative debates. The judicial branch not only interprets the law but also influences its creation. And the president's influence on congressional policymaking is contingent on many factors.

House and Senate

Members of the House are fond of a saying: "the members of the other party are our opponents; but our enemy is the Senate." This was certainly true for the campaign finance reformers in the House of Representatives. Even though the reformers overcame all the obstacles their opponents placed before them to achieve a majority victory in the House, the Senate, their enemy, was not likely to pass a reform bill. In fact, such institutional differences between the two chambers even affected the vote in the House. No matter how much the proreform House members wanted to believe that all who voted for the Shays-Meehan bill were doing so out of true support for the measure, they could never rid themselves of the uncertainty that this backing was not always genuine. For some, a vote for the Shays-Meehan bill was a safe vote by which legislators could appear to favor campaign finance reform with the confidence that it would not become law because the Senate was bound to kill the measure. Would all the House members who voted for the Shays-Meehan bill have done so if the Senate had been controlled by the Democrats and, therefore, much more likely to pass the reform bill? Probably not.

Likewise, sponsors of the Shays-Meehan bill knew that some lawmakers were voting for their measure only because they believed that the courts ultimately would see to its demise. Such a concern led Martin Frost, D-Texas, the chairman of the Democratic Congressional Campaign Committee, to introduce an amendment providing that if one part of the bill were struck down then the rest of it would be invalidated as well (see the discussion of severability in Chapter 5). Thus, predictions about what the courts were likely to do if the law were challenged influenced legislators' votes and behavior.

Legislators' motivations thus became blurred as some members voted strategically—that is, they voted for reform only because they were confident that it would die in the Senate or be struck down by the courts. They could take credit for supporting campaign finance reform and at the same time feel secure that the status quo, which generally benefits them as incumbents, would be maintained. Therefore, the campaign finance reform leaders were never certain about the level of support their bill actually had.

Procedural differences between the two chambers also affected the process and the outcome of the campaign finance reform policy debate. In the House, Republican leaders used the rules to try to restrict the process. For instance, even after the GOP leaders reached a consent agreement with the reformers to conduct a "fair and open" process for considering reform, Speaker Newt Gingrich still tried to maintain control of the process by allowing many poison pill amendments to be placed in the way of passing reform. Although the majority party had the formal ability to dictate the process and the rules, however, Shays, Meehan, and their cadre of core supporters led a House majority around the many legislative obstacles to pass their bill anyway. Indeed, rules do matter, but eventually the numeric majority can win out in the House, provided that the majority coalition can play successfully whatever game the leaders' rules establish.

Strategies that work in one chamber, however, are not necessarily successful or even viable in the other. The reformers in the Senate could not defeat the rules and tactics employed by the Republican leaders in that chamber. The House leadership's use of restrictive rules certainly presented a formidable challenge, but the outcome in the Senate was driven by procedures and rules, particularly the filibuster. In the Senate the filibuster obstructed the majority's will, resulting in defeat of the McCain-Feingold bill despite majority support for it. What became clear after multiple rounds of considering comprehensive campaign finance reform in the Senate was the generally obstructive effect of the use of unorthodox policy procedures in the upper chamber. As we have seen with this story of campaign finance reform through two Congresses, and as scholars have noted before, the use of unconventional procedures tends to make policymaking easier in the House, but more difficult in the Senate.[2] Indeed, the filibuster is an activity that is designed to stop action on some legislative item, whereas many of the unconventional procedures used in the House, such as special rules and the use of task forces instead of committee consideration, are often used to ease the path of legislation. For example, to control an issue, recent House Speakers have taken the issue out of the hands of a committee and given it to a task force of like-minded members to consider. Leaders are more likely to get their desired outcome with a hand-picked task force, particularly if the relevant committee is known to disagree with the leaders' viewpoint.[3]

In a comprehensive study of the use of filibusters in the Senate, the political scientists Sarah Binder and Steven Smith found an "explosive increase in the number of manifest filibusters since the late 1960s." They argue that the filibuster has become an "epidemic, used whenever a coalition can find 41 votes to oppose legislation." Binder and Smith attribute the increased use of the filibuster to many factors that "reduce the costs of filibustering and increase the rewards for obstructive behavior."[4] Some of those factors—namely, changes in Senate partisanship and the contemporary realities of running for reelection—help us better understand the case of campaign finance reform. Both of these factors exacerbated the formidable challenges faced by the Senate campaign finance reformers and increased the likelihood that they would face a filibuster.

Increased polarization between the two parties and increased unity within each party since the 1980s have encouraged congressional parties, especially the minority party, to use more filibusters. Both the majority and minority parties may try to stop the other from succeeding if there are vast differences between their views on a policy proposal; and with campaign finance reform there was definitely a wide gap between the two parties' views on the issue. These party filibusters have succeeded more often in the contemporary Congress in part because increased party unity has helped party leaders keep their members in line. Not only did the two parties fundamentally disagree on the campaign finance issue, but the party that wanted to kill reform controlled the chamber and, therefore, could exercise more control over the process than those who advocated reform. In the Senate these partisan and procedural obstacles were just too much to overcome. Four times the GOP leadership used both its majority party power and, in the face of majority support for reform, the filibuster to defeat the reform proposals offered by Senators McCain and Feingold.

Moreover, the demands of running for reelection to the Senate no doubt motivated Senate GOP leaders to do whatever they could to defeat reform in order to maintain their party's fund-raising advantage and majority status.

The Republican Party has long raised more money than the Democratic Party. And since the Republicans took control of both chambers of Congress in 1995 their fund-raising advantage has increased, primarily because most political action committees (PACs) and wealthy contributors tend to contribute more to the majority party to gain access to those who control the lawmaking process. The Republicans have been working to solidify their majority status, and party leaders will not easily give up this advantage. During the 105th Congress, GOP leaders were reluctant to make this purely strategic partisan argument, in part because they did not want to appear to oppose reform and, therefore, to favor what some argue is a corrupt system. Instead, they wrapped their objections to reform in the cloak of the First Amendment. Yet, as we saw in Chapter 7, when campaign finance reform reemerged as an issue during the 106th Congress, Republican Party leaders were determined to kill it for good and did not hesitate to appeal to their members' political ambitions with this bottom-line argument that presents campaign finance reform as an attack on the party's survival.

Although the 106th Congress did pass a narrow bill that requires disclosure of fund-raising and spending by secretive 527 groups, the law is likely to have little effect on either party's electoral fortunes, particularly if new loopholes are discovered to make up for the loss of this underground money channel. GOP leaders were willing to allow the 527 restrictions to pass also because they hoped this small victory for the reformers might slow their momentum for more comprehensive reforms. Of course, the reformers hoped it would do just the opposite.

Contemporary Senate elections are extremely expensive ventures, with the average cost reaching well over $3.5 million.[5] Senate elections also are less predictable and more competitive than House contests. Senators represent larger, more diverse constituencies than the generally homogeneous districts represented by their counterparts in the House, making it easier for a Senate challenger to piece together a winning coalition against a Senate incumbent. Moreover, since voter attachments to political parties have weakened in recent decades, Senate incumbents cannot rely on the loyalty of voters from their own party. These conditions motivated Senate Republican leaders as well as individual senators to oppose campaign finance reform to maintain their fund-raising advantage, thus making the political climate right for filibustering.

Clearly, differences between the two chambers can have an important effect on the outcome of legislative debates, and in some cases can thwart the will of a majority of lawmakers. A minority of senators defeated campaign fi-

nance reform over the objections of a majority of House members and senators. Granting such power to a minority in a representative democracy is said
to protect the rights of minority interests from the potential tyranny of the
majority and to ensure policy moderation rather than extreme measures that
might be passed by an overbearing majority. Yet Binder and Smith found that
the requirement for a supermajority to overcome a filibuster in the Senate
has not resulted in moderate policies that reflect the wishes of a popular majority.[6] Instead, filibusters often tend to protect the minority interests that
sponsor them and thwart policymaking that reflects the popular will. The
best example of these effects is the repeated use of the filibuster by southern
conservatives to defeat civil rights legislation for almost 100 years.[7] There
have been repeated calls for reform of the Senate rules to make it easier to invoke cloture to shut down a filibuster, but to date no blanket restrictions have
been adopted.[8] Thus, as long as campaign finance reform bills continue to
generate at least forty-one senators in opposition (the number of senators
needed to defeat a cloture vote), it is unlikely that reform will be enacted.

The Courts: Affecting Policymaking and Interpreting the Law

The campaign finance reform debates also emphasized the importance of
other institutions and political actors in the legislative process. For example,
questions about how the courts would view the measure if it passed were
raised first in the Senate. The debate demonstrated how the First Amendment might become a cover for the protection of potentially "corrupting
forces." Or would the courts agree with the reformers that protecting political speech was less important than combating corruption by allowing restrictions on issue advocacy communications and soft money? The debates
in Congress by no means settled these constitutional conflicts, and the
courts will continue to address these and other campaign finance issues independently of Congress.

For example, in October 1999 the Supreme Court heard oral arguments
in *Nixon v. Shrink Missouri Government PAC,* a case that addressed the
$1,000 contribution limit for individuals upheld in *Buckley v. Valeo.*[9] The
specific issue in the case involved whether the $1,000 contribution limit,
which Missouri adopted in 1994 for state elections, was valid given that inflation since the 1970s has greatly reduced the value of that $1,000. The
Eighth Circuit Court of Appeals previously ruled that Missouri's limits were
"too low to allow meaningful participation in protected political speech and
association."[10] Sen. Mitch McConnell, in an amicus curiae brief supported
by the Republican National Committee, the National Republican Senatorial
Committee, and the Missouri GOP, endorsed the Eighth Circuit's ruling.[11]

On January 24, 2000, the U.S. Supreme Court handed down a six to three decision in the *Shrink Missouri Government PAC* case upholding the limits on political contributions and rejecting the argument that the $1,000 limit it upheld in *Buckley* "no longer buys enough political speech to be constitutional."[12] Two key points emerged from this decision. First, in a dissenting opinion, Justice Anthony M. Kennedy declared that "*Buckley* has not worked," having "created a misshapen system" that has "forced a substantial amount of political speech underground."[13] Justices Stephen Breyer and Ruth Bader Ginsburg, in concurring opinions, suggested that discretion should be given to the legislative branches to decide this matter rather than leaving it to the courts. Justice Stevens's concurring opinion left the door wide open to reforms even beyond *Buckley* when he stated, "Money is property; it is not speech," essentially rejecting "the equation of money and speech that was the analytical foundation of *Buckley v. Valeo*."[14]

This case also presented the Supreme Court with a more fundamental issue, had it decided to consider it: Are large political contributions inherently corrupt? The *Buckley* Court apparently believed so, but the Eighth Circuit Court did not accept this view. Instead, the Eighth Circuit required that the State of Missouri provide sufficient evidence that large contributions corrupt in order to justify its restraints on speech.[15] The issue is still ripe for consideration. If and how the Supreme Court ever addresses the nature of contributions and political corruption, it has the potential to reshape the structure of the campaign finance reform debate for years to come.

As we saw above, lawmakers' views about what they thought the courts would do with a law such as the one proposed in the McCain-Feingold and Shays-Meehan bills may influence their decision making in Congress. For instance, such preemptive thinking was the basis of the most powerful argument against reform—that provisions of the bills were unconstitutional and would be struck down by the courts, so the bill should be defeated. To the extent that such forecasting about the courts' possible future treatment of laws influences how legislators actually vote, the judicial branch can have an important effect on the policymaking process. Many would argue that Congress should consider whether the legislation they contemplate will withstand constitutional and legal scrutiny by the courts, and that ignoring such considerations would be irresponsible. Yet, as was the case with campaign finance reform, sometimes lawmakers disagree about what they think the courts will do. Or they might purposely push the envelope to trigger a legal challenge to force the courts to reconsider a previous ruling. Indeed, some legislators believed that the Supreme Court was ready to overturn its narrow interpretation of express advocacy in *Buckley v. Valeo*. When there are such disagreements or when the constitutionality of proposed laws is a matter of dispute, then judicial factors such as the ones featured in the debates over campaign finance reform may greatly affect the course of congressional debates and the eventual outcome of legislative battles.

Presidential Influence

A president potentially can affect the outcome of congressional lawmaking to a large degree. One of the most obvious examples of presidential influence, and perhaps a president's most effective tool for swaying Congress, is the threat of a presidential veto. Such a veto threat often prompts Congress to modify the legislation to satisfy the president's objections. In the case of campaign finance reform, however, President Clinton favored the bills before the House and the Senate and therefore wanted to build support for the legislation in Congress. Thus, a veto threat was useless.

Clinton's efforts on the issue were helpful, but most reformers were disappointed that he did not do more. He provided media time to the issue by, for example, mentioning campaign finance reform as a priority issue in his State of the Union address in January 1998. He also made other public comments in support of reform. The president helped gain support for reform in general, and for the Shays-Meehan and McCain-Feingold bills in particular, by writing to House members and senators asking them to support reform and praising them when they voted in ways that moved the debate along.

Yet President Clinton's proreform efforts were somewhat tainted by the congressional investigations into his and his party's fund-raising practices in the 1996 election and by the emerging scandal over his affair with a White House intern that hit the news in January 1998. The case of campaign finance reform and, of course, the timing of the issue demonstrate the contingency of presidential influence in Congress. How much a president can influence the actions of Congress is dependent on many factors, not the least of which is his own reputation. Other considerations include the partisan makeup of government, whereby a divided government presents more formidable challenges for presidents to overcome.

The issue itself may affect the level of influence a president can have. Presidents generally receive more support from Congress on foreign policy issues than on issues of domestic policy. An issue with little public support and meager media attention also will diminish a president's ability to affect congressional decision making in that area, although a president can raise the profile of a sleeper issue more quickly and generally more effectively than any legislator can because of his ability to command media attention. This extraordinary media attention helps explain why President Clinton's efforts on behalf of reform were not completely nullified by his own campaign finance and other troubles.

Understanding Congressional Leadership

Leadership can come in many shapes and forms—many of which were displayed in Congress's consideration of campaign finance reform. Certainly, both House members and senators empower the majority party's formal leaders to shape the legislative process in their respective chambers. Yet leadership in Congress also can come from policy entrepreneurs, those issue leaders who forge strong legislative coalitions and effective issue networks around specific proposals. Understanding why and how some legislators become policy entrepreneurs helps us understand more about the nature of leadership in Congress.

During the legislative process involving campaign finance reform, the formal majority party leaders in the House and Senate were consumed with the desire not to lose control of their respective chambers to the Democrats. This was not only symbolically important, but it was also important for promoting party objectives and maintaining an air of strength. GOP leaders tried to use formal yet unconventional mechanisms to control the process. Whether it was the Republicans' repeated use of the filibuster, Senator Lott filling the amendment tree in the Senate, or the use of a structured rule to stifle progress on reform in the House, the ends were the same: stop comprehensive campaign finance reform. Reform leaders also used unorthodox procedural tactics, such as discharge petitions and negotiated deals, in pursuit of their goal. The timing of such procedural strategies was also quite important. Controlling not only how but when the issue would come on the agenda was key to the respective sides' strategies. And the extent to which leaders on both sides accomplished their goals using these strategies reflects not only the merits of their arguments, but also their abilities as leaders.

Understanding why certain legislators champion the issues they do also reveals much about the dynamics of leadership in Congress. For example, maverick politicians such as McCain and Shays apparently choose issues like campaign finance reform not simply because of some expected electoral payoff but because these issues allow legislators to pursue other goals. In this case, reform leaders wanted to enact good public policy. They were also focused on the institutional maintenance of Congress, whereby passing campaign finance reform might help restore the public's confidence in government. The importance of congressional institutional maintenance was best explained by political scientist David Mayhew in 1974. Mayhew argued that the primary goal of all legislators is reelection, but that "[e]fficient pursuit of electoral goals by members gives no guarantee of institutional survival." Institutional maintenance is important to all legislators because if they want to make a career in Congress "they have a stake in maintaining its prestige as an institution. . . . But if every member pursues only his own electoral goals, the prestige and power of Congress will drain away." Lawmakers are concerned about the public's confidence in their activities, because a lack of confidence indicates a lack of legitimacy. If Congress's legitimacy is called into question, it could endanger the government's ability to enact and implement laws as well as pose a threat to each legislator's reelection. Mayhew contends that institutional maintenance is such an important goal for members that it grants legislators who work to build the reputation of the institution special power and prestige: "Members are paid in internal currency for engaging in institutionally protective activities that are beyond or even against their own electoral interests."[16]

In this case, the majority party leaders in both chambers did not view campaign finance reform as an institutional maintenance issue, but many other legislators did. Some lawmakers, therefore, believed that Shays, Meehan, McCain, and Feingold deserved special recognition for their efforts. Therefore, the reform leaders were not only pursuing good public policy, they also were enhancing their reputations among their colleagues in Congress and potentially improving the electoral climate for themselves and their fellow legislators by enhancing the reputation of the institution. Opposing their own party's leaders may have made it more difficult for Shays and McCain to lead the campaign finance reform effort in their chambers, but support from other lawmakers and from groups and citizens outside of Congress helped insulate them from the potential consequences of working at odds with their party. The increasingly decentralized nature of Congress also helps explain why issue leaders are now freer and more likely to endure the high cost of pursuing institution-building legislation.

Still, being a policy entrepreneur remains risky, particularly if the legislator goes against his or her own party's leaders. Although the tools available to party leaders to induce party loyalty are not as powerful as in the past, there are still ways to punish legislators for disloyalty. Rep. Linda Smith lost her post as chair of a subcommittee after aggressively pursuing campaign finance reform in the 104th Congress. Some GOP members of Congress called on their leaders to punish Shays and the other Republicans who had signed the Blue Dog Democrat discharge petition. And one party leader may have actually tried to encourage someone to run against Representative Shays by giving that potential challenger money to mount a challenge against the GOP leader of the reform movement. Policy entrepreneurs also commit a great deal of their energy and resources to a single issue perhaps at the expense of other issues, some of which may need their attention if they are to maintain their electoral advantage back home. This is probably why most policy entrepreneurs are electorally secure and, therefore, free to pursue issues that may not directly affect the folks back home. Yet this potentially limits the number of lawmakers willing to become policy entrepreneurs, for virtually all members of Congress believe their reelection is at risk no matter how big their margin of victory was in the last election.[17] This story of campaign finance reform illustrates how difficult it can be to be a policy entrepreneur in a political climate that is hostile to one's efforts.

Party Developments

The campaign finance reform debates also reveal some interesting characteristics about congressional parties. For example, the debates over reform clearly illustrate the growing importance of moderate Republicans in Congress. It is only because of the support of Republican moderates that the Democratic reformers were able to build majorities in support of their bills in both chambers. The growing influence of the Tuesday Group (a group of about forty House GOP moderates who meet weekly to discuss strategies for moderating their party's position on various issues) had a clear impact on the reform process, as GOP House members such as Connie Morella of Maryland, Nancy Johnson of Connecticut, Marge Roukema of New Jersey, and Steve Horn of California signed onto the Democratic discharge petition and actively supported campaign finance reform within their party's conference and on the House floor. Of course, all the Republicans who voted for reform were certainly not moderates, but it was the GOP moderates who produced the numbers to make a difference.

Some conservative Republicans also lent their support to the reform effort. Shays himself is considered a conservative on many issues, as is McCain. Perhaps the most effective conservative Republican advocate of campaign finance reform in the House was Rep. Zach Wamp of Tennessee, who helped recruit other conservatives to the reform effort. Wamp and other conservatives sat at the table with some of the most liberal members of the House, such as Barney Frank, D-Mass., and worked together to pass the Shays-Meehan bill. One of the most articulate GOP advocates of reform was Tom Campbell of California. Campbell is considered a conservative on economic issues and more liberal on many social issues. Campbell was a fixture on the House floor during the debates and made some of the most well-reasoned and eloquent arguments in favor of the Shays-Meehan bill.

These moderate and conservative Republicans defied their party's leaders to form a crosspartisan majority coalition with the Democrats to pass campaign finance reform legislation in the House. Such diverse crosspartisan coalitions are rather rare in the heightened partisan climate that characterizes the contemporary Congress. Yet campaign finance reform presents an example that may work for other issues that face similar challenges such as opposition from the majority party leaders. The ability to form such coalitions may even help overcome some of the possible gridlocks that result from the increased use of unorthodox policy procedures.

From Iron Triangles to Issue Networks

In the past, the "iron triangle" model often was used to explain congressional policymaking. The iron triangle model suggests that policies are crafted by a small group of legislators who specialize in a certain policy area, related bureaucratic agencies, and some of the interest groups that have a vested interest in the legislation (usually representing only one side of the issue). The policies that came out of these iron triangles tended to benefit the participants at the expense of nonparticipants and the public at large. A classic example is policymaking involving atomic energy in the 1950s, whereby a single congressional committee and the representatives from the atomic energy industry and the Atomic Energy Commission developed policies that promoted the new industry at the expense of safety concerns.

The campaign finance reform process, however, demonstrates that these old iron triangles have been replaced by more free-flowing issue networks.[18] To at least some degree, iron triangles have expanded into issue networks that open up the process to more participants and to more views on an issue. These participants permeate the halls of Congress more than ever before as a variety of interest groups and the media take policymaking out of the back rooms and into a more public forum. For instance, interest group lobbyists openly work with staff to develop proposals and alternatives. The media now attempt to observe all stages of the legislative process and are particularly interested in policy battles that pit traditional allies against one another, such as the campaign finance reform debate in which Shays challenged his own party leaders—a David and Goliath story ready-made for the front pages.

Moreover, in today's media-savvy political world, political actors often have great incentives to use the media as a tool to influence the policy process. More people using the media to gain political leverage means that more of the policymaking process is subject to the media's scrutiny. Thus, controversies that in the past would have been worked out behind closed doors are now public events, making private bargains and deals, as well as strong-arm tactics, more difficult to accomplish.

When an effective policy entrepreneur inside of Congress can build a strong issue network of interest group support and positive media attention outside of Congress, the policy debate becomes a much more public deliberation, which may greatly enhance the chances of legislative success. As we saw in Chapters 4 and 6, the external issue network developed and maintained by Representatives Shays and Meehan contributed to passage of the Shays-Meehan bill in the House. This issue network that was developed during the 105th Congress was ready to take up campaign finance reform again in the 106th. The reformers did not have to start from scratch to build external support for their proposals. This established issue network also easily crossed chambers to provide assistance to the Senate effort and valuable institutional memory for new network members as well as policymakers inside of Congress. Often, issues will continue on the agenda from Congress to Congress.[19] It is vital, therefore, that issue networks also survive to carry on from one Congress to the next. Otherwise, the issue may drop off the congressional agenda for lack of sufficient external support and pressure. Policy entrepreneurs must work hard to ensure that their coalition of supporters, both inside and outside of Congress, remains intact. There have been several congressional efforts to reform the campaign finance system since the last major reforms were enacted in the 1970s. Each year's proposals have built on the earlier ones, and although the issue leaders may have changed over time, the external issue network of many of the good-government groups, especially Common Cause, has been a constant.

The Triumph of Unorthodox Lawmaking

One of the most potent lessons to learn from this examination of a policy debate over a single issue is the extent to which legislators use unorthodox methods to achieve their policy goals in the modern Congress. For example, against a slim GOP majority in the House, reformers tried discharge petitions and sought assistance from outside participants to push for campaign finance reform. House Republican leaders worked to bury the issue by stalling, trying to pass other so-called reform bills, attempting to amend the Shays-Meehan bill to death with multiple poison pill amendments, and requiring the bill to survive a complex and difficult Queen-of-the-Hill rule, whereby it had to compete with other popular reform bills. In the Senate, GOP leaders used the filibuster and other unorthodox procedures repeatedly to defeat the issue.

We also saw a legislative process that generally bypasses the traditional committee system of consideration. One prominent reform measure emerged completely outside of the traditional structure from rather unexpected quarters. The Freshman bill was developed by the freshmen's own task force, the ultimate alternative to committee consideration, and it was sponsored by first-term legislators who normally do not propose major legislation. Thus, the freshmen challenged the conventional notions of seniority that have characterized the chamber since seniority rules were instituted in 1910.

The GOP leaders did use the committee system, but in nontraditional ways. For example, committees in both the House and the Senate led investigations of alleged campaign finance abuses committed by President Clinton, Vice President Gore, and the Democratic Party. These investigative committees did not propose or consider legislation to address the campaign finance abuses they highlighted. Instead, the investigations served only one real purpose—to focus negative attention on the Democrats. House Republican leaders also used the committee system to rubber-stamp their handpicked legislation so that their bills would proceed to the floor to compete with the reformers' measures (see, for example, the discussion of the Thomas bill in Chapter 3).

When examined as a whole, the unorthodox methods used in the campaign finance reform debates help us better understand the impact of such unconventional lawmaking procedures. First, as we noted above, the use of unorthodox methods tends to make policymaking more difficult in the Senate but easier in the House. This case of campaign finance reform, therefore, confirms Sinclair's findings that both houses of Congress are using more diverse and unorthodox methods of lawmaking.[20] If this trend continues, the consequences could be quite negative. For example, as senators become more willing to use obstructive unorthodox methods, especially the filibuster, policymaking in Congress may become more incremental and may result in deadlock more often. Consequently, Congress will have a more difficult time addressing pressing policy problems, and the public will have more reason to become frustrated with the institution and its members. This situation, of course, will be exacerbated if there is divided government, whereby the parties are forced to work with each other to achieve any policy goals at all. We may already be seeing evidence of Congress's inability to deal with important policy issues. For example, legislators have recently disagreed about if and how issues concerning Social Security and Medicare, health care, and taxes should be addressed.

Since unorthodox methods are available to virtually any legislator, the traditional breeding grounds for leaders in Congress—the committees and the party leadership structure—are no longer the only places from which an ambitious lawmaker might emerge as a leader. Issue leaders can emerge from outside of the committee and party structures and generally do not need to rely on those institutions within Congress if they have enough support in the chamber for their policy proposals. Instead, issue leaders can become effective policy entrepreneurs by using the tools of unorthodox policymaking. For example, the discharge petition helped raise the profile not only of the issue of campaign finance reform but also of the reformers themselves.

Finally, unorthodox policy procedures may, at the same time, give those who already have quite a lot of power even more power. For instance, the Speaker of the House already controls many aspects of the legislative process. Add to that arsenal the ability to use a variety of unorthodox methods and the Speaker's power is limited only by imagination or, of course, by a majority of House members. The Speaker and the other GOP leaders were eventually defeated by the reformers. Yet many reformers were convinced that the GOP leaders' ability to stall the process significantly so that the Shays-Meehan bill did not pass the House until late in the second session of the 105th Congress and well into the 106th Congress contributed to defeat of the bill in the Senate. Thus, the effects of unconventional processes may transcend one chamber when they are used to affect deliberations in the other chamber.

We are convinced that unorthodox procedures are here to stay and we predict that legislators will continue to create new ways to bypass the traditional system of lawmaking. Unorthodox procedures allow legislators to get things done but also raise grave questions about what some of these shortcut tactics might be doing to the traditional structures of the institutions. In other words, do these unorthodox procedures place the institution's maintenance and long-term survival in jeopardy? For example, as committee chairpersons lose more control over the lawmaking process to these unconventional methods practiced by party leaders and other legislators outside of their committees, they are likely to come up with their own unorthodox methods for reasserting their control over legislation under their jurisdiction. Indeed, one of the complaints about Speaker Newt Gingrich articulated by the conservative Republicans who tried to depose him was that he had bypassed the traditional committee system for consideration of legislation. These GOP agitators tried to use the extremely unorthodox technique of toppling their leader in a coup, a strategy that had not been seen since the ouster of Speaker Joe Cannon in 1910. Although unsuccessful, the attempted coup against Gingrich did result in some changes, one of which was the return of some power to committee chairs and a decrease in the use of task forces for policy development.

Campaign Finance Reform Policy

Campaign finance reform politics itself has undergone a transformation. Its meaning and what it entails are dictated by the prevailing political context at the time. For example, earlier attempts at reform, as well as the early days of reform in the 105th Congress, focused on the undue influence of PACs on the political process. Reform proposals included public financing, free airtime for candidates' campaign advertisements, and limits on bundling. But shortly into Congress's consideration of reform in 1997, the debate turned to soft money and campaign-like issue advocacy advertisements, so that only the undertones of the previous debate remained. For now, reformers have chosen to define the reform debate as one about these two issues, which, not surprisingly, are the issues that received the most press as the most egregious violations of the spirit of fair campaigns during the 1996 elections. We may see even more unacceptable campaign finance practices in future elections that will make soft money and issue ads look like minor loopholes in the law, and future reform efforts will probably shift to these new practices. Future reformers are well advised, therefore, to expect campaign finance reform to be an ongoing policy problem as candidates, parties, interest groups, labor unions, corporations, and wealthy individual contributors are likely to find new ways to get around the law as well as any new laws that may be enacted (such as the new disclosure requirements for stealth 527 groups, discussed in Chapter 7). Moreover, the face of opposition to campaign finance reform may change. If, for example, new questionable campaign finance practices greatly benefit the Democratic Party and its candidates and are detrimental to their GOP opponents, then Democrats in Congress may be reluctant to curb or ban these new practices.[21]

The judicial branch first became a key player in the campaign finance policy area with the Supreme Court's *Buckley* decision in 1976, and it continues to be an important participant in the ongoing debate over campaign finance reform. If comprehensive reform legislation continues to fail in Congress, then the courts will become more important arbiters of campaign finance regulations as more cases go to court. An important case, *Republican National Committee v. Federal Election Commission,* which is now pending before the federal district court in the District of Columbia, could have a great effect on current campaign finance reform debates.[22] The plaintiffs in the case are challenging soft money regulations and seeking a ruling that would substantially limit the ability to restrict soft money as called for in the McCain-Feingold and Shays-Meehan bills.

As the courts rule on more aspects of campaign finance, their interpretations of the law and the Constitution will prevail, and Congress will have less to decide if it ever amends the Federal Election Campaign Act. This means that political responsibility for the financial conduct of American campaigns increasingly may belong to the undemocratic judicial system, whereby judges who are not elected, and, therefore, cannot be held accountable by the public, make the decisions that shape the regulation of campaign finance activities. For some in Congress this is a convenient reality, for the court system can be an easy scapegoat for what is wrong with the campaign finance system or why reforms proposed in Congress should not be enacted (that is, because such reforms would be struck down as unconstitutional by the courts anyway). However, the courts will continue to play a major role in campaign finance policymaking whether Congress passes new reform laws or not, for any new laws are bound to be challenged, particularly by those who think the statutes put them at an unfair disadvantage.

Campaign finance reform policy also will continue to be affected by the federal bureaucracy responsible for implementing the Federal Election Campaign Act, the Federal Election Commission (FEC). The FEC's regulations are supposed to carry the weight of the law, but its rulings often create more controversy than the infractions that triggered them. For example, the FEC's own rules often are blamed for creating today's soft money problem. Moreover, the structure of the agency and its level of funding make it difficult for the FEC to pursue aggressively those who break the law. Consequently, some contend that the rules are often broken, because those who raise and spend money for campaigns know that there is very little chance that they will be punished for relatively minor, and sometimes not so minor, infractions. The FEC is also a point of contention between the two parties on Capitol Hill, where the agency is often derided by Republicans and defended by Democrats. Many recent reform bills have featured provisions to provide more funding to the FEC and to alter its leadership structure to make it less partisan, and any future reforms are bound to affect how the agency does its job.[23]

The Future of Campaign Finance Reform

Campaign finance reform is fundamentally a process that aims to alter who will have power in our electoral and thus, eventually, governing systems. Those in favor of the reforms proposed in the McCain-Feingold and Shays-Meehan bills would argue that the wrong people have too much power. Therefore, soft money should be banned to take power away from corporations, labor unions, and wealthy individuals. Issue advocacy communications should be restricted if they mention candidates for federal office because groups that sponsor these communications are influencing elections without having to play by the rules. As long as there are areas of perceived imbalances of power, there are likely to be calls for some form of campaign finance reform.

The issue of soft money continues to receive attention, and new methods of using soft money concern legislators. During the 106th Congress, Representatives Shays and Meehan expressed their concern about the potential abuse of soft money presented by congressional leadership PACs. Additionally, a federal district court judge in Colorado struck down a federal law that limits the amount that political parties may spend on candidates.[24] Some observers believe that this ruling could open the door for federal parties to funnel unregulated soft money through state parties to promote federal candidates.[25] Furthermore, the fund-raising practices of those who sought the presidential nominations, particularly Senator McCain, demonstrate that the Internet can be a powerful fund-raising tool and a potential area of further exploitation and, as a consequence, additional regulation.[26]

Despite the potential growth in the use of soft money that these examples suggest, however, soft money has been curbed in other ways. For instance, on November 18, 1999, Time Warner, Inc., announced that it would "no longer make unregulated donations to political parties," saying such soft money contributions "distort the electoral process and sully the givers."[27] Whether other large corporate contributors will follow suit remains to be seen.

Issue advocacy advertisements also will continue to attract criticism when they skirt too close to being outright campaign ads. Perhaps as more and more congressional candidates are subjected to the attacks of outside groups that are virtually impossible to identify and that are not required to disclose their spending, more and more senators and House members will be motivated to reexamine the law that allows such attacks without any funding limits or public disclosure. Indeed, as more candidates were targeted in advertisements run by 527 groups, such as the Republicans for Clean Air ads run against John McCain during his presidential campaign, momentum grew for requiring these stealth groups to disclose their fund-raising and spending activities. There is nothing to suggest that the questionable use of these unregulated issue ads will not continue to increase. Thus, the number of "victims" of issue ads is likely to increase, potentially broadening the support for more comprehensive reform in Congress.

The proreform leaders in Congress, Shays and Meehan in the House and McCain and Feingold in the Senate, are not likely to back down soon from their efforts to change the nation's campaign finance system, and others will promote reform as well. For example, Sen. Chuck Hagel, R-Neb., introduced his "Open and Accountable Campaign Financing Act of 2000" on October 28, 1999, less than two weeks after the Senate defeated the McCain-Feingold bill and Majority Leader Lott declared the issue dead for the year. Hagel's bill has since been killed in committee, after the passage of the stealth 527 legislation, but his and others' efforts indicate the continued search to find the right vehicle for more comprehensive campaign finance reform. Campaign finance reform is an issue that may well continue on until a critical supermajority in the Senate finds a way to pass comprehensive reform. Although prospects for this seem dim, many hold out hope that the political landscape will be shaken up enough by future elections to enact reform.

Perhaps a scandal or a dramatic shift in public opinion in which citizens demand reform will finally bring about the momentum necessary to overcome the obstacles to reform, especially the supermajority needed to end the inevitable filibuster of reform in the Senate. The campaign finance scandals of 1996 apparently were not enough to build that supermajority. And even though 83 percent of Americans think that it is at least somewhat important for Congress to address campaign finance reform, not enough senators were moved to do so (see *Washington Post*/ABC News poll discussed in Chapter 7).[28] Conceivably, a presidential candidate will push this issue as an agenda item of importance, much as Republican senator John McCain and former Democratic senator Bill Bradley tried to do in the 2000 presidential election. Their focus on the issue prompted the two major party nominees, Al Gore and George W. Bush, to announce their own plans for campaign finance reform.[29] Or, perhaps campaign finance reform advocates must wait until a time when (and if) the Democrats control both Congress and the presidency, and hope that they pass reform while they are in the majority. Yet reform was not enacted when the Democrats were in charge during the 103d Congress (1993–1995). Since both the Democrats and the Republicans will be ever watchful for the potential partisan consequences of particular reform proposals, the issue will continue to be politically charged and hard fought. Given the many impediments to passage of *comprehensive* campaign finance reform, incremental changes are more likely to gain enough support to pass Congress.

These what-ifs can make political science a daunting task, for a scholar's ability to predict may be only as good as the current political context allows. We do know that there is a core group of committed legislators, interest groups, and citizens who will continue to push for reform. What we cannot guess, however, is when or whether a political climate ripe for change will arrive to allow these reform advocates to take advantage of a policy window of opportunity and successfully navigate the legislative labyrinth to enact changes to the campaign finance system.

NOTES

Chapter 1 (pages 1–34)

1. See especially Barbara Sinclair, *Unorthodox Lawmaking: New Legislative Processes in the U.S. Congress* (Washington, D.C.: CQ Press, 1997).
2. The "dance of legislation" refers to Eric Redman's classic book about a bill's journey through the U.S. Senate in 1969–1970: Eric Redman, *The Dance of Legislation* (New York: Simon and Schuster, 1973). The phrase is from Woodrow Wilson's *Congressional Government* (1885), quoted at the beginning of this chapter.
3. See Karen Foerstel, "From Teddy Roosevelt On: A Century of Changes." *CQ Weekly*, May 13, 2000, 1090.
4. When making independent expenditures, there can be no coordination or consultation with the candidate, and these expenditures must be paid for with funds raised in accordance with the FECA and reported to the Federal Election Commission.
5. For a thorough history of federal campaign finance laws, see Anthony Corrado, "Money and Politics: A History of Campaign Finance Law," in *Campaign Finance Reform: A Sourcebook,* eds. Anthony Corrado et al. (Washington, D.C.: Brookings Institution Press, 1997).
6. *Buckley v. Valeo,* 424 U.S. 1 (1976).
7. A helpful discussion of *Buckley v. Valeo* and relevant sections of the Court's ruling can be found in Daniel R. Ortiz, "The First Amendment at Work: Constitutional Restrictions on Campaign Finance Regulation," in *Campaign Finance Reform: A Sourcebook,* eds. Anthony Corrado et al. (Washington, D.C.: Brookings Institution Press, 1997).
8. See Corrado, "Money and Politics," 33–34.
9. See the Federal Election Commission's Advisory Opinion 1976-72, which allowed the use of nonfederal money (that is, soft money) to pay for a portion of a party's general overhead and administrative costs. The Federal Election Commission's Advisory Opinion 1978-10 allowed parties to use soft money to finance a portion of party-building activities such as voter registration and get-out-the-vote drives.

10. For a thorough discussion of soft money, see Anthony Corrado, "Party Soft Money," in *Campaign Finance Reform: A Sourcebook,* eds. Anthony Corrado et al. (Washington, D.C.: Brookings Institution Press, 1997).

11. Corrado, "Money and Politics," 33.

12. Federal Election Commission, "FEC Issues Semi-Annual Federal PAC Count," news release, July 20, 1999.

13. Federal Election Commission, "FEC Releases Information on PAC Activity for 1997–98," news release, June 8, 1999.

14. Staff allowances are approximately $500,000 a year for House members and larger budgets based on the population size of the state for senators. Information provided by the Clerk of the House, 1999.

15. See Diana Evans Yiannakis, "House Members' Communication Styles," *Journal of Politics* 44 (November 1982): 109–1073.

16. Informally, the frank is defined as a "member's legal right to send official mail postage free under his or her signature; . . . [t]echnically, it is the autographic or facsimile signature used on envelopes instead of stamps that permit members and certain congressional officers to send their official mail free of charge. The franking privilege has been authorized by law since the first Congress, except for a few months in 1873. Congress reimburses the U.S. Postal Service for the franked mail it handles." Walter Kravitz, *American Congressional Dictionary* (Washington, D.C.: Congressional Quarterly 1993), 115.

17. William Connelly and John Pitney, *Congress' Permanent Minority? Republicans in the U.S. House* (Lanham, Md.: Rowman and Littlefield, 1994). Of course, the 1994 elections, in which the Republicans took control of the House of Representatives for the first time in forty years, challenged these explanations.

18. Some PACs, called ideological PACs, do distribute their contributions according to candidates' positions on the issues. For example, the National Abortion Rights Action League would not give a contribution to a candidate who was not pro-choice, just as the National Rifle Association would not contribute to a candidate who favored strict gun control measures. Other PACs tend to favor one of the parties. For instance, labor unions give almost exclusively to Democratic candidates. Yet, although business PACs tend to favor Republicans, they did support Democratic candidates when the Democrats controlled Congress, evidence of the access strategy pursued by most PACs.

19. See, for example, John R. Wright. *Interest Groups and Congress: Lobbying, Contributions, and Influence* (Boston: Allyn and Bacon, 1996), 137–157.

20. See Frank J. Sorauf, *Inside Campaign Finance* (New Haven: Yale University Press, 1992), 197–203.

21. Philip M. Stern. *The Best Congress Money Can Buy* (New York: Pantheon, 1988); Dan Clawson, Alan Neustadt, and Denise Scott, *Money Talks: Corporate PACs and Political Influence* (New York: Basic Books, 1992); Brooks Jackson, *Honest Graft: Big Money and the American Political Process* (New York: Knopf, 1988); Sara Fritz and Dwight Morris, *Gold Plated Politics: Running for Congress*

in the 1990s (Washington, D.C.: Congressional Quarterly, 1992); David B. Magleby and Candice J. Nelson, *The Money Chase: Congressional Campaign Finance Reform* (Washington, D.C.: Brookings Institution, 1990); Greg D. Kubiak, *Gilded Dome: The U.S. Senate and Campaign Finance Reform* (Norman: University of Oklahoma Press, 1994).

22. Donna Cassata, "Bipartisan Overhaul Measure Meets an Unsurprising End," *Congressional Quarterly Weekly Report,* June 29, 1996, 1858.

23. Bundling involves an intermediate agent, usually a PAC or interest group, whereby the PAC, for example, collects checks that are made payable to a specific candidate and delivers those checks to the candidate. Both the individuals who write the checks and the PAC or interest group that collects and bundles them get credit for the donations. See the discussion of bundling later in this chapter.

24. The cloture, or debate-ending, rule in the Senate permits three-fifths of the Senate (sixty senators) to end a filibuster (that is, to end debate on an issue). Once cloture is invoked, thirty hours of additional debate time is provided before a final vote. The use of filibusters and cloture in the Senate has increased significantly. We discuss this trend and its relevance to campaign finance reform in Chapter 8.

25. Kim Mattingly, "Campaign Task Force Can't Reach a Deal," *Roll Call,* September 11–17, 1989.

26. See Frank J. Sorauf, *Inside Campaign Finance: Myths and Realities* (New Haven: Yale University Press, 1992), 195.

27. For an insightful discussion of the 1991 campaign finance reform effort, see ibid., 192–203.

28. "GOP" stands for "Grand Old Party," a name used for the Republican Party.

29. Sorauf, *Inside Campaign Finance,* 243.

30. Ruth Marcus, "Clinton Faces Floodgate of Probes; Campaign Fund-Raising Inquiry Looms; DNC Returns Questioned $325,000 Contribution," *Washington Post,* November 7, 1996, A28; Leslie Wayne, "Politics: Campaign Finance; Loopholes Allow Presidential Race to Set a Record," *New York Times,* September 8, 1996, A1; Elizabeth Shogren, "Dole Blasts Clinton Silence on Funds; Campaign: GOP Candidate Says President's Failure to Address Democrats' Acceptance of Illegal Donations Is an Admission of Wrongdoing," *Los Angeles Times,* October 20, 1996, 20.

31. Corrado, "Party Soft Money," 167.

32. Jonathan D. Salant, "Presidential Race Resuscitates Campaign Finance Debate," *Congressional Quarterly Weekly Report,* November 9, 1996, 3196.

33. For a comprehensive look at the allegations, particularly those against the Democrats, see the final report of the Committee on Governmental Affairs of the United States Senate, *Investigation of Illegal or Improper Activities in Connection with 1996 Federal Election Campaigns,* vols. 1–6 (Washington, D.C.: U.S. Government Printing Office, 1998).

34. Salant, "Presidential Race Resuscitates Campaign Finance Debate," 3195.
35. Leslie Wayne, "Campaign Finance: Common Cause Accuses Parties of 'Massive' Violations," *New York Times*, October 10, 1996, B12.
36. The term *twin evils* was used by various congressional reformers throughout the effort to pass campaign finance reform during the 105th Congress.
37. Elizabeth Drew, *Politics and Money: The New Road to Corruption* (New York: Macmillan, 1983).
38. For a thorough discussion of soft money, see Corrado, "Party Soft Money."
39. Ibid., 172.
40. Federal Election Commission, "FEC Reports Major Increase in Party Activity for 1995–1996," news release, March 19, 1997, 9. The first year for which data on soft money receipts and disbursements are available is 1992. Prior to 1992, the parties were not required to report soft money activity.
41. For an informative review of issue advocacy, see Trevor Potter, "Issue Advocacy and Express Advocacy," in *Campaign Finance Reform: A Sourcebook*, ed. Anthony Corrado et al. (Washington, D.C.: Brookings Institution Press, 1997).
42. *Buckley v. Valeo*, n. 52.
43. Anthony Corrado, "Financing the 1996 Elections," in *The Election of 1996: Reports and Interpretations*, ed. Gerald Pomper (Chatham, N.J.: Chatham House, 1996), 147.
44. Deborah Beck, Paul Taylor, Jeffrey Stanger, and Douglas Rivlin, "Issue Advocacy Advertising during the 1996 Campaign" (Philadelphia: Annenberg Public Policy Center, 1997), 32.
45. Ibid., 54.
46. Ibid., 10.
47. Potter, "Issue Advocacy and Express Advocacy," 227.
48. See the relevant law at 11 C.F.R. 109.1(a).
49. *Colorado Republican Federal Campaign Committee v. Federal Election Commission*, 116 S.Ct. 2309 (1996).
50. Norman J. Ornstein, Thomas E. Mann, and Michael J. Malbin, *Vital Statistics on Congress, 1999–2000* (Washington, D.C.: AEI Press, 2000), 111.
51. Each bill was named for its primary sponsor from each party: Sens. John McCain and Russ Feingold and Reps. Christopher Shays and Marty Meehan. Representatives Shays and Meehan originally introduced their bill in the 105th Congress as H.R. 493. Later, they split the bill into two: H.R. 1776 and H.R. 1777. In their primary push in 1998, Shays and Meehan introduced a pared-down version of their reform bill as H.R. 3526. The Shays-Meehan bill eventually passed as a substitute to another bill, H.R. 2183.
52. Sinclair, *Unorthodox Lawmaking*.
53. Ibid., 72.
54. Ibid., 50.
55. David R. Mayhew, *Congress: The Electoral Connection* (New Haven: Yale University Press, 1974).

56. See, for example, Edward V. Schneier and Bertram Gross, *Congress Today* (New York: St. Martins Press, 1993).

57. See, for example, John W. Kingdon, *Congressmen's Voting Decisions,* 3d ed. (Ann Arbor: University of Michigan Press, 1989); and Sinclair, *Unorthodox Lawmaking.*

Chapter 2 (pages 35–61)

1. Alison Mitchell, "Bill Lacks 9 Votes: Supporters Vow to Keep Issue Alive and to Use It in Next Elections," *New York Times,* February 27, 1998, A22.

2. Amy Keller and Ed Henry, "Will the Campaign Finance Reformers Finally Prevail in '98?" *Roll Call,* January 26, 1998, A36.

3. Rep. John Lewis, D-Ga., who was a leading civil rights activist and worked closely with Dr. Martin Luther King, also enjoys this special kind of respect from his colleagues and others.

4. The term *pork barrel* generally refers to special projects or other benefits that elected officials bring back to their districts and states. They are said to "bring home the bacon."

5. *CQ's Politics in America, 2000: The 106th Congress,* ed. Philip D. Duncan and Brian Nutting (Washington, D.C.: Congressional Quarterly, 1999), 41.

6. A full chronicle of the allegations against Republicans can be found in the final report of the Senate Committee on Governmental Affairs, *Investigation of Illegal or Improper Activities in Connection with 1996 Federal Election Campaigns,* Report 105–67 (Washington, D.C.: U.S. Government Printing Office, 1998); see the section entitled "Minority Views."

7. An earlier version of the McCain-Feingold bill was introduced in 1995 and was defeated with a filibuster in 1996.

8. Paul Farhi, "GOP Hill Leaders Oppose FCC on Free Air Time," *Washington Post,* March 7, 1998, A8. For examples of the positive press, see "The Cleansing Power of Free TV," *New York Times,* editorial, March 11, 1998, A30, and David Broder, "The Broadcasters and Their Friends on the Hill," *Washington Post,* March 10, 1998, A17.

9. *Communications Workers of America v. Beck,* 487 U.S. 735 (1988).

10. Senator John McCain and Senator Russell Feingold, "McCain, Feingold Introduce Modifications to Campaign Finance Reform Bill," press release, September 29, 1997.

11. Amy Keller, "Without House, Senate Reform Deal Doesn't Matter," *Roll Call,* September 25, 1997, 14.

12. Amy Keller and Ed Henry, "Senate Goes Another Reform Round Today," *Roll Call,* October 9, 1997, 1.

13. See Charles Tiefer, *Congressional Practice and Procedure: A Reference, Research, and Legislative Guide* (New York: Greenwood Press, 1989), 671-679. For examples of drawings of the amendment tree structure, see Floyd Millard Riddick, *Riddick's Senate Procedure: Precedents and Practices* (Washington, D.C.: U.S. Government Printing Office, 1992), 74, 75, 84, 89.

14. The number of first- and second-degree amendments for any given bill is dictated by the rules established for consideration.
15. See Tiefer, *Congressional Practice and Procedure,* 676–679.
16. Ibid., 679.
17. Keller, "Parliamentary Moves Thwart Reform, Burton 'Filling the Tree' Blocks McCain Bill," *Roll Call,* February 26, 1998, 1. According to Sen. Byron Dorgan, D-N.D., "[t]his is a rarely used approach. It is true that this approach has been used by the Majority Leader a couple of times last year, but in history, it has been rarely used in the Senate. And the reason is, it is almost exclusively used to block legislation."
18. "Nickles Vows to Fight Limits on Corporate Political Action," *National Journal's Congress Daily,* January 5, 1998, 2.
19. Keller and Henry, "Senate Goes Another Reform Round Today," 1.
20. Ibid.
21. Keller, "Will the Campaign Finance Reformers Finally Prevail in '98?" *Roll Call,* January 26, 1998, A37.
22. "Nickles Vows to Fight Limits on Corporate Political Action," 2.
23. See Tiefer, *Congressional Practice and Procedure,* 573–583.
24. Keller, "Senator Snowe Works to Save Campaign Finance Reform on Eve of Senate Vote," *Roll Call,* February 19, 1998, 3.
25. "Hill Briefs." *National Journal's Congress Daily/A.M.,* February 6, 1998, 5.
26. "Excerpts from Draft of Senate Report on Improper Fund-Raising," *New York Times,* February 8, 1998, sec. 1, p. 20. See also the full report: Senate Committee on Governmental Affairs, "Investigation of Illegal or Improper Activities in Connection with the 1996 Election Campaigns," Report 105–167 (Washington, D.C.: U.S. Government Printing Office, 1998).
27. "Hill Briefs," *National Journal's Congress Daily/A.M.,* February 10, 1998, 7.
28. Alison Mitchell, "Bill Lacks 9 Votes: Supporters Vow to Keep Issue Alive and to Use It in Next Elections," *New York Times,* February 27, 1998, A1.
29. For a useful reference addressing *Buckley* and the other cases discussed here, see Corrado et al., *Campaign Finance Reform.*
30. In footnote 52 of the *Buckley v. Valeo* decision, the court listed some terms of express advocacy (the "magic words"): "vote for," "elect," "support," "cast your ballot for," "Smith for Congress," "vote against," "defeat," and "reject."
31. Ruth Marcus, "When the Opposition Isn't on the Ballot; Candidates Expect Another Fall of 'Issue Advocacy' Spots; Outside Groups Anxious Too," *Washington Post,* June 30, 1998, A4.
32. *Federal Election Commission v. Massachusetts Citizens for Life, Inc.,* 479 U.S. 238 (1986). 2 U.S.C. § 441b(a) prohibits corporations from making expenditures in connection with any federal election.
33. *Colorado Republican Federal Campaign Committee v. Federal Election Commission,* 518 U.S. 604 (1996).
34. *Federal Election Commission v. Furgatch,* 807 F.2d 857 (1987), *cert. denied,* 484 U.S. 850 (1987).

35. *Furgatch*, 807 F.2d 864.

36. *Maine Right to Life Committee, Inc. v. Federal Election Commission*, 914 F.Supp 8 (D. Me. 1996), affirmed 98 F.3d 1 (1st Cir. 1996).

37. *Faucher v. Federal Election Commission*, 928 F.2d 468 (1st Cir. 1991), *cert. denied*, 502 U.S. 820 (1991).

38. Ibid., 472.

39. *Federal Election Commission v. Christian Action Network*, 110 F.3d 1049, 1064 (4th Cir. 1997).

40. Ibid., 1064.

41. The word *codify* is used here because it is the term used by the reformers when discussing their approach to *Beck*. Namely, they sought to take the *judicial* decision and make it part of a *legislative* reform package. In formal, legalistic jargon, however, a codifying statute is "a law that purports to be exhaustive in restating the whole of the law on a particular topic, including prior case law as well as legislative provisions" (*Black's Law Dictionary*, 7th ed.). Thus, the reform bills technically did not "codify" the *Beck* decision.

42. Note that unions may, and do, raise money separately through political action committees for political activities.

43. 144 *Congressional Record*, 981 (1998).

44. Ibid., 869.

45. Ibid., 997.

46. Ibid., 972.

47. Ibid., 998.

48. Ibid., 985, citing *U.S. v. Harriss*, 347 U.S. 612 (1954).

49. Ibid., 974.

50. Ibid., 805. (emphasis added).

51. Ibid., 988.

52. Ibid., 982.

53. Ibid., 869–870, 997.

54. Ibid.

55. Ibid., 869.

56. Ibid., 1046.

57. Peter H. Stone, "Uphill Struggle for Campaign Reformers," *National Journal*, August 22, 1998, 1983.

58. Barbara Sinclair, *Unorthodox Lawmaking: New Legislative Processes in the U.S. Congress* (Washington, D.C.: CQ Press, 1997), 50.

Chapter 3 (pages 63–113)

1. E. J. Dionne Jr., "Guinea Pigs in California," *Washington Post*, January 20, 1998, A15.

2. Ibid.

3. Alan Greenblatt, "California House Race Shapes Up As a Duel of Interest Groups," *Congressional Quarterly Weekly Report*, January 17, 1998, 137.

4. 144 *Congressional Record,* 5833–5836 (1998).

5. Roger H. Davidson and Walter J. Oleszek, *Congress and Its Members,* 6th ed. (Washington, D.C.: CQ Press, 1998), 235.

6. Ibid.; see also Barbara Sinclair, *Unorthodox Lawmaking: New Legislative Processes in the U.S. Congress* (Washington, D.C.: CQ Press, 1997), 87.

7. Davidson and Oleszek, *Congress and Its Members,* 235.

8. House Resolution 259 provided for consideration of the Blue Dog bill, with several amendments that could be offered as a substitute. The rule provided for one hour of debate on the base bill (the Blue Dog bill) and then one hour on each of seven amendments. Those who would be able to offer amendments under this rule were Reps. Scotty Baesler, R-Ky.; Sam Farr, D-Calif.; John T. Doolittle, R-Calif.; Richard A. Gephardt, D-Mo.; Dick Armey, R-Tex.; Asa Hutchinson, R-Ark., and anyone who offered the text of a bill passed by the Senate. The amended rule later introduced by Baesler added Shays and Rick White, R-Wash. A letter to Shays from Baesler and John Tanner, D-Tenn., stated they would ask for unanimous consent to replace the original rule with this substitute. In addition, Baesler agreed that he would offer the Shays-Meehan bill if the discharge petition were enacted.

    The rule called for any substitute bill that passed to become the base text, and if more than one passed, the one with the highest number of votes would become the base text. There would then be ten additional hours of open debate, during which time any member would be able to offer any germane amendment to the base bill. Staff to Representative Shays, memorandum, April 7, 1998.

9. Press release issued by House Speaker Newt Gingrich's office following the November 13, 1997, press conference.

10. As cited in Joseph E. Cantor, *CRS Issue Brief—Campaign Financing,* report no. IB87020, updated October 16, 1998, i.

11. The amount that parties can spend on behalf of House and Senate candidates, known as coordinated expenditures, is increased each election cycle by a cost-of-living adjustment. For the 2000 elections, the limit for House candidates was $33,780, except in states with only one congressional district, where the limit was $67,560. Federal Election Commission, "FEC Announces 2000 Party Spending Limits," news release, March 1, 2000, online at http://www.fec. gov/press/441ad2000.htm. The Freshman bill would have removed the limit altogether.

12. Joseph E. Cantor, "Campaign Finance Bills in the 105th Congress: Comparison of H.R. 2183 (Hutchinson-Allen), H.R. 3526 (Shays-Meehan), and Current Law," *CRS Report for Congress* (Washington, D.C.: Congressional Research Service, 1998), 2.

13. Cantor, "Campaign Finance Bills in the 105th Congress," 2.

14. "Campaign Finance to Be Centerpiece of GOP Reform Week," *National Journal's Congress Daily,* May 7, 1996; U.S. House Democratic Policy Committee,

"The Republican Leadership Record on Campaign Finance Reform: Promises Made, Promises Broken," July 17, 1998, 2.

15. House Republican Conference, *Legislative Digest,* February 27, 1998, 12.
16. Sen. Fred Thompson to Honorable Dan Burton, March 9, 1998.
17. Ibid.
18. The Democratic Caucus is the organization of all Democrats in the House.
19. For an example of opinion poll data regarding campaign finance reform, see Chapter 7.
20. Steven A. Holmes, "House G.O.P. Shifts on Campaign Bills," *New York Times,* March 28, 1998, A8.
21. "The Ebb and Flow of Reform: Mr. Gingrich Retreats," *New York Times,* editorial, March 27, 1998, A18.
22. Indeed, about 50 percent of the bills passed by the House are considered under suspension of the rules today, whereas only about 8 percent were passed from the suspension calendar in the 1970s. See Davidson and Oleszek, *Congress and Its Members,* 229.
23. 144 *Congressional Record,* 1684 (1998).
24. Melinda Henneberger, "Republican Lawmaker Is Caught in the Middle," *New York Times,* March 31, 1998, A18.
25. "The Plot to Bury Reform," *New York Times,* editorial, March 30, 1998, A16.
26. David Lightman, "Shays Talks Back to GOP," *Hartford Courant,* March 28, 1998.
27. See Henneberger, "Republican Lawmaker Is Caught in the Middle." Common Cause and others pointed out that the Republican bill would not, after all, ban all soft money for federal elections, because it wouldn't touch the use of soft money for issue ads, one new way the parties have gotten around the limits.
28. "Hypocrisy on Campaign Funds," *Washington Post,* editorial, April 1, 1998, A18.
29. As quoted in a press release from the U.S. House Democratic Policy Committee, "The Republican Leadership Record on Campaign Finance Reform: Promises Made, Promises Broken," July 17, 1998, 5.
30. "A Joke," *Fort Worth Star-Telegram,* editorial, April 1, 1998, 12.
31. Meehan quoted in "Election Reform: A Sham Vote," *Virginian-Pilot,* editorial, April 1, 1998, B10.
32. Henneberger, "Novel Petition Drive May Save House Campaign Finance Bill," *New York Times,* March 31, 1998, A8.
33. See Lizette Alvarez, "Campaign Finance Backers Petition to Force House Vote," *New York Times,* April 18, 1998, A8.
34. Ironically, making discharge petitions public was pioneered in an earlier Congress by Newt Gingrich himself. See press release, "Leadership Statement on Campaign Finance Reform," April 22, 1998.
35. By "critical mass" we mean a number sufficient to make the Republican leadership fear that they would lose control of the House floor. As one GOP source close to the leadership noted in mid-April, "Once we get to 10 Republicans [signing the petition], there will be concern." Quoted in Lisa Caruso, "Moder-

ate Republicans Ponder Discharge Petition Route," *National Journal's Congress Daily,* April 16, 1998.

36. "The Backlash in the House," *New York Times,* editorial, April 1, 1998, A22.
37. Rep. Tom Campbell, R-Calif., played an important intermediary role between the Shays-Meehan reformers and the leadership to broker this deal. In addition, meetings with the other Republican discharge petition signers, led by Zach Wamp, pushed the leadership into contemplating such an agreement.
38. See "Leadership Statement on Campaign Finance Reform," April 22, 1998.
39. Jim VandeHei and Amy Keller, "DeLay Forms Team to Kill Reform Plans," *Roll Call,* May 14, 1998, 32.
40. Press release issued by Representative Shays, May 11, 1998.
41. Each letter, dated May 29, 1998, was personally addressed and on White House stationery.
42. Rep. Gerald Solomon, R-N.Y., House Rules Committee chair, met with Shays and promised to be fair. The GOP leadership had placed pressure on the committee to make reform difficult, and therefore the definition of fair meant "everyone" would be heard. This outcome played right into the hands of the Republican leadership, who, in consultation with reform opponents in the Senate, were advised to delay the process until after the August recess.
43. VandeHei and Keller, "DeLay Forms Team to Kill Reform Plans," 32.
44. The "motor-voter" law was passed in 1993 and required states to give citizens the opportunity to register to vote when they acquired or renewed their driver's license.
45. VandeHei and Keller, "DeLay Forms Team to Kill Reform Plans," 1. The Free Speech Coalition included DeLay and Reps. Anne M. Northup, R-Ky.; Bill Paxon, R-N.Y.; Edward Whitfield, R-Ky.; Roy Blunt, R-Mo.; Roger Wicker, R-Miss.; and John Doolittle, R-Calif.
46. A "Dear Colleague" letter is written by a member of Congress to his or her fellow members regarding a particular bill, policy, or position. This is a form of communication used by members of Congress to converse with one another. Some letters are sent to all members; others are targeted to specific delegations, parties, or members.
47. VandeHei and Keller, "DeLay Forms Team to Kill Reform Plans," 32.
48. The Democratic Congressional Campaign Committee, or DCCC, is the national political party organization that assists Democrats running for the House of Representatives. The Republican counterpart is the National Republican Congressional Committee (NRCC).
49. Peter H. Stone, "Hammering Campaign Reform," *National Journal,* June 13, 1998, 1366.
50. This included originally fifteen Democrats and twelve Republicans although the number grew as the process progressed. Briefing books are often used, but the extent of their use as well as their content was much more vast than the standard sort used in congressional debate.

51. See "Congressional Notebook: Why GOP Delays on Campaign Finance Reform?" Associated Press, May 3, 1998; "Tactical Delay," *CQ Update,* May 5, 1998.

52. By voting "present," the Commission bill sponsors did not have to vote against their own bill. Thus they ensured that the bill would not receive more "yea" votes than the Shays-Meehan bill.

53. The Committee of the Whole has the same membership as the entire House but only 100, rather than 218, members are required for a quorum in order to do business.

54. The Republican reform members were Christopher Shays; Michael Forbes, R-N.Y.; John Edward Porter, R-Ill.; Jim Ramstad, R-Minn.; Sue Kelly, R-N.Y.; Zach Wamp; Nancy Johnson, R-Conn.; Fred Upton, R-Mich.; Jim Greenwood, R-Pa.; Jack Metcalf, R-Wash.; Amos Houghton, R-N.Y.; Jim Leach, R-Iowa; Mike Parker, R-Miss.; and Tom Campbell, R-Calif.

55. Armey also allowed the group to use one of his offices right off the floor of the House of Representatives for the meeting.

56. A July 1998 letter from L. Anthony Sutin, acting assistant attorney general, to Gingrich stated that the Department of Justice "strongly opposed these amendments": Doolittle Amendment 61, Doolittle Amendment 62, Peterson (of Pennsylvania) Amendment, Wicker Amendment 31, and Goodlatte Amendment.

57. Jack W. Germond and Jules Witcover, "A Flash of Hope for Reformers," *National Journal,* July 11, 1998, 1643.

58. Thomas helped broker a deal that was in part designed to regain some input into the process. As the chairman of the committee of jurisdiction (the House Oversight Committee), he had lost some face with the removal of most of the process from his committee's consideration, his failure to broker an earlier deal that led to the suspension votes, and the sound defeat of his own reform effort.

59. Amendments sponsored by Reps. Bob Barr, R-Ga.; Bob Schaffer, R-Colo.; Fred Upton, R-Mich.; Tom DeLay; and Dan Miller, R-Fla., were not offered.

60. At this point the Shays-Meehan bill had enough votes to be Queen of the Hill. Therefore the Freshman and Doolittle bills were now offered as substitute bills to the Shays-Meehan bill.

61. Helen Dewar, "House Approves Campaign Finance Limits," *Washington Post,* August 7, 1998, A1. Dewar also notes that the House Republican leaders "came to power under a reform banner, but found themselves defending a system that many of their own members described as corrupt."

62. E. J. Dionne Jr., "A Chance for Campaign Reform," *Washington Post,* August 7, 1998, A25.

63. Ibid.

64. See Sinclair, *Unorthodox Lawmaking,* chap. 6.

65. One of the strategies that supporters of reform tried to use early on in the process in the 105th Congress was to persuade those in the Republican majority who had voted for campaign finance reform while in the minority in 1992 to do so again. Some suggested that the bill that was passed in the 102d Con-

gress and later vetoed by President George Bush be reintroduced or at least used as a base to achieve Republican support. What proponents of this strategy failed to mention is that the 1992 process was filled with its own partisanship, and passage then was called into question as a political ploy by the Democrats in an election year. The Democrats controlled both chambers of Congress in 1992 and passed a bill that reflected their views in part because they expected Bush to veto it, making it a "free vote" for the Democrats and allowing them to claim that the Republican president had killed reform.

66. John W. Kingdon, *Agendas, Alternatives, and Public Policy* (Glenview, Ill.: Scott, Foresman, 1984).

Chapter 4 (pages 115–139)

1. This discussion is based in part on David E. Price, *Who Makes the Laws? Creativity and Power in Senate Committees* (Cambridge, Mass.: Schenkman, 1972). Price identified six functions associated with a legislator being "responsible" for a bill: instigation and publicizing, formulation, information-gathering, interest aggregation, mobilization, and modification.

2. See Richard Fenno Jr., *Home Style: House Members in Their Districts* (Boston: Little, Brown, 1978), for his discussion of careerism and why members of Congress pursue different goals at different times in their careers. Also see John R. Hibbing, "Contours of the Modern Congressional Career," *American Political Science Review* 85 (1991): 405–428.

3. See the discussion of transformational leadership in James McGregor Burns, *Leadership* (New York: Harper and Row, 1978).

4. Price, *Who Makes the Laws?* 297.

5. John W. Kingdon, *Agendas, Alternatives, and Public Policies* (Boston: Little, Brown, 1984).

6. Michael Mintrom, "Policy Entrepreneurs and the Diffusion of Innovation," *American Journal of Political Science* 41 (1997): 738–770. See also Frank R. Baumgartner and Bryan D. Jones, *Agendas and Instability in American Politics* (Chicago: University of Chicago Press, 1993); Paula J. King, *Policy Entrepreneurs: Catalysts in the Policy Innovation Process* (Ph.D. diss., University of Minnesota, 1988); Kingdon, *Agendas, Alternatives, and Public Policies;* and Nelson Polsby, *Political Innovation in America: The Politics of Policy Initiation* (New Haven: Yale University Press, 1984).

7. Mintrom, "Policy Entrepreneurs and the Diffusion of Innovation," 739.

8. For further discussion see King, *Policy Entrepreneurs;* Kingdon, *Agendas, Alternatives, and Public Policies;* and James A. Smith, *The Idea Brokers* (New York: Free Press, 1991).

9. For further discussion of issue or policy networks, see Hugh Heclo, "Issue Networks and the Executive Establishment," in *The New American Political System,* ed. Anthony King (Washington, D.C.: American Enterprise Institute, 1978);

Michael W. Kirst, Gail Meister, and Stephen R. Rowley. "Policy Issue Networks: Their Influence on State Policymaking," *Policy Studies Journal* 13 (1984): 247–263; and Jack Walker, "The Diffusion of Knowledge, Policy Communities, and Agenda Setting: The Relationship of Knowledge and Power," in *New Strategic Perspectives on Social Policy,* ed. John E. Tropman, Milan J. Dluhy, and Roger M. Lind (New York: Basic Books, 1981).

10. Note, however, that Tom Allen also supported the Shays-Meehan bill.

11. Public opinion on campaign finance reform was a somewhat confusing matter. Although voters did not place campaign finance reform at or near the top of their list of policy priorities, when asked, most Americans said that the campaign finance system should be reformed.

12. Melinda Henneberger, "Republican Lawmaker Is Caught in the Middle," *New York Times,* March 31, 1998, A1.

13. Eric Friedman, "Shadowing Super Shays," *Fairfield County Weekly,* May 21, 1998; James Dao, "An Uneasy Republican Maverick; Shays's Rebellion on Campaign Finance Angers Party," *New York Times,* June 22, 1998, B2.

14. For example, one recurring comment from many Republican staff members was that Shays should become a Democrat, a sentiment that Republican representatives themselves often implied as well.

15. Dao, "An Uneasy Republican Maverick," B2.

16. David Lightman, "Shays May Pay for His Rebellion," *Hartford Courant,* April 1, 1998, A1.

17. Lisa Caruso, "House GOP Moderates Debate Party Loyalty System," *National Journal's Congress Daily,* June 24, 1998, 7. Ehrlich circulated a letter among Republican House members stating that the Republican Conference has "a right to expect all members, particularly committee chairmen, subcommittee chairmen and members of leadership to refrain from signing discharge petitions, to refrain from voting against the previous question [on rules], and to always sustain the rulings of the chair." In expressing support for Ehrlich's letter, Majority Leader Tom DeLay stated that Republicans who act in such ways effectively are "turning the floor over to the minority," which would be "the beginning of the end for the majority." In response to Ehrlich's letter, Rep. Wayne Gilchrest, a moderate Republican from Maryland, wrote a letter to Speaker Gingrich that was signed by other Republican members "express[ing] our deep concern over recent reports of efforts to revert to a system of punishment and retribution against members who express views in opposition of leadership positions."

18. Lightman, "Shays May Pay for His Rebellion," A1. Shays placed his arm around Gingrich as he put this question to him. Gingrich indicated that he had no problem but was not pleased with Shays's efforts on campaign finance reform. Shays replied that the next time Gingrich was angry he should, "Just call me on the phone."

19. Dear Colleague letter signed by Reps. Christopher Shays, R-Ct.; Martin T. Meehan, D-Mass.; Nancy L. Johnson, R-Conn.; Jim Leach, R-Iowa; James C.

Greenwood, R-Pa.; Bill Luther, D-Minn.; Paul McHale, D-Pa.; and Thomas M. Barrett, D-Wis.

20. Martin T. Meehan to Campaign Reform Staff.

21. Ibid.

22. Tom Campbell and Charles Stenholm, Dear Colleague letter, May 19, 1998.

23. Christopher Shays and Brian Bilbray, Dear Colleague letter, May 21, 1998.

24. Christopher Shays and Martin T. Meehan, Dear Colleague letter, May 13, 1998.

25. Samuel Kernell, *Going Public: New Strategies of Presidential Leadership* (Washington, D.C.: CQ Press, 1986).

26. John B. Bader, *Taking the Initiative: Leadership Agendas in Congress and the "Contract with America"* (Washington, D.C: Georgetown University Press, 1996), 108–112.

27. Remember that bills brought to the floor on the suspension calendar are allowed only forty minutes of debate (twenty minutes for each side) and need a two-thirds majority vote to pass. The process is usually reserved for noncontroversial issues, and campaign finance reform certainly was not a noncontroversial issue.

28. "Voters Must Insist on Change," *Hartford Courant,* editorial, May 1, 1998, A24.

29. See, for example, "Republican Leaders Kill Reform," *Hartford Courant,* editorial, April 1, 1998, A14; "The Backlash in the House," *New York Times,* editorial, April 1, 1998, A22; "Hypocrisy on Campaign Funds," *Washington Post,* editorial, April 1, 1998, A18; and "Their Cheatin' Hearts," *Palm Beach Post,* editorial, April 1, 1998, 12A.

30. Linda Smith, R-Wash., had once stated that the discharge petition "would only waste precious time on a fruitless effort and heighten the understandable cynicism Americans feel about this issue." Lisa Caruso, "Moderate Republicans Ponder Discharge Petition Route," *National Journal's Congress Daily,* April 16, 1998.

31. By the time the Shays-Meehan bill was sent to the Senate, there was very little time left in the session to act upon it.

32. Paycheck protection was a controversial measure advocated by the Republican leadership to limit the ability of labor unions to collect and use union dues. Although Republican leaders and some GOP reformers called this measure "paycheck protection," the Democratic leadership had dubbed it the "worker gag rule" (see Chapters 2 and 3).

33. Kingdon, *Agendas, Alternatives, and Public Policies.*

Chapter 5 (pages 141–166)

1. See Roger Davidson and Walter Oleszek, *Congress and Its Members,* 6th ed. (Washington, D.C.: CQ Press, 1998), 182–183.

2. The handshake agreement between President Clinton and House Speaker Newt Gingrich on June 11, 1995, in Claremont, N.H., was a pledge to work to-

gether to establish a bipartisan commission that would recommend a reform proposal that Congress would have to vote up or down without any changes.

3. Davidson and Oleszek, *Congress and Its Members,* 259–260.

4. Initially, the Contract with America called for passing two measures regarding congressional process: the first was to require Congress to end its exemptions from eleven workplace laws, and the second was to revise House rules to cut committee budgets and their staffs, impose term limits on committee chairmen, end proxy voting, and require three-fifths majority votes for tax increases. Then the Contract contained ten "planks": the balanced-budget amendment and the line-item veto; anticrime measures; welfare reform; protections for families and children; tax cuts; enhancement of national security; repeal of the tax increase on Social Security; reduction of federal regulations; change in liability laws; and imposition of congressional term limits. The constitutional amendment to impose term limits on federal legislators received a majority in the House but failed to get the two-thirds vote required for a constitutional amendment.

5. The Senate vote on the president's economic plan was a tie, and Vice President Al Gore had to cast the deciding tie-breaker vote.

6. Nicol C. Rae and Colton C. Campbell, "From Revolution to Evolution: Congress under Republican Control," in *New Majority or Old Minority? The Impact of Republicans on Congress,* ed. Nicol C. Rae and Colton C. Campbell (Lanham, Md.: Rowman and Littlefield, 1999), 5.

7. Adam Clymer, "Reshaping Medicare: The Overview; House Votes to Curb Costs of Medicare by $270 Billion; President Promises a Veto," *New York Times,* October 20, 1995, A1.

8. Jim VandeHei and Francesca Contiguglia, "A Year Later, Rebels' Work Isn't Done," *Roll Call,* July 13, 1998, 1.

9. For example, the Republican Party was able to enact much of its policy agenda from 1980 to 1986, when the party controlled the Senate and the White House, in part because many conservative Democrats voted with the Republicans on numerous issues in the House.

10. Norman J. Ornstein, Thomas E. Mann, and Michael J. Malbin, *Vital Statistics on Congress, 1999–2000* (Washington, D.C.: AEI Press, 2000), 193–194, 201.

11. For an excellent discussion of the electoral motivations of legislators, see David R. Mayhew, *Congress: The Electoral Connection* (New Haven: Yale University Press, 1974). For an insightful discussion of the three goals of lawmakers—reelection, gaining influence, and making good public policy—see Mayhew, *Congress: The Electoral Connection,* and Richard F. Fenno Jr., *Congressmen in Committees* (Boston: Little, Brown, 1973), chap. 1.

12. See, for example, Anthony Downs, *An Economic Theory of Democracy* (New York: Harper and Row, 1957), chap. 2.

13. Mayhew, *Congress: The Electoral Connection,* 16.

14. Fenno, *Congressmen in Committees,* chap. 1.

15. Ibid.

16. Jim VandeHei, "Gingrich May Punish Rebels: Moderates Targeted Over Votes," *Roll Call,* May 25, 1998, 1, 17.

17. Lisa Caruso, "Gingrich Hits Leach on Petition," *National Journal's Congress Daily AM,* April 23, 1998, 1.

18. VandeHei, "Gingrich May Punish Rebels," 17.

19. Under the seniority system, the committee member from the majority party with the most years of continuous service on the committee becomes its chairperson.

20. In fact, the GOP was quite pleased to leave the campaign finance laws alone, for the status quo does appear to benefit them more than the Democrats.

21. *CQ's Politics in America, 2000: The 106th Congress,* eds. Philip D. Duncan and Brian Nutting (Washington, D.C.: Congressional Quarterly, 1999), 651.

22. Indeed, the Reagan tax cuts substantially reduced taxes for wealthy taxpayers and for corporations.

23. Joseph Cooper and Garry Young, "Partisanship, Bipartisanship, and Crosspartisanship in Congress since the New Deal," in *Congress Reconsidered,* eds. Lawrence C. Dodd and Bruce I. Oppenheimer, 6th ed. (Washington, D.C.: CQ Press, 1997).

24. Ibid.

25. The Jeffords, Snowe, Dodd, and Murphy bill was S. 1037, the CIDCARE Act (Creating Improved Delivery of Child Care Act).

26. Jeanne Cummings, "GOP Devises New Ways to Kill Campaign-Finance Bills," *Wall Street Journal,* June 2, 1998, A24.

27. *Congressional Quarterly's Politics in America, 1998: The 105th Congress,* eds. Philip D. Duncan and Christine C. Lawrence (Washington, D.C.: CQ Press, 1997), 278.

28. Senate Committee on Government Affairs, *Investigations of Illegal or Improper Activities in Connection with 1996 Federal Election Campaigns: Final Report* (Washington, D.C.: U.S. Government Printing Office, 1998), vol. 6, see "Minority Views."

29. Note that after ACLU leaders had publicly announced that they opposed such campaign finance reforms, many of the organization's former board members just as publicly threw their support behind the Shays-Meehan bill, saying it did not, in their opinion, violate free speech rights (see Chapter 6).

30. Of course, the Democrats did these things as well, but because the Republicans had more soft money they could run more issue ads.

31. Alison Mitchell, "G.O.P. Leadership in House Rebuffed on Election Funds," *New York Times,* June 20, 1998, A1.

32. "Stretch-Out in the House," *Washington Post,* editorial, June 21, 1998, C6.

33. Albert Hunt, "The Bipartisan Money Chase," *Wall Street Journal,* July 23, 1998, A17.

34. Mitchell, "After Hours Debate on Fund-Raising Rages," *New York Times,* July 20, 1998, A1.

35. "Christopher Shays's Moment," *New York Times,* editorial, June 15, 1998, A26.

36. Alison Mitchell, "Some House Democrats Balancing Doubts and Party Loyalty in Fund-Raising Debate," *New York Times,* June 8, 1998, A14.

37. Tom DeLay, "Protect the NAACP's Scorecards: Vote for the Doolittle Amendment," Dear Colleague letter, no date (early July 1998).

38. Ibid.

39. Eighteen Democrats voted for the Doolittle amendment. Some of them were antiabortion members who also voted against the Shays-Meehan bill, such as Collin C. Peterson, D-Minn., and Nick J. Rahall II, D-W.V.

40. Instead, as discussed in Chapter 3, before the petition had the needed 218 signatures, the GOP leadership agreed to allow votes on campaign finance reform bills, effectively nullifying the need for the discharge petition.

41. Proreform lobbyist to the authors, June 6, 2000.

42. Samuel Kernell, *Going Public: New Strategies of Presidential Leadership* (Washington, D.C.: CQ Press, 1986).

43. Ed Henry and Amy Keller, "Reform Debate Is Joined but Bill Is Filibuster Bait," *Roll Call,* September 29, 1997, 1.

44. *Politics in America, 1998,* 1527; Amy Keller and Jim VandeHei, "GOP Agonizes on Reform Vote as Shays Rebels," *Roll Call,* October 27, 1997, 20.

Chapter 6 (pages 167–199)

1. Most contemporary textbooks on Congress devote one chapter to the role of interest groups and lobbyists in Congress, and some have no separate section to consider these important players; see, for example, Matthew C. Moen and Gary W. Copeland, *Contemporary Congress: A Bicameral Approach* (Belmont, Calif.: West/Wadsworth, 1999). Other scholars, however, have acknowledged the importance of external players; see, for example, Timothy Cook, *Making Laws and Making News: Media Strategies in the U.S. House of Representatives* (Washington, D.C.: Brookings Institution, 1989), and Samuel Kernell, *Going Public: News Strategies of Presidential Leadership* (Washington, D.C.: CQ Press, 1986).

2. For a contemporary look at how interest groups use money to affect the policy process, see Darrell M. West and Burdett A. Loomis, *The Sound of Money: How Political Interests Get What They Want* (New York: W. W. Norton, 1999).

3. See, for example, Clyde Wilcox, "The Dynamics of Lobbying the Hill," in *The Interest Group Connection,* eds. Paul Herrnson, Ronald Shaiko, and Clyde Wilcox (Chatham, N.J.: Chatham House, 1998).

4. See Mark J. Rozell and Clyde Wilcox, *Interest Groups in American Campaigns: The New Face of Electioneering* (Washington, D.C.: CQ Press, 1999).

5. Jeffrey M. Berry, *The Interest Group Society,* 2d ed. (New York: HarperCollins, 1989), 53.

6. Many organizations use telephone banks to contact the public as well as legislators' offices to advocate their position.

7. Lizette Alvarez, "Campaign Finance Backers Petition to Force House Vote," *New York Times*, April 18, 1998, A8.

8. Lisa Caruso, "The Friday Buzz," *National Journal's Congress Daily*, April 24, 1998, 4.

9. Rep. Asa Hutchinson, "Reformers Urge Common Cause Not to Threaten Chances of Success for Campaign Finance Reform This Year: Group's 'Scorched Earth' Strategy Gives Congress an Excuse to Walk Away from Reform," news release, June 5, 1998.

10. Cited online at http://www.lwv.org/, July 11, 1999.

11. Cited online at http://www.citizen.org/, July 11, 1999.

12. Ibid.

13. Cited online at http://www.pirg.org/, July 11, 1999.

14. The report was issued on November 25, 1997, and entitled "The Big Picture: Money Follows Power Shift on Capitol Hill." This report looked at the 1996 campaign and documented how the money had followed the Republicans into leadership and the explosion of soft money and its effects. On November 29, 1997, *Congressional Quarterly Weekly Report* highlighted the CRP's findings in an article by Ronald Elving, "New Study Confirms Big Jump in 1996 Campaign Spending," 2957. Shays and Meehan sent the CRP report and the Elving article out as a "Dear Colleague" letter on December 10, 1997.

15. Aspen Institute, online at http://www.aspeninst.org, July 2, 2000.

16. Jack W. Germond and Jules Witcover, "A Flash of Hope for Reformers," *National Journal*, July 11, 1998, 1643.

17. Warren E. Buffett to members of Congress, July 13, 1998.

18. Wright, *Interest Groups and Congress*, 46–47. See also David B. Truman, *The Governmental Process: Political Interests and Public Opinion* (New York: Knopf, 1955), 46.

19. Wright, *Interest Groups and Congress*, 46–47. See also Truman, *The Governmental Process*, 353–362.

20. Alison Mitchell, "Some Democrats Torn over Fund-Raising Curbs," *New York Times*, June 8, 1998, A12.

21. National Right to Life Committee, online at http://www.nrlc.org, July 3, 2000.

22. National Right to Life Committee to members of Congress, February 24, 1999, online at http://www.nrlc.org/federal/Free_Speech/shayslet.htm, July 3, 2000. See also Norman J. Ornstein, "Message to Members: Look beyond Rhetoric before Voting on Campaign Finance Reform," *Roll Call*, May 21, 1998, 8.

23. Ibid.

24. Christian Coalition to members of Congress, July 7, 1998, as quoted in Amy Keller, "Reform Debate Shifts to Voter Guide Controversy," *Roll Call*, July 13, 1998, 12.

25. National Right to Life Committee to House members, February 24, 1999.

26. Christian Coalition, online at http://www.cc.org/about.html, July 3, 2000.

27. Christian Coalition, online at http://www.cc.org/issues/campaign–finance. html, July 3, 2000.

28. Common Cause to members of the House of Representatives, July 13, 1998.

29. American Civil Liberties Union, online at http://www.aclu.org/library/pbp1. html, July 3, 2000.

30. American Civil Liberties Union, "ACLU Campaign Finance Reform Fact Sheet #4: What's Wrong with H.R. 3526, the Shays/Meehan Bill?" June 16, 1998, online at http://www.aclu.org/congress/cfr0611698.html.

31. "Big Mo at Last," *New York Times*, editorial, June 21, 1998, sec. 4, p. 14.

32. American Civil Liberties Union, "ACLU Campaign Finance Reform Fact Sheet #4."

33. Davidson and Oleszek, *Congress and Its Members*, 404.

34. Ibid., 409.

35. Cook, *Making Laws and Making News*, 82–83.

36. Davidson and Oleszek, *Congress and Its Members*, 184.

37. For further reading on the role of media in politics, see Thomas R. Dye and L. Hannon Ziegler, *American Politics in the Media Age* (Monterey, Calif.: Brooks/ Cole, 1983), and Doris A. Graber, *Mass Media and American Politics*, 5th ed. (Washington, D.C.: CQ Press, 1997).

38. Thomas E. Patterson, *We the People: A Concise Introduction to American Politics*, 3d ed. (New York: McGraw-Hill, 2000), 280.

39. See Shanto Iyengar, "Shortcuts to Political Knowledge: The Role of Selective Attention and Accessibility," in *Information and Democratic Processes*, eds. John A. Ferejohn and James H. Kuklinski (Chicago: University of Illinois Press, 1990).

40. The seven other reformers were the Democrats Lois Capps, Lloyd Doggett, Carolyn Maloney, George Miller, and Charles W. Stenholm, and the Republicans Brian P. Bilbray and Jim Leach.

41. Celinda Lake, "Polls Say Public Has Prescription for Reform," *Roll Call*, March 23, 1998, 5.

42. "Shays Leads Battle in House for Campaign Finance Bill," *New York Times*, editorial, June 22, 1998, A19.

43. See, for example, Glenn F. Bunting, "Clinton's Hard and Fast Ride on Donation Trail," *Los Angeles Times*, December 22, 1997, A1.

44. Patterson, *We the People*, 285; see also James Fallows, *Breaking the News* (New York: Pantheon, 1996).

45. "Plotting against Reform," *New York Times*, editorial, March 14, 1998, A30.

46. "Mocking Campaign Reform," *Washington Post*, editorial, March 22, 1998, C10; "Plotting against Reform"; "Embarrassment II," *Roll Call*, April 2, 1998, 4.

47. "The Plot to Bury Reform," *New York Times*, editorial, March 30, 1998, A16.

48. "196 Names . . . and Counting," *Washington Post*, editorial, April 3, 1998, A30.

49. "Gingrich's Empty Victory: Watering Down of Campaign Reform Causes House Backlash," *Los Angeles Times*, editorial, March 31, 1998, B6.

50. Mark Shields, "The Politician Who Won't Wobble," *Washington Post,* June 22, 1998, A21.

51. James Dao, "Shays Leads Battle in House for Campaign Finance Bill," *New York Times,* June 22, 1998, A19.

52. Shays and his fellow farmers had been promised that they would not lose their land because of unpaid debts and taxes that accumulated while they were away fighting in the Revolutionary War. The event, and other protests like it, was a catalyst in replacing the Articles of Confederation with the Constitution, which would provide a stronger central government to ensure public order and preserve the union. The title "Shays's Rebellion" was picked up by reporters covering campaign finance reform in 1998. See, for example, James Dao, "An Uneasy Republican Maverick: Shays's Rebellion on Campaign Reform Angers Party," *New York Times,* June 22, 1998, B1. Also see Amy Keller and Jim Vande-Hei, "Shays's Rebellion Irks Gingrich, Sparks Campaign Reform War," *Roll Call,* March 30, 1998, 1.

53. "A Sign-Up List for Reform," *New York Times,* editorial, April 6, 1998, A26; "196 Names . . . and Counting."

54. David Lightman, "Shays Talks Back to GOP," the *Hartford Courant,* March 28, 1998.

55. "Embarrassment II," 4.

56. Guy Gugliotta, "Campaign Reform: Death by Debate?" *Washington Post,* July 13, 1998, A19.

57. Alison Mitchell, "House G.O.P. Opens Floodgates on Campaign Finance," *New York Times,* May 22, 1998, A16; Jill Abramson, "When $10 Million Is in Trough, Few Want to Overturn It," *New York Times,* June 15, 1998, A1.

58. Mitchell, "Bill to Overhaul Campaign Finance Survives in House," *New York Times,* July 31, 1998, A1.

59. "Plotting against Reform," *New York Times.*

Chapter 7 (pages 201–225)

1. Alison Mitchell, "6 Republicans Break Ranks on Campaign Finance Issue," *New York Times,* May 27, 1999, A28.

2. Rep. Christopher Shays, "Shays Joins Bipartisan Group of Legislators to Open National Debate on Campaign Finance Reform," press release, February 25, 1999.

3. Rep. Martin J. Meehan, "Marty Meehan: Fighting for True Reform," online at http://www.house.gov/meehan/cam.htm.

4. House Democratic Policy Committee, "Outrage of the Week, April 12, 1999: Republicans: Struggling to Save Their Marriage to Big Money," online at http://www.house.gov/democrats/welcome.html.

5. Ibid.

6. Mitchell, "6 Republicans Break Ranks."

7. Ibid.

8. Frank Bruni, "Tightrope for Republicans on Campaign Finance," *New York Times,* April 23, 1999, A22.

9. Alison Mitchell, "House G.O.P. Urges a Vote of No on Ban on Donations," *New York Times,* September 14, 1999, A20.

10. Bruni, "Tightrope for Republicans."

11. Ibid.

12. U.S. House Democratic Policy Committee, "Outrage of the Week, May 7, 1999: Speaker Rejects Appeal to Move On Campaign Finance Reform," online at http://www.house.gov/democrats/welcome.html.

13. Amy Keller, "Campaign Finance Reform in Turmoil—Vote Deadline Unclear; Doolittle Blasts Moderates," *Roll Call,* Thursday, May 13, 1999, 1.

14. Alison Mitchell, "Campaign Finance Put on Back Burner," *New York Times,* May 22, 1999, A9.

15. Ibid.

16. Ibid.

17. The six Republican signers were: Michael N. Castle, Del.; Michael P. Forbes, N.Y.; Greg Ganske, Iowa; Nancy L. Johnson, Conn.; Constance A. Morella, Md.; and Christopher Shays, Conn. It is interesting to note that Michael Forbes later switched to the Democratic Party.

18. Rep. Christopher Shays, "Shays Signs Discharge Petition," press release, May 26, 1999.

19. Mitchell, "6 Republicans Break Ranks."

20. Testimony of Christopher Shays and Marty Meehan before the House Administration Committee on H.R. 417, the Bipartisan Campaign Finance Reform Act, June 29, 1999.

21. Mitchell, "House G.O.P. Urges a Vote of No on Ban on Donations."

22. Online at http://www.soc.american.edu/campfin/ and http://www.brookings.org/gs/campaign/cfr_hp.htm, respectively.

23. Robert Lewis, "Shays Keeps Battling Election-Law Abuses," *AARP Bulletin,* July–August 1999, 4.

24. Don Van Natta Jr., "Soft Money's Multifaceted Foe," *New York Times,* October 17, 1999, sec. 3, p. 2; Don Van Natta Jr., "Executives Seeking Caps on Donations Stand Strong," *New York Times,* October 5, 1999, A22.

25. Van Natta, "Executives Seeking Caps on Donations." The CED also recommended that the limit on individual contributions be raised from $1,000 to $3,000 and that there should be partial public funding for congressional elections with voluntary spending limits.

26. Edward A. Kangas, "Soft Money and Hard Bargains," *New York Times,* October 22, 1999, A27.

27. Rep. Christopher Shays, "Shays, Meehan Applaud CED's Call for Reform," press release, July 14, 1999.

28. Van Natta, "Executives Press for Political Finance Change," *New York Times,* September 1, 1999, A1.

29. Ibid.

30. Van Natta, "Soft Money's Multifaceted Foe."
31. John Kruger and Alysson Ford, "Pro-Life Group Puts Pressure on Campaign Reform," *Hill,* July 7, 1999, 1. See also Michael Grunwald, "Campaign Finance Issue Divides Abortion Foes," *Washington Post,* September 14, 1999, A1.
32. Kruger and Ford, "Pro-Life Group Puts Pressure on Campaign Reform."
33. Grunwald, "Campaign Finance Issue Divides Abortion Foes."
34. Ibid.
35. Ibid.
36. Rep. Christopher Shays, "Shays Statement on Campaign Finance Reform Debate," press release, September 13, 1999.
37. David Rosenbaum, "A Day of Debate and Forced Allusion," *New York Times,* September 15, 1999, A22.
38. Ibid.
39. Helen Dewar, "Campaign Reforms Pass House," *Washington Post,* September 15, 1999, A1.
40. Ibid.
41. At the time the amendment was proposed, First Lady Hillary Rodham Clinton was exploring a possible Senate bid in New York State. She later was nominated as the Democratic candidate for the seat vacated by Sen. Patrick Moynihan, D-N.Y.
42. Rep. Christopher Shays, "Shays on Passage of Bipartisan Campaign Finance Reform Act," press release, September 14, 1999.
43. Sen. John McCain, "McCain Says Conservative Reform Hinges on Campaign Finance Reform," press release, May 24, 1999.
44. McCain, "McCain Responds to Majority Leader on Campaign Finance Reform," press release, July 1, 1999.
45. Helen Dewar, "McCain to Seek Action on Campaign Finance," *Washington Post,* July 19, 1999, A4.
46. Robin Tone, "The 'Designated Spear Catcher' on Campaign Finance," *New York Times,* October 18, 1999, A12.
47. Ibid.
48. McCain, "McCain, Feingold Introduce Revised Campaign Finance Reform Bill for October Debate," press release, September 16, 1999.
49. Alison Mitchell, "2 Senators Revise Measure to Limit Campaign Money," *New York Times,* September 16, 1999, A20.
50. 145 *Congressional Record,* S12585–S12586 (1999).
51. Ibid., 12592.
52. Ibid., 12589.
53. Mitchell, "McCain Outmaneuvered in Vote on Campaign Finance Change," *New York Times,* October 19, 1999, A20.
54. Mitchell, "Republicans Pillory McCain in Debate over Soft Money," *New York Times,* October 15, 1999, A30.

55. Further complicating the process was the additional burden that filibusters regarding rule changes require a two-thirds vote (sixty-seven) for cloture instead of the sixty required to end a filibuster during normal debate.

56. Mitchell, "McCain Outmaneuvered."

57. On roll-call vote no. 330, taken on October 9, 1999, a "Motion to Invoke Cloture on Daschle Amdt. No. 2298," was rejected by a vote of 52–48. Senate roll-call vote no. 331, taken on October 19, 1999, a "Motion to Invoke Cloture on Reid Amdt. No. 2299," was rejected by a vote of 53–47. Senators Brownback, R-Kan., Hutchinson, R-Ark., and Roth, R-Del., all voted for cloture on vote no. 331, but not on vote no. 330. Conversely, Senators Chafee, R-R.I., and Specter, R-Pa., voted against cloture on vote no. 331 and for cloture on vote no. 330.

58. Quoted in Jim Drinkard, "Campaign Reform 'Dead' for Another Year," *USA Today*, October 20, 1999, 8A.

59. John M. Broder, "The 2000 Campaign: The Money Fight; Suit by Democrats Attacks Republican's Fund-Raising," *New York Times*, May 3, 2000, A24.

60. Ibid.

61. Ibid.

62. The 1994 Supreme Court case to which Guerra was referring as support for this current suit is *National Organization for Women, Inc. v. Joseph Scheidler*. In this case the Court ruled that the "National Organization for Women [could] proceed with its RICO lawsuit against anti-abortion protesters who were allegedly engaged in extortion by threatening violence against abortion-clinic workers and patients in an effort to shut down the medical facilities." Greg McDonald and Steve Lash, "Democrats' Lawsuit Takes Aim at DeLay; Extortion, Money Laundering Alleged," *Houston Chronicle*, May 4, 2000, A1.

63. "McCain Catches Leaders Off Guard with Campaign Finance Victory," *CQ Weekly*, June 10, 2000, 1383–1384.

64. Ibid.

65. Republicans voting with McCain were Spencer Abraham, Mich.; Conrad Burns, Mont.; Lincoln Chafee, R.I.; Susan Collins, Maine; Mike DeWine, Ohio; Chuck Hagel, Neb.; Kay Bailey Hutchison, Texas; James M. Jeffords, Vt.; Richard G. Lugar, Ind.; Olympia J. Snowe, Maine; Gordon H. Smith, Ore.; Arlen Specter, Pa.; and Fred Thompson, Tenn.

66. Andrew Taylor. "Support Grows for Curbing Secrecy of '527' Political Groups," *CQ Weekly*, June 17, 2000, 1447–1448.

67. Ibid., 1448.

68. Ibid.

69. Lawrence L. Knutson, "Banning Secret Money: Clinton Signs Law Closing Campaign Finance Loophole," online at http://www.ABCNEWS.com, July 1, 2000.

70. Eric Schmitt, "Congress Moves toward Disclosure Requirement for Tax-Exempt Groups," *New York Times*, June 29, 2000, A21.

71. Sen. John McCain, "McCain Vows to Continue to Push for Votes on Campaign Finance Reform," press release, October 19, 1999.

Chapter 8 (pages 227–246)

1. John W. Kingdon, *Agendas, Alternatives, and Public Policies* (Boston: Little, Brown, 1984); Barbara Sinclair, *Unorthodox Lawmaking: New Legislative Processes in the U.S. Congress* (Washington, D.C.: CQ Press, 1997).
2. Sinclair, *Unorthodox Lawmaking.*
3. Ibid., 16–17.
4. Sarah A. Binder and Steven S. Smith, *Politics or Principle? Filibustering in the United States Senate* (Washington, D.C.: Brookings Institution, 1997), 9, 6, 13.
5. Norman J. Ornstein, Thomas E. Mann, and Michael E. Malbin, *Vital Statistics on Congress, 1999–2000* (Washington, D.C.: AEI Press, 2000), 86.
6. Binder and Smith, *Politics or Principle?* 203.
7. Ibid., 136–141.
8. Senators have imposed antifilibustering rules on certain types of bills in recent decades. For example, senators have banned the use of unlimited debate (the filibuster) on certain budget matters. See Binder and Smith, *Politics or Principle?* 205.
9. *Nixon v. Shrink Missouri Government PAC,* 120 S.Ct. 897 (2000).
10. *Shrink Missouri Government PAC v. Adams,* 161 F.3d 519, 523 (8th Cir. 1998).
11. Helen Dewar, "GOP Urges High Court to Scrap Contribution Limit," *Washington Post,* June 8, 1999, A4.
12. Linda Greenhouse, "Justices Uphold $1,000 Cap on Campaign Contributions," *New York Times,* January 25, 2000, A1.
13. *Nixon,* 910.
14. Ibid., 905.
15. See *Shrink Missouri,* 522.
16. David Mayhew, *Congress: The Electoral Connection* (New Haven: Yale University Press, 1974), 141, 145, 146.
17. See Thomas E. Mann, *Unsafe at Any Margin: Interpreting Congressional Elections* (Washington, D.C.: American Enterprise Institute, 1978).
18. Jeffrey M. Berry, *The Interest Group Society,* 2d ed. (New York: HarperCollins, 1989), 184–187.
19. For further discussion of the notion of continuing agenda items, see Charles Jones, *Presidency in a Separated System* (Washington, D.C.: Brookings Institution, 1994).
20. Sinclair, *Unorthodox Lawmaking.*
21. In July 2000, four months before the 2000 presidential election, the Democratic Party had more cash on hand than the Republican Party. Some suggest if

this trend were to continue, the Democrats' resolve for pursuing campaign finance reform might not remain so strong.

22. No. 98-CV-1207 (WBB) (D.D.C.).

23. Currently, the law requires that the FEC board be split evenly between Democratic and Republican members.

24. *Federal Election Commission v. Colorado Republican Federal Campaign Comm.*, 41 F. Supp. 2d 1197 (D. Colo. 1999). This case was on remand from the Supreme Court's decision in *Colorado Republican Federal Campaign Committee v. Federal Election Commission,* discussed in Chapter 2.

25. Mary Boyle and Michele Ames, "Colorado Ruling Could Affect Election Funding," *Arlington Star-Telegram,* April 11, 1999, A31.

26. Within forty-eight hours of winning the New Hampshire primary, Senator McCain had raised $5.6 million in online contributions. Tracy Westen, "Online Fundraising: Campaign Finance Solution or Gasoline on the Flames?" *National Voter,* June/July 2000, 20–22.

27. Time Warner owns Cable News Network, Warner Brothers, and *Time* magazine. According to their estimates they have "given roughly $1 million to the Republican and Democratic Parties in each of the last two elections." John M. Broder, "Time Warner to End Gifts of Soft Money," *New York Times,* November 18, 1999, A28.

28. Poll results reported in the *Washington Post,* September 9, 1999; online at http://www.washingtonpost.com/. Poll results have a margin of error of ± 3 percent. See poll questions in Chapter 7.

29. Al Gore's plan called for banning soft money, requiring greater disclosure by lobbyists, mandating Congress to post monthly information on the Internet, and requiring groups that run issue ads within sixty days of an election to disclose their sources of funding. Gore also suggested a $7.1 billion fund to support general election candidates who do not accept private donations and free broadcast air time for candidates targeted by issue ads. George W. Bush's plan called for indexing hard money contribution limits to inflation, banning soft money donations from labor unions and corporations but not individuals, and instantaneous disclosure of contributions. Bush also called for restricting the use of union dues (from both members and nonmembers) for political purposes, prohibiting contributions from lobbyists to members of Congress while Congress is in session and preventing incumbents from transferring funds from one federal race to another. See Derek Willis, "Proposals to Overhaul Campaign Finance," *CQ Weekly,* May 13, 2000, 1092.

INDEX